MAKING
MAGIC

MAKING MAGIC

HOW ORLANDO WON AN NBA TEAM

PAT WILLIAMS
WITH
LARRY GUEST

A publication of *The Orlando Sentinel*
Sentinel Communications Company

Edited by Stephen R. Vaughn
Designed by Bill Henderson
Cover photo by George Remaine / *The Orlando Sentinel*
Authors' photo by Red Huber / *The Orlando Sentinel*
Additional photographs courtesy of the Orlando Magic,
the Associated Press, Fort Lauderdale *Sun-Sentinel* and
Gary Bogdon, Joe Burbank, Tom Burton, Bobby Coker, Tom Spitz,
Judy Watson Tracy, Chris Usher, Steve Vaughn, *The Orlando Sentinel.*

Printed in the United States by R. R. Donnelley

First Edition October, 1989

Library of Congress Cataloging-in-Publication Data
Williams, Pat, 1940-
Making magic / by Pat Williams and Larry Guest. -- 1st ed.
     p. cm.
"A publication of the Orlando Sentinel."
ISBN 0-941263-11-8
1. Orlando Magic (Basketball team) -- History. I. Guest, Larry, 1942- . II.
Orlando sentinel. III. Title.
GV885.52.075W55 1989
796.323'64'0975924--dc20   89-38769
                         CIP

DEDICATION

On behalf of the hundreds who helped to nurture our Magic dream into reality, to six men in particular — Mayor Bill Frederick, Orange County Commissioner Tom Dorman, *Sentinel* Publisher Tip Lifvendahl, Greater Orlando Chamber of Commerce Executive Vice President Jacob Stuart, SunBank Chairman Buell Duncan, late Disney World Vice President Bob Allen and late civic leader Jim Greene.

Pat Williams

To Mary, who lovingly understood why I couldn't turn off the computer and come to bed, and to Steve Vaughn, who embraced this project with a passion and filtered every cliche through his spleen.

Larry Guest

OTHER BOOKS by Pat Williams include
The Gingerbread Man, The Power Within You,
We Owed You One, Nothing But Winners, Rekindled,
Keep the Fire Glowing, Kindling, and *Love Her Like Him.*

CONTENTS

MAKING MAGIC

FOREWORD

When Pat Williams formally was introduced to Central Florida in June, 1986, as the point man for an NBA franchise chase, Orlando sports attorney Robert Fraley attended the press conference at the Expo Centre. Like most in the city, Fraley was curious but skeptical. To convince any major league that fast-growing Orlando was ready for prime time and to upgrade the natives' own fragile self-image as a sports city would require a man of unusual enthusiasm and energy.

Williams seemed to qualify. "That was the first time I laid eyes on Pat Williams and his enthusiasm that day was most apparent," recalls Fraley. "If you don't see that, you don't see Pat." The scope of that trait didn't really hit Fraley, though, until a few weeks later after Williams established a temporary base of operations in an extra office of Fraley's law suite. A partner, Greg Hyde, burst in on Fraley one day, shock spread across his face.

"To the day I die, no matter what Pat Williams does or what he has already done, the thing I'll remember most about Pat is what Greg described that day," says Fraley. Hyde had opened the men's room door to discover Williams down on the ceramic floor, doing pushups. Fraley was unsure whether to throw an arm around Pat's shoulders or a net over his head. "To me, Pat will never be any different from the man doing pushups in the men's room," he says.

"I do pushups wherever I have to," Pat said later with a matter-of-fact shrug, providing a peek at his extraordinary will. If he decides to do 60 pushups a day and the men's room floor is the only available gymnasium, then so be it. In this particular gymna . . . , uh, men's room, Pat figured he could crank out 60 quick ones devoid of prying eyes that might not appreciate his resolve. When Hyde swung open the door, Pat looked up with a weak smile but kept pumping.

"I was a little embarrassed," Pat remembers, sheepishly."but I finished the 60 pushups."

Dragging Orlando into the big leagues would require that brand of resolve and dedication. Big-time sports in Orlando to that point had consisted of a couple of PGA Tour stops, the Florida Citrus Bowl college post-season game and Minnesota Twins spring training. As far as having its own team, Orlando had experienced a bittersweet procession of off-Broadway football leagues. There had been the Orlando Panthers of the old Continental League, the Florida Blazers of the short-lived World Football League, the Orlando Americans of the anonymous American Football Association and, finally, the Orlando Renegades of the impatient and Donald Trumped USFL. Orlando particularly had given its heart to the Panthers and the Renegades, only to be jilted by the failure of the leagues they were in.

The one season of medical magnate Don Dizney's Renegades demonstrated Orlando was hungry for a sports entity of its own, but the locals continued to have trouble thinking of themselves in the same vein as accepted sports datelines like Detroit, Kansas City, Milwaukee, Houston. "A big league franchise? In *Orlando?* G'wan, shoo!"

Williams was the key in changing that mindset. This infectious pied piper with the Stan Laurel countenance and innocence would soon convert those football-steeped naysayers, miraculously, into can-do zealots. "An NBA franchise in Orlando? Of course we can! And start clearing off a spot for the NFL and major league baseball."

I knew Pat had hit for the cycle in marshaling all possible forces when I listened in astonishment from my pew one Sunday morning in the mammoth First Baptist Church as he delivered an unabashed ticket sales pitch from the pulpit. Pat insists his sole mission that day was to briefly extol the virtues of the Christian school being considered as a church project. But as he bounded toward the pulpit, the Rev. Jim Henry, First Baptist's pastor and leading Pat Williams disciple, leaned close and whispered, "Sell some Magic tickets while you're at it." It was like offering a lamb chop to a wolf.

Though clearly the central figure, Pat Williams was hardly the only hero in this civic transformation. There was a visionary mayor. A Pollyanna named Hewitt. A vigorous young du Pont heir who found himself swept into the drive as 11th-hour angel. And dozens of community leaders who threw a shoulder to the dream, starting with Pat's list back there on the dedication page.

But each aspect, each role was inextricably tethered to this unique and upbeat newcomer as the charming little citrus/tourist community began to take its first, tentative steps on big-city legs. It took an outsider to see Orlando's dynamic sports potential and his decision to bail out of a secure, prestigious position as GM of the Philadelphia 76ers to chase a vision in Orlando spawned a sobering reassessment by the locals. Said eventual majority owner Bill du Pont: "Pat struck me as having a real cheerleader type of personality and could generate enthusiasm in almost anybody in almost anything."

Jimmy Hewitt, an FSU football devotee, was struck the same way after a 1985 chance encounter with Williams and recognized this was the man to lead Orlando's breakthrough. Even if it was *basketball*.

The day after brainstorming the possibility with his new friend, destiny led Hewitt to another chance encounter while the notion was warm. He drove into the back parking lot at Lake Highland Prep late on a Monday afternoon to pick up his son, Ben, after soccer practice. There in the car parked just ahead was a friend, Mayor Bill Frederick, also waiting for his son. Hewitt turned off the ignition and walked up to the mayor's window.

"Bill, I'm glad to run into you," he said through an ever-present wide smile, and proceeded to recount his conversation of the previous day with Williams. "Bill, Pat told me the NBA is going to expand. And he thinks it could be as early as '87-'88. I told him our arena is planned for the early '90s and he said that would be too late. But he said the NBA is interested in expanding into Florida. As far as I'm concerned Central Florida is the only place to put it."

Frederick had seen the Blazers and the Renegades and the others come and go, so was somewhat jaded by the carpetbaggers of pseudo big-time sports. Hewitt emphasized that the NBA is one of the big three of major league team sports. "Jim, I don't know anything about it," confessed Frederick, "but if you really think there is a chance of getting an NBA team, we'll try to work with the county to get the arena timetable moved up. You go for it. We'll get it done."

The rest, as they say, is history.

That's where I come in. As this saga began to unravel, Williams recognized a need to record the story. I can't really remember how I was drafted to co-author this account. It may have been the suggestion of *Orlando Sentinel* Publisher Tip Lifvendahl. It may have been Pat's own idea after absorbing the whimsical threads common to the ramblings of my columns in the *Sentinel.* Pat is a man attracted to the lighter side.

In August, 1988, we launched the project, laboriously wading through more than a dozen legal-pad diaries that would form the foundation of this book and also afford me a fascinating window into

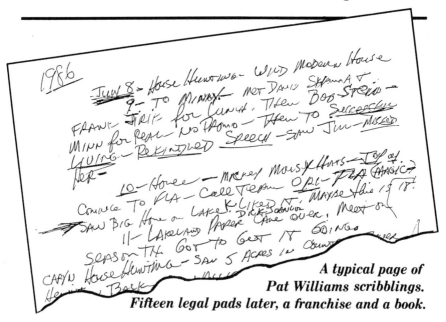

A typical page of
Pat Williams scribblings.
Fifteen legal pads later, a franchise and a book.

a most unusual life. The daily notations he jotted while stopped at a red light or awaiting a Little League game highlighted not only heavy decisions in NBA boardrooms and the consummation of million-dollar contracts, but also the forgotten school lunches and other adventures in a frenetic household containing an international array of children and a truckload of love.

I laughed through the foibles of Ulysses and Julia, Pat and Jill's neighborhood-hopping pet peacocks (named after Gen. and Mrs. Grant), and was touched by the Williams' emotional struggle with whether to add four homeless Filipino brothers to the eight children already crowded around their breakfast table.

While the exercise chained me to a word processor for countless days, transcribing more than 50 hours of tapes and shaping the events into a narrative, it provided insight into the breed-apart character there at the wheel of Orlando's most important sports entity. Here's a guy who never met a one-liner he didn't like or a necktie he did. He's proper, but casual. Highly organized, but adamantly non-computerized. Often pauses for mid-afternoon naps, but refuses to stop for lunch.

The challenge was to weave the narrative in Pat's vernacular. One of the passages where I failed miserably describes du Pont frantically sprinting through Manhattan to meet an appointment, "his Countess Mara flapping in his wake." While reading the galleys, Pat looked up, blinking, and asked, "What's a 'Countess Mara?'" I laughed at the realization that here no doubt was the only major-league general manager who actually might not be familiar with the last name in neckwear.

The Pat Williams style leans heavily toward his professional role model, Bill Veeck, the flamboyant baseball owner and GM who died in 1986. As a management rookie, Williams sought and was given a lasting primer on sports administration during a memorable visit to Veeck's home in Easton, Maryland, in the fall of 1962. The session was made possible by Miami Marlins' GM Bill Durney, for whom Williams labored first as a weak-hitting catcher, then as an eager young business manager for the Phillies' Class A farm club. Veeck's delightful autobiography, *Veeck, As In Wreck*, came out during Pat's first summer in Miami. He bought a copy in a downtown Burdine's and devoured it cover-to-cover in one enchanted sitting. His boss, Durney, had been Veeck's road secretary for the old St. Louis

Browns, and the first chapter was filled with funny references about him.

"Durney was 6-feet-5, 350 pounds and he physically picked up Eddie Gaedel, Veeck's famous midget pinch-hitter, and stuffed him into a giant birthday cake," Williams cites from the book. "It was Durney who threatened to choke Gaedel if he swung at a pitch.

"As I read this book, my life was being radically transformed. Never had I been so caught up in a man's life as I was with Veeck's. At season's end, I told Bill Durney I would really like to meet Bill Veeck, so he told Veeck I'd be calling."

Young Williams dialed his new idol a few days after returning home to Wilmington, Delaware, scared to death. Veeck invited Pat to make the 90-minute drive to his river estate the next day.

"It was a beautiful fall afternoon. I'll never forget it," Williams recalls. "As I drove up the entrance circle, there was Bill Veeck, sitting with a pair of khaki shorts on, no shirt. His aritificial leg was off. Sunning himself and reading a book on civil war poetry. His reading habits were both indiscriminate and voracious.

"I got out of the car and began to chat. It was wonderful and the time just flew by. Suddenly, he said, 'Bill Durney would be very upset with me if I didn't invite you to lunch.' The next thing I knew, Mary Frances Veeck is delivering BLT sandwiches on the front porch. Then, almost instantly, it was five o'clock in the afternoon. I was absolutely mesmerized.

"The one thing I do remember that came out of it was I asked for his advice to any young man wanting to get into pro sports administration. He offered three suggestions. One: Learn how to type, because you'll start at the lowest level of sports and you'd better know how to type. Two: Learn all you can about accounting. You'll need to know how to do that. Three: Get as much training and knowledge as you can about advertising. Those are going to be the three things starting out in which you'll need some skills and insights."

As the years rolled by, the relationship between Veeck and his promising pupil flowered. As he rose in sports management from business manager of the Marlins to general manager of the Spartanburg Phillies, business manager of the 76ers and GM of three NBA teams, Williams constantly bounced ideas off the still-imaginative old master.

Those memories came rushing back one day in 1987 when Veeck's son, Mike, called Williams about the possibility of a marketing position with the fledgling Magic franchise. Nothing worked out, but then the Magic already had one Veeck on board — one named Williams.

Pat was heartened by the retelling of my own last encounter with his hero at the '85 World Series, where Veeck was assigned a seat next to me in the auxiliary press box in St. Louis. He had accepted an invitation to serve as a guest columnist during that Series for *USA TODAY,* but, like Williams now, was a fervent holdout to the computer age. The "real" sportswriters were lugging lap-top word processors, but Veeck showed up with an old Olympia portable typewriter in a tattered case and tapped out his reports in hunt-and-peck style.

The typical, contemporary forest of computer terminals can be found in all Orlando Magic offices — save one. When the club moved into its gleaming suite in the new Orlando Arena and was outfitted with a computer system, Pat suspiciously asked where his terminal would go. He is a stickler for keeping his desk top bare. When told the terminal could be situated on the credenza behind his desk, Williams fended off the electronic threat by announcing: "Nah, I don't want all that clutter up there. I'll just try to get along without one. I just figured out how to work my Viewmaster."

Instead, Pat leans on his trusty assistant, Marlin Ferrell, to store information in conventional files. He communicates with other members of the staff not by electronic messaging but via scribbled notes on memo pads, backs of envelopes and newspaper margins. When they were both with the Sixers, Pat routinely jotted down agreed-upon terms of players' contracts on the back of a coffeeshop placemat and handed it to finance officer Danny Durso to convert into a formal contract.

After rejoining Williams in Orlando, Durso knew nothing had changed when Pat walked into his offices and handed him a jagged scrap of paper bearing the basic contract terms of new assistant coach Bobby Weiss.

But where Williams most resembles his one-legged guru is in the area of dogmatic persuasion and unabashed publicity-hounding. The former proved invaluable in selling Orlando on pro basketball and the NBA owners on Central Florida. Orlando chamber exec Jacob Stuart, himself an accomplished arm-twister, watched in awe as

Williams worked the vital October, 1986, NBA owners meeting when this round of expansion was first considered.

Stuart: "Pat personalized basketball in this community. He became the focus of the effort and became like a political candidate. I've never worked with a more charismatic or energetic candidate. He came in and took the town by storm and never looked back.

"Part of his gift is that he's a consummate actor. You have to determine when he's on stage and when he's not. When we flew home from Phoenix, he mumbled something about being cold during our layover in Houston and went off to put on an extra shirt. I didn't think anything more about it until after we were greeted in Orlando by a battery of TV cameras. He whipped off his shirt to reveal the 'warming' T-shirt, emblazoned with a Magic slogan, that he had pulled on in Houston. I shook my head and marveled at the apparent spontaneity of it all. When the children around the world were learning table manners, Pat Williams was learning photo opportunities."

Just before the deadline for this book, Williams converted one of those photo opportunities in a Veeckian coup that tweaked the vulnerable noses of his Miami detractors while also turning up his pet rivalry with the Heat two more notches. Under the playful premise that he was in jeopardy as Public Enemy No. 1 in Miami when attending a Summer League rookie game between the Magic and the Heat, Williams entered the Miami gym wearing a zany disguise of orange-horned cap, fake glasses with Groucho eyebrows and rubber duck nose. Print and TV photographers swarmed around him throughout the game and the next morning's *Miami Herald* sneered at the stunt, but nevertheless carried a quarter-page photo of the "incognito" Magic general manager.

The Prince of Overkill, Pat's only problem is recognizing too much of a good thing. I had to talk him out of wearing an elaborate werewolf mask to the games the next night.

This foreword has been Larry Guest talking, from the outside looking in, but from here on is written in Pat Williams' first-person narrative as he takes you behind the closed doors of the adventure. There's history here, maybe even some sociology and divine inspiration. But the real intent is simply to provide a fun read. Enjoy.

HE AIN'T HEAVY, HE'S MY BUBBA

July 21, 1989. A few minutes after 9 a.m. Twenty players running routine drills, their sneakers squeaking on the gym floor to the whistle commands of three coaches. On the surface, it was only a basketball practice there on the University of Central Florida campus.

It was much, much more. These were Orlando Magic players and these were Orlando Magic coaches. At long last, this was reality, the fruition of years of efforts by hundreds who believed Orlando was fertile for a big league sports franchise.

As I watched from my perch in the pull-out bleachers, a sense of arrival swept over me. The talking, the begging, the planning, the hypothetical at last was giving way to basketball in the flesh. There was Jerry Reynolds, the four-year vet plucked from the Seattle Supersonics, firing over the hands of game old pro Otis Birdsong. Mark Acres, the former Celtic, jostled for rebound position against seven-footer Wallace Bryant. They were all sweating in practice uniforms with the block lettering, "MAGIC BASKETBALL." In just a couple of months, some would be wearing fancier, pin-striped Magic uniforms in the dazzling, new Orlando Arena.

Nick Anderson, our No. 1 draft pick, sat to my left, two rows down. David Steele, our radio play-by-play man was to my right, intently studying players he would be describing on a statewide network. This was heavy stuff to me. Long-awaited. You can only sell tickets for so long. You can only watch construction crews pound pilings into the ground so long. You can only speak to so many Kiwanis clubs before the real basketball had to start.

At last, the dream was springing to life nearly four years after it had begun . . .

For me, the Philadelphia summer of 1985 was long and hot. My 11th season as general manager of the Philadelphia 76ers had been cut short in the playoffs by the Boston Celtics. It was the fourth year after the franchise had been bought by Harold Katz, the ultimate hands-on owner, and I felt restless and uneasy. I wanted to do something different.

Katz basically is a good person. Very involved. He would love to be a player, the general manager, the coach, the business manager, the promotions director, the trainer and the team doctor. A street kid from South Philly, he made millions in the weight-loss business. Short, curly hair, banty-rooster type, tough outer fiber, basketball fanatic. Prides himself on knowing every player, every move, every development.

On the last Sunday in August I called an old friend, Norm Sonju, general manager of the Dallas Mavericks. My family was away for the

Harold Katz, the ultimate hands-on owner, loved to be involved in absolutely every phase of the 76ers' organization.

Norm Sonju, one of my closest friends and the best executive in pro sports. The first time we talked about an NBA team in Florida, Orlando never came up.

weekend and I was alone on the phone in the living room near the front door of our rambling, eight-bedroom, 200-year-old farmhouse in the Philadelphia suburb of Moorestown, New Jersey.

Norm, best man at our wedding, lived through expansion with the Mavericks. He went to Dallas on his own in '79 with little more than a dream. He forced the lords of the NBA to react. And he dragged football-crazy Dallas kicking and screaming into big league hoops. I called to talk about what he'd gone through. I was thinking about trying it.

"You've got to go where it's untapped, where it hasn't happened before," he said. Florida? We kicked around the names of a few potential owners and locations. He listed some things to avoid. We honed in on Tampa. Orlando never came up.

That phone call revved my engines. The next weekend I was part of a sports show at the Expo Centre in downtown Orlando. The show's basketball contingent included Celtics Coach K.C. Jones and Adrian Dantley, then playing for the Utah Jazz. Willie Stargell, Archie Griffin and Larry Csonka also were there.

Earlier I called an old friend, John Tolson, associate pastor of the First Presbyterian Church of Orlando, whom I'd met in 1982 on a trip to China. He invited me to share some experiences with his Sunday School class and attend church.

On that fateful first Sunday in September, 1985, I was picked up at my motel by Tolson, spoke at Sunday School, then strolled into the

Jimmy Hewitt and I revisit the place it all began in September of '85 — that pew at First Presbyterian Church.

sanctuary for the morning service. John found a spot for me on a front pew next to a friendly man with a warm smile. Motioning toward the man, John said, "Pat, you remember Jimmy Hewitt."

Ever wonder how Sears met Roebuck? Did a chance encounter bring together Rodgers and Hammerstein? Would Oregon be nothing but beavers and evergreens if destiny hadn't joined Lewis and Clark?

I doubt it. And perhaps it would be too far-fetched to suggest the existence of the Orlando Magic hinged on a chance seat next to Jimmy Hewitt. Who knows? — maybe Jimmy and I would have bumped heads leaning over the water fountain after the service. Besides, there would be too many other hairpin turns during the next three years on Orlando's thrill-ride into the NBA to know if that pew seat were the make-or-break, coincidental fulcrum for it all. But it certainly was the launching pad.

A year earlier Tolson had invited me to speak in San Antonio. Jimmy Hewitt was with him. The three of us ate together and Jimmy took me to the airport. Moving toward that church seat a year later I had to think a minute, but, yes, I did remember him. I remembered how he talked a mile a minute and had just sold his string of day-care centers.

We were in the car no more than 30 minutes at San Antonio and I knew the man's life history. An accounting and finance major at Flor-

ida State University, he went to work as an accountant for Martin
Marietta, the huge defense contractor in Orlando. Then he was an account executive with Merrill Lynch. In 1970 he started the eight day-
care centers he sold at a handsome profit just about the time he and
his brother, Robert Hewitt, began forming limited partnership investments. The Hewitts created 30 of them, ranging up to $8 million, in
apartment complexes, warehouses and land holdings.

Jimmy is totally transparent. No hidden agenda. An almost pixielike
air swirls around him. A graying man with a hawkish nose, Jimmy's the
kind of guy who would call Henry VIII "Hank" if he met him. Everybody else he calls "Bubba." Probably even his wife, I figured. (Thankfully I was wrong.) Unique. Compelling. You couldn't help but like him.
His passions were his family, his faith, his Seminole football and his
golf.

So when we were reunited a year later, he acted like I'd known him
100 years. That's Jimmy. I was told he was a big hitter, but he seemed
too nice a guy to be a big hitter. I was used to big hitters as grim,
aloof, Darth Vader types. Jimmy exudes a happy, innocent glow. Could
there really be a Bambi with bucks?

After the final session of the sports show that afternoon, John Tolson
and Jimmy Hewitt offered another airport ride. Orlando seemed a nice,
growing little community but there was no real skyline in 1985. No Du
Pont Plaza, no SunBank Center. Orlando was not part of my simmer-
ing notion of a Florida NBA franchise. As we settled into Jimmy's car I
asked if pro basketball would fly in Florida. They thought for a moment and agreed it would.

"Yeah, but where would you put the franchise?," I asked, "Tampa or
Miami?" They stiffened and gasped as if I'd just spilled a pitcher of
Kool-Aid down their skivvies. Jimmy, behind the wheel, and John, in
the back seat, caught one another's eyes in the rear-view mirror. They
blinked in disbelief. "Neither place. Here. The future of Florida is
here," they blurted, almost in unison.

"You really believe that?" I challenged.

"Without question, Bubba," said Bubba.

I mentioned the expansion talk around the NBA and suggested that
if they thought Orlando would be receptive, they'd better get working
on it. No cities had come forward, though there had been some casual
noise from the mayor of St. Louis, some quiet talk out of Minneapolis,
and rumors of others. I advised Jimmy to contact NBA Commissioner

David Stern.

"Bubba, I'll check that out and let you know," he said. That was the end of the conversation. I flew back to Philadelphia to prepare for the '85-'86 season, frankly not expecting to hear from him again.

But in a few weeks I began getting briefings from Jimmy — long, upbeat phone conversations. He'd met with Orlando Mayor Bill Frederick and with Tom Dorman, Orange County Commission chairman. They suggested the planned Orlando Arena might be fast-tracked, though a city-county financial agreement would be difficult. He met with *Orlando Sentinel* publisher Tip Lifvendahl to solicit support and ask for help preparing a market report. He retained Orlando sports attorney Robert Fraley as his legal guru. And he began putting together an ownership group. The Orlando thing was starting to build, but I told him to forget it unless the arena got started soon.

"Don't worry, Bubba. It's done. We've got it on track. C'mon down," he said. Had I realized the only track the new arena was riding then was Jimmy's boundless optimism, I'm not sure I would have made the jump.

If I needed a sign, I got it after a December speaking engagement in Orlando. I had a remarkable call from a friend named Bill Gaither, the Babe Ruth of gospel singers. He lives in Indiana and is an Indiana Pacers season ticket holder. Big hoops fan. He said his fantasy was to get into my business — to own and run a pro basketball team, preferably an expansion franchise. He had no idea I was thinking of leaving Philadelphia for Orlando. I said, "Bill, if you could pick any place in the country, where would you put your team?"

Without hesitation he said, "Orlando, Florida."

I was just dumbfounded. I asked why. He said of all the places he and his group traveled around the country, they got the best reception and felt the most electricity in Orlando.

Jimmy Hewitt's first big step was meeting David Stern in New York on January 22, 1986. I called Russ Granik, NBA executive vice president, to help get Jimmy an audience. I told Jimmy the key to whether Stern thought he and Orlando were for real would be if the commissioner recommended he go to Dallas to talk to Norm Sonju. Dallas had been the last NBA expansion franchise and Sonju was chairman of what was then the league's rather inactive expansion committee.

Jimmy, John Tolson and Don Dizney, the United Medical chief executive officer who had been owner of the Orlando Renegades of the United States Football League, walked into NBA headquarters on the 14th floor of Olympic Towers in midtown Manhattan. Jimmy was impressed by the raised NBA logo on the double doors, by the rich, green carpeting in the reception area, and even by the framed memorabilia in David Stern's executive washroom.

"You could go in there and spend a couple of hours reading the stuff on the walls," he reported.

Bubba, I'll take your word for it.

Standing before this powerful sports figure, he said he felt excitement, awe and overwhelming responsibility to Orlando in this opportunity to crack the select company of big league datelines. Stern warned that the league might not expand at all and that Jimmy could spend time and resources for nothing. But *should* the league expand, Stern detailed the basic needs of a franchise — an arena, good management and an ownership group able to come up with, for starters, more than $20 million for the yet-undetermined expansion fee. The last previous franchise transaction, Kansas City-to-Sacramento, had been $18 million. So the commissioner was sure the price for a new club would be "at least" $20 million.

That the figure might increase considerably (which it did) during the next madcap 12 months was not on Jimmy's mind as he sat, intoxicated by a dream, before David Stern. Jimmy's thoughts wandered back to what I said would be the key response and found himself transfixed on Stern's lips, trying to *will* the word "Dallas" from them.

Stern digested the rhetoric and leaned back for a few thoughtful moments. He puffed on his cigar. He said, "Well, we've listened and we feel you do mean business and that you potentially could make it happen. So after hearing what we've said, if you still want to move forward, we recommend you make a trip to Dallas."

Be still my Bubba heart.

"Pardon the pun," Jimmy remembers, "but those were the magic words."

The first of a hundred litmus tests had been passed. Within a week, Jimmy and four principals in his embryonic group were in Dallas to grill Norm Sonju and watch a Mavericks game. But not just any game. Is this destiny or what? They saw Dallas' first-ever victory over the mighty Boston Celtics, sending that alleged football-focused Texas outpost into ecstasy and turning up the flame within Jimmy Hewitt. The travel party included Robert Fraley, another who would play an important role in creating the Magic.

Fraley: "I remember how excited Jimmy Hewitt and the others were about going after a franchise and how exciting that game was. It got everyone pumped on the prospect of big league sports. Most of the group had been involved in the Orlando Renegades and could see this was different, a step above.

"The next morning we met with Sonju. My impression was, one, Norm Sonju knew what he was doing; two, that he ran maybe the best franchise in the NBA, maybe even the best sports franchise I'd ever seen; and three, that he was approachable and open about everything."

Sonju: "I felt an immediate compassion for the whole group. I really liked those guys. But they seemed to be more fans than owner candidates. I got the feeling they were here mainly to collect pennants and autographs."

Throughout that season I heard from Jimmy every couple of weeks. I was intrigued. I was finishing my fifth year under Harold Katz, still feeling somewhat like a fifth wheel and knowing I had more drive and creativity to devote to something. Expansion talk was up a few more decibels.

In February, a couple of Minneapolis businessmen announced an effort to get a team with big Hall of Famer George Mikan as ambassador. Former Sixers player and coach Billy Cunningham and theater promoter Zev Bufman were up and running in Miami. Charlotte joined the chase.

As these stories broke I was being drawn into the expansion movement. I wondered about that little Orlando thing. Did it fit in? The clock was ticking and the other cities were launching. I told Jimmy things were moving rapidly and if Orlando was going to be a factor, something was going to have to trigger it.

He called one night in April. I was in the kitchen at home, pacing back and forth to the limits of the long telephone cord. The gist of the hourlong conversation was this: "Bubba, we have everything you ask — the ownership group and the arena on the way. I've gone as far with it as I can. The next step is that you're going to have to come and make it happen. Or we're not going any farther with it. You come and head it up or we're not going to do it."

My wife, Jill, was ready to take the next plane. She's an adventuresome, warm-weather type. But I was caught in a swirl of activity with the Sixers. We were back in the playoffs against Washington. Moses Malone, our big man, was out with an eye injury. We were scraping by with a patchwork lineup but beat Washington and advanced to the next round against the Milwaukee Bucks.

Eight years earlier, in 1978, we traded for Cleveland's first draft choice in the 1986 draft. That choice turned out to be a pick in the draft lottery in which the seven teams not making the playoffs are drawn randomly for the top college picks. But those teams can trade those picks for live players years in advance.

That's how the Sixers and the Boston Celtics, teams with two of the best records in the league that year, were drawing for the top two picks, players who otherwise would've been helping teams at the bottom of the standings.

I went to New York for the lottery draw at the Grand Hyatt on the same Sunday we were in the seventh and final game of our series with Milwaukee. The draw was at halftime of the game's telecast. The lottery teams were picked in reverse order. The final and No. 1 pick came down to either us or Boston. There was Red Auerbach, the Celtics institution, puffing cigar smoke. The air pollution was so bad I took a deep breath and chipped a tooth. The next pull was ... Boston. Philadelphia had won the lottery and first pick.

I talked to the press for an hour then rushed to a hotel room to see the last 10 seconds of the Milwaukee game. The Sixers were down by one. My mind was racing with everything Jimmy Hewitt had been saying.

Julius Erving, the inimitable "Dr. J," worked the ball down the floor and rose majestically for a 16-footer that could win the game and advance us to the Eastern final against Boston. The ball bounded off the iron. The horn sounded. Was this Orlando's next hairpin turn? Had Dr. J's shot gone in to extend our season, would it have meant backing off on Jimmy Hewitt? *Sorry, Bubba, but I'm just too tied up to get involved right now. Better move on without me.* Is that what would have happened?

I needed to talk to David Stern about expansion. The league was guarding its intentions like a rare recipe. It was known only that a general discussion of expansion was scheduled for the owners' October meeting in Phoenix. My chance to see Stern came at the lottery draw. I captured him just after lunch when we went to the men's room at the same time. Had even my bladder teamed with destiny? On the way out I asked David for a private moment. We stepped to a secluded corner of the hallway.

"David, this thing in Orlando is brewing, as you know, and they're talking to me. Can you tell me anything? Can you give me any advice at all?"

"I really can't," said Stern. "I can't predict what's going to happen. But if you're willing to take a chance, a warm-weather site isn't the worst thing in the world. There's a major risk, but if you don't mind taking a chance and you don't want to stay in Philadelphia, well, what have you got to lose?"

He didn't encourage or discourage. But he was saying that if I gambled on a city like Orlando, a good place to live, it might not be all that bad. I needed that. I virtually had made up my mind to hold my nose and take the plunge. But winning that lottery made it tough. Drafting high is fun and exciting and I wanted to stick around another month to let that be my curtain call to 12 years as GM of the Sixers.

But I should have gone right then. We traded both Malone and the No. 1 draft pick. Malone's departure to Washington was greeted by howls from the Philly media and fans. The No. 1 pick went to Cleveland, which used it to grab North Carolina's Brad Daugherty who quickly developed into an all-star. The kid we got in exchange from Cleveland, Roy Hinson, didn't pan out in Philly. Everything went wrong.

The week after the lottery draw, Jill and I slipped off to Orlando to talk with Jimmy Hewitt. Jimmy and I met for three or four hours while Jill went on a tour of neighborhoods with Rosemary Hewitt, Jimmy's wife. Jill's introduction to Orlando was memorable: Rosemary's car got stuck in the sand at some new housing development and had to be towed.

More important was a one-hour meeting Jimmy set up with Tip Lifvendahl, president and publisher of *The Orlando Sentinel*. His views on Central Florida were invaluable. I had a thousand questions. I sensed he was a man's man. He had a real presence about him, a vibrancy and enthusiasm for life. He was a sports buff and incurable Chicago Cubs fan. He moved from Chicago some years earlier, elevated by Tribune Company, which owns the *Chicago Tribune,* the Cubs and media hold-

From the very first time I met the Sentinel's Tip Lifvendahl it was obvious he'd play a big role in bringing the NBA to Orlando.

ings around the country, including the *Sentinel.*

I felt nervous walking right into a newspaper office on what was something of a clandestine mission. That ain't typical. I'd told Katz I wanted to investigate Orlando and he understood. Otherwise, this was supposed to be strictly Deep Throat stuff. Tip put me at ease. We sat on couches in his office and I fired off all the hard questions. Would the community respond? Is the time ripe? How did you like moving here from Chicago? Do you feel like it's your home? What support could the paper give? I left feeling this guy was going to be a key player if the project were going to work. That instinct proved correct with oak leaf clusters.

Jimmy and I then met in the employee cafeteria with Larry Guest, lead sports columnist for the *Sentinel.* Guest was privvy to Jimmy's approaches to me and agreed to sit on the story as long as he could. But word was leaking in Philadelphia that I was in Orlando. Larry broke the story in the next morning's *Sentinel* that I was close to becoming the point man in pursuit of an Orlando NBA franchise. It was a speculative story, but as Jill and I flew home that night we knew what we'd do. We liked Orlando and felt good about Bubba.

A major part of this adventure was to pick up six children, sell that wonderful house in Moorestown and move to Orlando not knowing if the October owners meeting would launch a great new adventure or turn into a dead end.

I stayed in Philly through the June 17 draft, on the eve of which we traded the No. 1 pick for Hinson. The deal was my last act with the Sixers and came after a pie-in-the-sky comment to the Cleveland general manager. Taking a wild shot, I told the guy, "Kick in $1 million and you've got a deal." Katz didn't know about it. The Cleveland guy said the money was a bit steep. He'd have to call back. He did and said he'd go $800,000. I was stunned he'd even go that high. When I told Harold he said, "Why didn't you get a million?"

I had agreed to introduce Dr. J at a charity event the day after the draft. I was itching to launch the Orlando adventure, what with Miami announcing it already had sold 3,000 season tickets. I told Jimmy that every day was crucial and that I'd fly all night to get there if he were ready to hold a press conference the morning of the 19th. "Bubba," he said, "strap on your helmet."

I introduced Dr. J on the night of the 18th, rushed to the airport and flew Philly-to-Houston-to-Orlando, a trumped-up connection that got me there at 7 a.m., three hours before the press conference. Up all night, I jogged that morning around Lake Adair near Jimmy's home in College Park and was ready.

"We've got good news and bad news," I said from an Expo Centre podium. "We're in the chase, but we're way behind."

We were fourth in. Minneapolis, Miami and Charlotte were up. Toronto, Orange County, Calif., and St. Petersburg came later. And at that point we expected the league to add just one expansion team, maybe two at the most.

Jill went to a mall near Philly the day before and had a T-shirt lettered on the front: "ORLANDO: ON THE WAY TO THE NBA." On the back: "TOGETHER WE CAN DO IT." I wore the prophetic shirt beneath my suit and at the right moment during the press conference peeled off my coat, tie and dress shirt.

With no major league sports track record, the only way Orlando was going to make it was season tickets, commitments up front. We announced we would take $100-per-year season ticket deposits for up to three years. We had to demonstrate something to the NBA. At the end of the press conference, Tip Lifvendahl walked up to Jimmy with a big smile and stuck out his hand. "Put us down for 100 tickets," he said, "and a sky box."

We also said that day that Jimmy had rented post office box No. 76. He thought box 76 would be appropriate because of my coming from the 76ers. I'd just as soon have avoided any connection with the Sixers. The next morning, Jimmy didn't expect much response on such short turnaround. Still, he thought he'd find more than just *one* item in the box. It was an official notice instructing him to check with a clerk. Curious, he thought. He'd paid in advance. Had he left blank some nebulous item on the application? The clerk disappeared, then returned with more than 400 letters that had overrun P.O. Box 76. Jimmy was flabbergasted.

"If only David Stern could be standing here right now!" he thought.

He took the sack of mail to lunch at Morrison's Cafeteria on East Colonial and dumped it on a table in a corner of the main dining room. He excitedly tore through the responses, openly giggling as passing diners cut a wide berth around this curious person. Most responses went the distance, attaching checks for three-year commitments. One of the first Jimmy opened included a $1,800 check for six tickets for six

That first press conference in Orlando, June 19, 1986, was something worth staying up all night for. No time for a formal dress code.

years. The Bubba Grin began to stretch all the way from the molded gelatin salads to the tray of fried shrimp.

Meanwhile, I had returned to Philadelphia the previous afternoon for a press conference to announce my departure from the Sixers. Harold Katz himself was there at the Airport Quality Inn to share the moment. I poured out mixed emotions from the excitement of venturing into the unknown to the melancholy of ending a major segment of my professional life. Then I parted with a playful zinger.

"I've been trying to think of some gift I could give to Harold to symbolize our five years together," I deadpanned, "but there was no way I could get an ulcer framed."

WILLIAMS VS. NBA BOARD OF GOVERNORS, BEST OF THREE FALLS

At the press conference in Orlando, Channel 6 sportscaster Rod Luck, whom I knew when he worked for a Philadelphia station, noted that Miami also was going after a franchise and asked why I felt the league instead might choose Orlando. Trust me, but in total innocence I listed all the good things I knew about Orlando and added: "We all know the problems Miami has."

That was the opening shot in a Florida rivalry as spirited as Macy's vs. Gimbel's. Six cities would vie for the NBA's attention and four ultimately would be selected, creating waves of comparison and competition among them. But none of them — indeed, few rivalries with decades of league history — would touch the sniping, one-upmanship, civic-mudslinging, territorial skirmishing and downright feuding that marked the Miami Heat-Orlando Magic relationship, even *before* the franchises would meet at the center-jump circle.

Back in Philadelphia the next morning, I answered the phone and Billy Cunningham, my former Sixers coach and now Miami point man, was mad enough to melt several thousand miles of AT&T fiber optics. The headline on his *Miami Herald* that morning was something like, "Orlando Enters Chase, Williams Blasts Miami." I as-

*My former coach with the 76ers,
Billy Cunningham was furious
over what I said about Miami
at our first Orlando press
conference.*

sured Billy my last intention was to have a name-calling contest and
hadn't said anything really controversial. But I hadn't anticipated
how pro basketball would create a Grapefruit Wall between the ri-
val areas.

My first week on the job was bonkers. Season ticket deposits
were flying in and I launched a civic club speaking schedule that
would have left Howard Cosell hoarse. The paid staff consisted of
me and a Kelly Girl. The phone rang constantly and we hardly had
a place to hang a hat. Robert Fraley provided a spare office in his
law suite in the Atlantic Bank Building. For the next 12 months I
used his phones, leaned on one of his employees, Betty Johnson, to
coordinate my speaking engagements and regularly packed up and
moved to another vacant corner in Robert's fast-expanding kingdom. As a new lawyer arrived I'd shift to another empty office. People kept coming into one nice little room and asking for the brooms.

Later I operated from one end of a conference table. I'd be at my
end of the table on the phone while lawyers huddled around the
other end working on Orel Hershiser's next million or Howard
Schnellenberger's new pipe contract.

Robert, one of the nation's top sports lawyers, detests being
called an agent. His impressive portfolio includes Hershiser, a herd
of top running backs and, at various times, a quarter of the NFL's
head coaches. From Winchester, Tennesee, he played quarterback
at Alabama, mostly backing up Richard Todd and Jeff Rutledge,

but started a half-dozen games. He got a law degree from Alabama and a masters in tax law from Florida.

After working in firms in Nashville and Lakeland, Florida, he started his own business in Orlando in 1982. Robert is a gracious spirit and has a great reputation in his field. But with his unbelievable client list and travel schedule, he's often a vapor. He handled most of our franchise, sponsorship and personnel contracts.

My first priority was to do anything to impress NBA owners who would meet in October, just four months away. That meant obtaining a towering stack of season ticket reservations, fast-breaking the arena construction and whipping Central Florida into a four-alarm basketball fury. We needed a nickname. We couldn't be just Orlando Professional Basketball, Ltd. People would sooner cheer for Smith Barney. Tip Lifvendahl put me in touch with two of his *Sentinel* marketing people, Bert Lacey and Hartwell Conklin, who had run a name contest with the Renegades. Within days the *Sentinel* launched a contest and — presto! — our nickname committee was buried alive under 4,000 suggestions.

The word came. Four words, actually: Heat, Tropics, Juice and Magic as finalists. Heat was eliminated because (no offense, Billy) it wasn't one of our more embraceable assets. Tropics was scratched because it's geographically incorrect for Orlando. And Juice was out because the citrus industry had just been frozen and cankered out.

The Sunday before we were to settle on *the* name, I took my daughter Karyn, then 7, to the Orlando airport. Down for her birthday weekend, she visited Disney and Sea World and swam and went boat riding at the late Bugsy Engelberg's home. By the end of this wonderful weekend she didn't want to go home. As I put her on the plane she said, "Daddy, it's really great down here. This place is magic."

That was all I needed.

This Magic was not black magic, not magician's magic, not rabbit-out-of-a-hat magic. We were sensitive to that. It was the "magic" of Central Florida — the sunshine, the orange juice, the golf, the spring baseball. The good life. The magic life. I called Disney PR executive Diana Morgan to check on any potential conflict with the Magic Kingdom. She ran it around the Disney front offices and called back. "We love it!" she gushed.

The NBA required a $100,000 deposit to make our application of-

ficial. We were to make it July 2, 1986. I was in Philly and would
meet Mayor Frederick, state Sen. George Stuart and Jimmy Hewitt
at David Stern's office. Newspapers and TV would be there so we
planned to make a big show of the formal check presentation. From
Philly I called Jimmy and told him to pick up a Mickey Mouse hat.
For some reason he bought two.

The commissioner fell victim to the fastest promotional hands in
the NBA. As the flashbulbs popped and the TV lights went on I put
a Mickey hat on Stern, but he whipped it right off. So, boom, I put
the second one on him and that's the one the photographers
snapped. He just couldn't get the second one off in time. The picture was nationwide in hours.

The guy on the left, holding the oversized check and wearing
mouse ears, was David Stern, distinguished commissioner of the ex-
alted National Basketball Association. Poor David. He didn't need

*David Stern whipped off Mickey Mouse hat No. 1 (in his left hand)
but wasn't fast enough to get rid of hat No. 2.*

mouse ears at this point, not with other cities popping up every other day. He knew the expansion derby was growing warm. And you could sense from Day One the neutrality of the NBA office. They were trying to be Switzerland and here I was trying to turn them into Barnum & Bailey.

Besides sticking mouse ears on the commissioner, I was flooding league pooh-bahs with regular waves of news clippings and other printed material about Orlando and Central Florida. Norm Sonju began calling my little packages, "Pat's double-hernia mail."

Said Russ Granik: "We try not to be too stuffy but we do try to be business-like. There were periods during expansion when we told Pat if he sent us any more clippings we immediately would disqualify Orlando. He can be relentless. At the same time, everybody could appreciate his enthusiasm and it does get infectious at times. It provided a little humor, although some of the owners started saying they didn't have room for all the stuff Pat was sending out."

Granik also had a leading role in the loops and spins of expansion during the next two years. And he was a vital player in the 11th-hour scramble resulting in Orlando's franchise approval. A Harvard Law School grad, he was learning to be a tax lawyer in a large New York City firm where one of the senior associates was the son of former NBA Commissioner Larry O'Brien.

In 1977 the younger O'Brien tipped Russ that the NBA was look-

Russ Granik warned: Any more clippings from me and Orlando would be disqualified.

ing for an attorney. Granik, just 28, got the job and climbed to the league's No. 2 position when David Stern succeeded O'Brien. Granik was there the day Jimmy Hewitt stepped into the NBA office in January, 1986.

"By that time we were starting to listen to people," Granik recalled. "Until then we'd been turning expansion candidates away, feeling we weren't ready to expand. Pat called and asked if we'd meet with Jimmy. He seemed like a very nice guy, very sincere in wanting to get this thing done. Our first reaction, as with Charlotte, was, how are you going to put an NBA team in a small town? Hewitt seemed serious enough about it and we were going to take him seriously, at least for a while.

"I'm sure it helped to have Pat on board if for no other reason than he has known most of us for a long time and could pick up the phone and deal on a more personal basis than some applicant we didn't know. The key thing for us always was who the principal owner would be. But it certainly didn't hurt to have Pat in there pitching."

In one sense that familiarity hurt. The view by too many in Orlando was that here was a guy who left the mighty Philadelphia 76ers after 12 years. He must have a secret commitment from all the muckety-mucks or he wouldn't have done this. A guy who would make that gamble would fail all his ink blot tests, right? I kept denying I had any sure thing up my sleeve and kept showing them my ink blot tests. Everyone kept chuckling out of the sides of their mouths, winking and saying, "Sure, Pat, sure."

Sure, I had checked with a number of GMs and a couple of owners and some key newspaper guys just to see what they thought. The response was encouraging in a general sort of way, but nothing was promised. I was not holding the trump card so many seemed to think.

Well, maybe Jimmy Hewitt and I *did* have a few and didn't realize it. Our trumps were not chits in high league places but the unusual talents and selfless dedication of a batch of Central Floridians. Three near the top were Stewart Crane, a minority investor with an accounting background; Jacob Stuart, executive vice president of the Greater Orlando Chamber of Commerce; and a cuddly bundle of creativity named Doug Minear.

Stew Crane was one of Jimmy Hewitt's original investors who

*Jacob Stuart. The effort
really got moving when
he called out of the blue
and said, 'I want to
help you. You can't do
this alone.' The late
civic leader Jim Greene
told me, 'Jacob could
sell an anvil to a
drowning man.'*

gave his life for 18 months starting in June, 1986, as the numbers guy. An accountant by training, he became our volunteer controller-ticket manager-bookkeeper until we won the franchise and hired a staff. There's no way we could have done this thing without him. Stewart is a laid-back guy from an old-line Central Florida family. He'd show up in a Palm Beach shirt and Gucci loafers and if it were an important meeting he'd have on socks. If it were *really* important, the socks would match.

Jacob Stuart, also from a deeply rooted Central Florida family, called one day out of the blue and told me to meet him at the Radisson Hotel for breakfast the next morning. He said we needed his help, just kind of took me by the hand and advised that we were going to make it happen. Jacob brought in Orlando PR executive Jane Hames who took over marketing our ticket pledges, advised on my speaking schedule, created a political strategy for the arena push and helped plan our presentation to the owners in Phoenix.

Jacob is a firebrand with wide mood swings and a vivid imagination. He is opinionated, dominating, intimidating, clever and has an almost indescribable level of energy to the point of being scary. He took a sabbatical from his chamber duties for nearly two months to devote his high-voltage presence to the Magic infancy.

Says Jacob: "It's just something the chamber did, allowing its top staff executive to take off. That's how important the chamber officials thought it was for Orlando to acquire a big league sports franchise. Dropping everything to help Pat wasn't so much something I personally wanted to do — though I did — but something the chamber officials thought was vital. We had the unanimous approval of the board."

Future Magic communications director Cari Haught, then a member of Jacob's chamber staff, put me on to Doug Minear. Anxious to pick our logo and colors, I challenged Cari that there must be a graphics guy somewhere in town who was a cut above. She sent in Doug and, at first sighting, I figured we had a graphics person and mascot rolled into one. Here was a squat, curly-haired former Florida State wrestler, a zany creative guy with dancing, popping eyeballs. A live Disney cartoon character if I'd ever seen one. First impulse was to run around behind him to see if there was a huge, wind-up key.

Doug said he and a high school buddy back home in Colorado decided to attend college in Florida "because we figured we could meet chicks down here." He enrolled at Florida State in '67 and admits it took two months to discover the school's mascot was not a Gator. In addition to wrestling, he was announcer for the Marching Chiefs, FSU's band. "I was into everything except going to class," he said. "I had a great time."

After graduation Doug settled in Orlando and in just three years became creative director for an advertising agency. Something of a loose cannon in the graphics game, he started his own business, which escalated into a creative-based ad agency, The Advertising Works. Doug Minear may be the sharpest, most creative guy I've ever run into in that business. In all my wanderings through Philly and earlier in Chicago, where I was GM of the Bulls, there was nobody quite like him. He's really good.

He took the lead on our logo, floor design and uniform. He also helped with selection of a mascot design. We keep getting rave reviews on those and it mostly has been Doug Minear. But to avoid taking himself too seriously he keeps an electric hand with wiggling fingers and a windup disco dinosaur on his desk. He cranks them up to instantly become a kid again.

Doug Minear, the most creative guy I've run across anywhere.
Designer of uniforms, floors and logos.

In hundreds of early rap sessions Doug helped me understand the pulse and soul of Central Florida. He arrived in town just in time to experience Disney transforming Orlando from relatively sleepy citrus community to magic city of the '90s (pun intended). And he was savvy enough to distinguish the players from the pretenders.

Doug: "It was neat in the beginning because it was, like, Pat and nobody. We had these philosophical discussions and he had this theory that in every town, no matter how large or small, there are always a few key people. His idea of establishing an organization was to find those people and get them involved."

Norm Sonju told me the logo took more time than anything else in getting his Dallas team going. I remember looking at him kind of funny, but he held fast. He reasoned that the logo is the single identifying mark of a franchise and that you don't stop until you have it perfect. Sure, Norm, sure. Among the monumental tasks we faced, the logo seemed somewhat frivolous. But as we got into it I realized he was absolutely right.

USA Today ran an item announcing to artists and creative types that the Orlando Magic was looking for logo suggestions. Hundreds arrived, some with elements that influenced our eventual design. But they all fell short. After going through 500 proposals by November, 1986, I asked Doug to design a logo. He said, "Pay me and I will." I did. He did.

In 10 days Doug presented the logo and uniform designs that would be unveiled, with only a few minor changes, more than a year later. We'd think we had it then someone would say something to throw us out of whack. One guy walked in the office one day, pondered Doug's trail of shooting stars across the logo and asked if the stars weren't going the wrong way. That put us in a tizzy, though it shouldn't have. Think about it: How can stars be going the wrong way?

Dear Diary: This logo business is so confusing, how do you ever know when you've got the right one?

We were working with my favorite colors, black and yellow. I'm a Wake Forest man, after all. But I had few compatriots. John Christison, gifted manager of the Orlando Arena, turned up his nose at yellow. He said yellow showed up poorest on a basketball court. And there was the conflict with the local University of Central Florida, whose colors are black and gold. The killer was a thumbs-down much later from Bill du Pont after he became majority owner.

Back to the color board. We didn't want red. It seemed every club in the league had red. Doug proposed blue as the dominant color with silver and black trim. Doug didn't like navy blue, so he invented a blue. The result was Magic blue, quicksilver and midnight black. The colors and logo became a hit.

Bill Cosby performed in an Orlando Magic sweatsuit during the arena's opening night, January 31, 1989. After returning to Southern California with the suit, several of his entertainment friends said they *had* to have one of those great-looking suits for themselves. A check arrived from someone on Cosby's staff for five more Magic sweatsuits.

Some logo suggestions. We studied thousands of them before hitting on a final choice above. NBA merchandising types constantly are telling us it's the best in the league.

Opening night with
Bill Cosby at the arena.
Nice looking wardrobe,
huh?

A few weeks later, singer Tony Orlando was photographed performing in one of the suits. Tony Orlando Magic, indeed. Take a bow, Doug, and give Disco Dinosaur a spin.

Season ticket reservations, already brisk, became a torrent with Jacob's telemarketing phonebank cranking. We flew past 4,000 and hit milestones almost weekly. A ticket reservations competition erupted among the expansion candidates. Though beginning late, we broke in front by the end of August with 5,000. Miami had 4,700; Charlotte, 4,000. Minneapolis, which had said it would not get into the ticket pledge business, was advised by David Stern to reconsider.

Curly Neal of Globetrotter fame called one day in September. He had moved to Orlando and wanted to help. Curly bought our 7,000th ticket pledge in honor of the 7,000 games he played with the Globetrotters. *Seven thousand!* Half the existing teams in the NBA didn't have that many! And it got wilder. After a Rotary Club speech in Altamonte Springs I sold 47 tickets on the spot, including two to Billy Cunningham's roommate at North Carolina.

Curly agreed to a three-year promotional contract, adding his wonderful people talents. Curly can light up a room with the best of 'em. By the end of September we were at 8,000, including eight from a local golf pro named Arnold Palmer.

I even sold four tickets in the checkout line at Chamberlin's, the Winter Park health food store. Some guy recognized me and said he had been meaning to get tickets. I quickly fetched a form from my car. He filled it out and wrote a check for $400.

I tracked down Davey Johnson, the Mets manager who lives in Orlando, to buy No. 10,000. NBA star Otis Birdsong, from Winter Haven, became Mr. 12,500. Jacob Stuart created a huge banner with changeable numbers on one side of the chamber building, displaying our daily progress to I-4 motorists. It violated some city code or another, but we got away with it.

In October we trotted out another local hero, Tim Raines, who purchased two tickets, bringing us to 12,334 in honor of his .334 National League batting championship average. We reached for every angle. We passed the other expansion cities and turned to bigger game. We zipped by the LA Lakers in tickets and set a goal of 13,000, which would catch the Celtics.

A huge banner on the chamber building violated some city code but charted our ticket pledge progress.

It seemed every day we'd have another press conference announcing how we'd passed another milestone of season ticket deposits. Jacob Stuart would get a sign painted up and I'd rip it in half.

Dear Diary: They've got to let us in the league now, right? Huh?
Tell us, tell us. Puh-leeeeeze, tell us it's so.

There was a sobering moment amid this frenetic and apparent
success. Sixers Coach Matty Guokas called in late summer just to
talk basketball. It hit me how isolated I was after spending so many
years on the cutting edge. Matty was getting ready for the '86-'87
season and here I was schlepping around Kiwanis clubs trying to
sell tickets to a dream. Now I was on the outside, face pressed
against the glass. To the league I had become an adversary. I felt
marooned.

But it helped that by pure coincidence the annual preseason
league personnel meeting was in Orlando at the Grand Cypress resort. That gave me some salving contact with front-office types and
gave them a taste of the surfacing basketball interest in Central
Florida.

There was an unexpected appetizer on the day they arrived: *Sen-*
tinel headlines announced that arena construction would begin that
coming January. And there was unexpected dessert during a luncheon of league broadcast executives. Russ Granik was at the lec-
tern briefing them on league matters, including expansion possibilities. He ticked off the candidate cities. He mentioned Orlando and
was startled by an eruption of cheers from six busboys in the back
of the room. The audience laughed, Russ laughed.

"That made it seem like everybody in town was wired into the
effort," said Russ. "It showed Pat had done the job of letting everybody in town know what was happening." He playfully accused me
of planting the busboys. I didn't. Scout's honor.

But they were starting to take notice of my new city. Back home,
Jill was working with a moving company. "What's going on down
there?" the mover asked, "I'm moving seven families a month
there." I told that story a few days later at the Rotary Club in
Apopka, which is sort of the Mayberry of Central Florida. An elder-
ly gent harrumphed and said, "Tell those daggone Yankees to stay
up there. We've got enough of 'em here already."

Though everything was upbeat on the surface, the task seemed
enormous. I began to wonder if I was banging my head against
granite. A dinner at Church Street Station with Dr. Wendell Kemp-

ton, a missionary executive, helped. After hearing of my summer adventure, Wendell named my year "The Abraham Experience." He said, "Just like the Biblical character Abraham, you're hung out there just trusting in God, but He knows what He's doing."

Dear Diary: Just call me Anxious Abe.

One of our toughest converts was Rod Luck, the Channel 6 sportscaster and a member of Central Florida's particularly competitive media. A rascal of a character with a checkered background. An absolutely lovable rogue. I knew I'd arrived when Rod, a serious detractor throughout the first three months, jumped aboard. He finally declared himself a believer and became aggressive in reporting Magic developments. Rod Luck built his career around grass-roots stuff. He's there covering grade-school swimming, youth soccer, cheerleading trials. Pro sports are lower on his list.

Luck heard we'd lost some ticket orders and showed up one night at the little house in suburban Maitland we were renting while our permanent residence on Lake Killarney in Winter Park was being expanded to take on the growing Williams clan. It was about nine one night and I was headed out the front door with a big black bag of trash. Rod jumped out with his minicam to get to the bottom of it. I put the trash down and off we went. That's Rod. Just a bizarre, off-the-wall, unpredictable guy. You can't stay mad at him, though everything he does seems to get him in trouble.

The three major Orlando stations were at the pivotal owners meeting in Phoenix doing live reports. They had spent a lot of money to arrange satellite uplinks so their sports guys could trumpet the news live at 6 and 11. For the Channel 6 interview, Rod, Jimmy Hewitt and I stood among some cactus in the brown Arizona moonscape to one side of the Biltmore. One silhouette was swaying and it wasn't me, Jimmy or the cactus. During the daylong meetings, Rod was passing time in the bar. I had to anticipate the questions and tried as best I could to carry the interview, questions and answers. I think we got the basics covered and Rod threw it back to the studio, somewhat confused and momentarily unable to think of

Channel 6's news slogan as he signed off.

Buddy Pittman, then the lead sports guy at Channel 2 and now a backup to Marc Middleton, was a regular good ol' boy. Wouldn't say an unkind word about the Ayatollah. Or even George Steinbrenner. Through this early period his station was helpful, constantly making their shows available to us.

Channel 9, the ABC affiliate, dominated the Orlando television market. Sports director Pat Clarke had just arrived when our effort began. He's good-looking, glib, self-assured. Mr. Smooth. Very competitive. Clarke's sidekick is Greg Warmoth. Gosh, golly gee. Wet behind the ears. Good little reporter. His Sunday night long sports bit is probably best watched of any in Orlando. They give him 20 minutes. If you want to get the best mileage out of an interview, you want to get it on that program.

I learned in no uncertain terms that massive Don Coble, Magic reporter from the Cocoa-based *Florida Today* newspaper, did not want to be left out. If he wasn't part of a story we heard from him and he really took it hard. I had to keep reminding myself to stay in touch with the media in Cocoa and Lakeland and Daytona Beach and Ocala and the Tampa-St. Pete area because they were important to this whole thing.

Then there's the all-powerful voice of the market, *The Orlando Sentinel*, which I came to appreciate as a national-class newspaper, not just in sports but throughout. A tough, fair, investigative-type paper that at the same time supports the emerging city it serves. Early on, I thought Barry Cooper, the sports writer assigned to the Magic beat, might have been a little over his head covering an NBA team. But as time went on I think the guy grew with it. He turned out to be a far better writer than I first imagined. A good researcher. Listens well. Not afraid now to ask the tough question. He'll track down leads. Barry has landed most of the Magic's major scoops — getting the Orlando All-Star Classic, the rise of Bill du Pont to general partner and the naming of Matty Guokas as head coach. I'm impressed with what Barry has become.

Any examination of the Central Florida sports media, however, begins and ends with Larry Guest, the *Sentinel* sports columnist. He has the gift of addressing most any sport, but his passions have been golf, baseball and college football. At least until the Magic came to town. Admittedly basketball has never been his game, though he's acquiring a taste for it, even at the risk of his health. In the spring of '89 Larry was in the hospital reportedly for a brief attack of diverticulitis. But I accused him of having an adverse reaction after writing two basketball columns in a row.

When I arrived in Orlando a radio sportscaster, Chris Russo, told me Larry would be a key to our success "because he sets the tone for sports in this town." That was true. I discovered no writer in the country hungers more or digs deeper than the Round Man. Equally so, few sports writers in the country can put words together as effectively. In my 27-year pro sports career, I've met the brightest and best and Larry is right up there on my list as one of the best in the country.

Larry, who did most of the writing of this book, agreed to run those previous paragraphs verbatim. If he has changed a word, I'm bending his seven-iron.

In August, two months ahead of the Phoenix expansion talks, I planned a crucial owner-by-owner tour of the country to stump for Orlando. After I started calling for appointments, word filtered back to the NBA office, setting off an epidemic of seizures. The league countered with a telex urging owners not to participate in the Pat Williams Magical & Mystical Whistle-Stop Tour. I'd lined up 20 of the 23 owners. Now some were canceling. But 10 of them, bless 'em, hung in there — Philadelphia, New York, New Jersey, San Antonio, Houston, Chicago, Milwaukee, Golden State, Utah and Denver. Under the circumstances I was pleased.

I didn't even have to leave town for the first meeting. Sidney Shlenker, the straight-shooting Denver owner (who's since sold the team), was vacationing in Orlando and agreed to lunch at Hemingway's. This was an encouraging, landmark meeting. He liked three cities, Minneapolis, Orlando and Miami, and was the first actually to say "I believe expansion is going to happen."

I was off to see my former boss Harold Katz at his palatial home in Huntington Valley, Pennsylvania, a posh Philly suburb. From various podiums I have alleged that in Harold's neighborhood the IRS is a terrorist organization and the Salvation Army band has a string section. Harold's bird-feeder, I have been known to claim, has a salad bar. None of that is true, of course.

The truth is even more impressive: Behind Harold's stone security wall and stately white columns are such amenities as a $3 million gym. He's got a full-length basketball court, an Olympic swimming pool with the 76ers logo on the bottom, and tennis and squash courts. A houseboy let me in and I waited in a parlor. Harold was friendly and helpful. He'd said in June when I left the Sixers he'd be supportive if I did things properly. He liked the idea of Orlando.

I drove to New York to meet Nets owner David Gerstein in the Oak Room at the Plaza Hotel. Somehow we missed connections. He insisted he was there, but I paced the Oak Room for 90 minutes before giving up. Next day Jack Krumpe, president of Madison Square Garden and the Knicks, said the owners would be foolish to repel the Orlando groundswell. He seemed excited about Orlando.

I landed in Chicago the day baseball GM Ken "Hawk" Harrelson was fired by Jerry Reinsdorf who owns the NBA Bulls and American League White Sox. Tom Seaver's uniform hangs on Reinsdorf's office wall just above two seats salvaged from Ebbett's Field, the old Brooklyn shrine. Reinsdorf declared himself an Orlando fan.

In Milwaukee, Herb Kohl was intrigued with Orlando's cable TV potential. And Larry Miller, a big friendly bear who owns a batch of Salt Lake City auto dealerships and the Utah Jazz, praised our marketing efforts. I was pleasantly surprised when he offered to drive me to the airport. I thanked him and took a cab. I just wasn't accustomed to owners being so generous with their time.

I planned to return to Chicago to meet Golden State owner Jim Fitzgerald, who lives in Wisconsin, but got an emergency call that he was sick in Phoenix. He would see me in the hosptial in Arizona. I got lost, found the place and got up to his room. There was Jim in bed with tubes sticking out of him. Talk about a captive audience. He couldn't go anywhere or the tubes would fall out. He seemed glad to have somebody to talk to. I stayed more than two hours. Fitz was open to expansion and thought it was inevitable.

Off to San Antonio to see colorful Angelo Drossos, who spent four informative hours with me. He stressed what he was looking for: radio and TV deals, scoreboard and beverage contracts. Then a short hop to Houston and the Rockets' Charlie Thomas, who said he was open-minded on expansion.

Back home, I dashed to Fort Lauderdale to meet with Alan Aufzien, one of the principal owners of the Nets. It was his partner I'd missed at the Oak Room in New York. We had a friendly meeting in a diner, but my eyes were riveted on his breakfast, two of the most watery, undercooked, poached eggs I'd ever seen. Let us in the league, Allen, and I'll show you how to poach eggs.

Coast-to-coast for audiences with 10 owners was invaluable. In the first place, we were hanging on for any little kernel of good news, rumor or subtle clue. Anything to dupe us into thinking we were making progress. And here I was face-to-face with the very men who would decide our fate. Every word was golden. Every handshake. Every tube attached to poor old Jim Fitzgerald.

Those sessions also proved a great advantage a few weeks later in Phoenix when I would look into the hard, cold faces of 23 czars. Having been with many of them in casual settings greatly disarmed the situation, and I wasn't as intimidated as I might have been.

As Zero Hour for the six expansion groups approached, the NBA staff detected the need to head off a circus. Each expansion group was afraid of getting one-upped and the grapevine was abuzz with rumors of whistles and horns up their sleeves. League lieutenants could tell that the whole thing could get out of hand. We asked about a slide show. Someone else wanted permission for a hospitality suite. *Could we bring a three-piece band? The Spudettes? How would the commissioner feel about roman candles and skyrockets burning "TORONTO" into the ceiling?*

The NBA quickly tired of the whole thing and just said, "stop it." There was a sense of relief. If they were saying no to our slide show, they were saying no to whatever the others had dreamed up to knock the owners' socks off. The league ground rules: 30-minute oral presentations with printed materials bound in standard, three-ring notebooks. No other gimmicks. No bears to wrestle, no Tahitian dancing girls.

Now the competition was to see who could come up with the snazziest notebook. We had a beaut, a slick white binder with ORLANDO BELIEVES IN MAGIC on the cover. Inside were neatly organized market data, a detailed audit of our 14,046 ticket reservations, information on Jimmy Hewitt and his partners, a color rendering of the Orlando Arena, financial projections, and letters of support from dozens of political, civic, media and business entities.

October 18 — Phoenix departure day. Tip Lifvendahl had 60

copies of the Sunday *Sentinel* delivered to my house and Jill and I were up early clipping up-to-the-minute additions to the packets we'd give the owners the next day. One o'clock flight to Phoenix. Local TV covered our departure. On the flight there was tension among the Hewitt brothers, Stewart Crane (his socks matched) and the dummy who turned in his Philadelphia 76ers' keys for a pig in a poke. Lots riding on this. Only our lives and our futures.

We already had one strike on us. We had anticipated having an approved arena lease to impress the NBA owners, but brush fires of opposition to the tentative terms were breaking out on the city council. Sensing the whole proposal might be shot down, John Christison, the new arena manager, decided not to present it for a council vote at that time. Not having the lease in hand was a definite downer hiding there behind our shaky facade of optimism.

Jacob Stuart, who had flown out the previous day, set up an Orlando Magic room at the opulent, ornate Arizona Biltmore to host dinner that evening for the sizable Florida media group. The room turned out to be directly across the hall from where a committee of NBA owners had scheduled a working dinner. Pure coincidence, believe me.

Russ Granik didn't. Granik normally is an even-tempered guy. He showed up for the owners committee dinner, saw us a few feet away, and I know how his mind works. By now there was so much intrigue between competing cities that the league staff was absolutely paranoid. Russ figured we had scouted out where the dinner would be and deliberately booked the adjacent room so we could pick off owners one by one as they came down the hall and slip crates of oranges in their pockets.

The only guy picked off, though, was Jimmy Hewitt. By Granik. Russ turned on Jimmy and tore him apart, just screaming at him. Jimmy had walked up the hall, cheerful as a Dalmatian pup, tail wagging. He brightened at the sight of Granik's familiar face, even if it was arranged in an angry scowl. "Hi, Russ," he said, smiling.

"Don't talk to me right now, Jim Hewitt! You really teed me off!" Granik boomed.

Jimmy blinked in confusion. Bambi had just discovered that curious little trinket on the tree limb was a hornet's nest. "Wh-what in the w-world are you talking about?" he stammered.

"You *know* what I'm talking about!" Granik snapped.

"No, Russ, I don't know what in the world you're talking about," said

An airport farewell from Jill, then off to Arizona to find out our fate at the hands of the NBA owners.

Jimmy, his own temperature rising. "And whatever it is, you're wrong. So I suggest you get it figured out for your own benefit, not for mine."

Now Russ really jumped him, accusing him of everything in the book. Here was poor Jimmy, pinned against a wall with Russ exploding in his face for what seemed like five minutes.

"You purposely planned to eat right across the hall from the owners' meeting," he charged, "and that's ridiculous."

Jimmy explained the coincidence and the real purpose of the room. Russ backed down. But it took Jimmy three days to get over it. Granik looks back sheepishly on the misunderstanding.

"I felt awful about that because I was really giving Jim a hard time," he recalled. "I felt pretty embarrassed. But that's how careful we were trying not to let it get out of hand. We'd required everybody booking a conference room to come through our office. Apparently they weren't aware of that. I thought they'd done it to kind of surreptitiously entertain some of the owners."

The owners were staggered by the full-court press in Phoenix. They knew expansion was on the agenda but weren't prepared for dozens of print reporters and three TV crews from each expansion city. The parking lot was a forest of satellite dishes.

Granik: "You have to remember that when we did the Dallas expansion in '80-'81 we were actively seeking buyers and ended up with one. Most of the owners were still around five years later and suddenly saw people knocking on the door pretty vigorously."

October 19 — Zero Day. Up at 3:30 a.m. to rehearse my presentation, which I essentially had given roughly 599 times to every civic club and group of four or more. If four golfers took too long at the turn I'd suddenly appear and assail them with the wonders of the NBA in Central Florida. Surprisingly, the league granted my request to be the first presentation. I wanted them when they were fresh. At 8:30 we made our way to a little library holding room down the hall for a final run-through. At 9 a.m. sharp the owners were ready for Orlando.

Walking to that room was like walking from death row to the chair. What a tense moment. There were at least a dozen TV crews. Lights, action, heart beating, palms sweaty, knees knocking. Overwhelming. We were convinced the next 30 minutes would determine everything. The Hewitts and Stewart Crane stood to one side as I launched into repetition No. 600. Working without notes, I poured my heart out.

Reason One: Here's what happened with the tickets. Reason Two: Here's the potential for local television revenue. Reason Three: Here's the arena we're about to build. Here are Central Florida's phenomenal growth projections. Here's the corporate commitment. And on and on and on.

I felt as if I were outside my own body, listening in. I was watching for any sign of encouragement from those steely eyes around the room, any emotion that would give me a lift, anybody who seemed to be rooting for us. That's where Norm Sonju helped. Norm, a demonstrative guy, was face-walking me through it.

I kept talking. I felt I was getting through. They seemed to be listening. The ultimate downer would have been if some had been reading the paper or whispering some trade deal. And these guys are capable of anything.

I finished emotionally drained. I had been up early and had not eaten. I just wanted to go lie down. But the procedure was to go to an adjacent room and meet the press. Jacob Stuart was waiting. He grabbed me and screamed: "Stay up! Stay up! Stay high! Don't stop selling! Now sell your case to the national media!" Jacob never does anything quietly. Take No. 601. Cameras rolling ... action!

At least one owner was impressed that I had winged it. On the way to the men's room during a break, the owner told Sonju, "Did you notice that Pat Williams didn't use a single note? Wasn't that incredible?" Little did the guy know he had listened to spiel No. 600.

After the meeting, half the owners left their notebooks behind, under their chairs.

The expansion groups were invited to a poolside party that night. Four more owners praised our presentation — Alan Cohen of the Celtics, Alan "Poached Eggs" Aufzien of the Nets, Herb Simon of the Pacers and Don Carter of Dallas. Each compliment brought more color back to my face.

October 21 — The owners had a 9 a.m. session and the wait began. They had to digest everything from the day before. We sat around for three hours then were told to meet with David Stern at 1 p.m. with the other expansion candidates. The meeting room turned out to be the one where we staged the media dinner two nights earlier that turned Russ into a rumbling Mount St. Granik. The news from the commish could have been anything. From "We've decided not to expand" to a decision to expand by X number of teams to "We've narrowed it to this city and that and the rest of you are history." And then there was the chance they already had decided who would get a franchise. That was unrealistic, but we really didn't know what was about to hatch. You could have poured the anxiety over waffles.

David Stern started by kind of fumbling around, nervous, stammering. It took 3.4 years off my life. My reaction was, bad news. Then he said, "Well, I've got it right here. Why don't I just read it?" He pulled out a prepared release.

Great news! Hear, ye! Hear, ye! The NBA had formed an expansion committee and decided to expand by up to three teams. Minimum one, maximum three. He read the committee: Dick Bloch chairman, Herb Simon, Alan Cohen, Charlie Thomas, Bill Davidson and Norm Sonju. The committee would have six months to scout the aspiring cities and make recommendations to the full board in April in New York.

This 15-minute briefing came before the same announcement was

Great news from Phoenix: The NBA would expand by up to three teams. Bubba and I enjoy the moment in October of '86.

made to the press. That was thoughtful: At least they didn't make us stand in the back of the press conference to hear the news. It all meant that the six cities had done one thing: Convinced the NBA to expand. What an accomplishment! The owners hadn't seriously considered it before.

Nearly three years later, Bob Ryan, the noted basketball writer from Boston, looked back on what transpired during those two days in Phoenix and called it "the most important non-game event in the history of the NBA."

Just before the press session I got into it with Lewis Schaffel, general manager of the Miami Heat. A day earlier he called Orlando a "second-rate city" and questioned the honesty of our ticket count, taking one cheap shot after another. I always considered Lew a good friend — still do. He was a guest at our wedding exactly 14 years ago to that day. I pulled him aside and, to his surprise, went off in his face. I told him everything he was doing was wrong. I just popped him. He was taken aback and tried to deny it.

*While GM of the Nets, the
Heat's Lewis Schaffel told me
he'd choose Orlando as an
expansion site. We traded barbs
long before we started playing
games.*

Couldn't. But lo and behold, he went right out to the press and
apologized. Lewis showed me something by doing that.

Footnote: Remember in Philly when I was calling anybody who
would answer the phone to get a feel for Orlando's chances? I asked
the same question over and over. What city would you choose as an
expansion site? One of the respondents was an old friend, then GM of
the New Jersey Nets. "Orlando," he said without hesitation that day in
June. GM. New Jersey Nets. Lewis Schaffel, who jumped to the Miami
Heat the next month.

Gotcha, Lewis.

After Schaffel's apology I spent an hour in private with Harold Katz.
It was then I began to realize there might be a problem with the size of
our 32-investor group. Neither he nor the league were comfortable
with it. We didn't have that one powerful, financial entity. Still, Katz
was encouraging. He said, "I want to help you. You've gotten to this
point, you did a good job, people are impressed, they like your town.
But you've got to work on this ownership thing."

Norm Sonju also cornered me and mentioned our group. Obviously the owners had begun talking among themselves. When Orlando came up, our Cecil B. deMille ownership roster was troubling. If the roof caved in, the league wanted one person responsible for the bills.

I called Bill Frederick with the NBA's decision. He was enthusiastic and vowed to get moving on the arena. Meanwhile, I'd spent our wedding anniversary in Phoenix while Jill was home in Orlando. But the news was a great present.

Next morning on the flight to Orlando the whole conversation was about ownership structure. I told Jimmy what Katz and Sonju said. It was awkward. I couldn't tell Jimmy Hewitt he wasn't financially big enough for the NBA or that he was the one jeopardizing our chances. Not after he had given so much of himself to get this whole movement going. But we were beginning to realize the difficult reality ahead.

Bands, press and dignitaries greeted us at the Orlando airport. Back at the office, the triumphant moment was tempered by a dark little cloud. Stewart Crane, who had returned from Phoenix the previous day, pulled us aside for a grim bulletin: the Cake Man had disappeared.

Jacob Stuart had thousands of these buttons printed up. I pinned them on anybody who could sit up and take nourishment as we tried to whip Orlando into a furious frenzy before the Phoenix meeting.

GOODBYE CAKE MAN; HELLO EXPANSION COMMITTEE

We went into business with the Cake Man after talking to him in the parking lot at Lake Highland Prep near downtown Orlando. Jimmy Hewitt arranged for me to speak to the school boosters, and the Cake Man was to meet us there. He wore an ascot, which should have been the first clue. Short guy, ruddy complexion, silver gray hair. A smooth orator in his early 50s with a deep, resonant Southern voice. Engaging, self-assured, confident. R.P. Moore was the name on his business card, though it's anybody's guess what's on his birth certificate.

To the Magic's early inner circle he was known as the Cake Man because of his side business of selling cakes by telephone to kids on college campuses. Now he was angling to use the cake phones to sell Orlando Magic season tickets. I liked him right off. Jimmy disliked him right off. Score one for Bubba.

We misnamed him. The Cake Man turned out to be the Ultimate Flimflam Man.

This was the summer of '86. We furiously were pushing ticket pledges. With time so much a factor, telemarketing was a natural shortcut — a telephone sales staff clicking off calls to every man, woman and palmetto bug in Central Florida, selling the wonders of the pro basketball that, hopefully, would be played in Orlando during some not-too-distant winter. We checked out the Cake Man as best we could in the hectic pace of the moment and unleashed him. Sales had slowed near the end of summer and we needed a lift. He offered a deal we couldn't match. For every $100 ticket reservation he produced, the Cake Man and his lady partner would keep $15.

The next sign of a problem (after the ascot) I failed to heed was when the Cake Man began trying to keep $15 from orders he shouldn't have taken credit for. He arranged for me to speak to a Jewish men's group in Altamonte Springs and even drove me there. But after I spoke he was in the back of the room collecting orders from people who might have signed up anyway after my talk. A little red flag went up but I chalked it off to ingenuity.

He overstepped ingenuity the morning of August 22 when 900 down-town business people attended an Orange Juice Forum "Magic Rally" featuring Jerry West and Norm Sonju. Those interested in tickets were asked to fill out a form. Afterward, Jimmy Hewitt was talking with someone when he spotted the Cake Man across the room, scoop-

Two good NBA friends, Norm Sonju (left) and Jerry West at the Orange Juice Forum. This was the day the Cake Man crumbled.

ing up completed order forms and stuffing them into his briefcase.

Jimmy grabbed Stewart Crane. "Stewart! The Cake Man! He's about to go out the door with all of our orders from this morning!" It was instantly obvious to Jimmy and Stewart that the Cake Man was about to slip off with the forms, call the people who had filled them out and score a batch of gimmee $15 commissions for himself. Jimmy lurched around one side of the tables while Stewart flew around the other, determined to head off the Cake Man at the door like a pair of blitzing linebackers trying to meet at the quarterback.

"Waitaminit! Waitaminit!" Crane challenged. "Where you going with those forms?!"

"Oh, I was just picking these up for you fellas," the Cake Man cooed, his tones dripping with innocence. Jimmy and Stewart cut glances at one another as if to say, "Yeah, right."

If you're scoring at home, each gets credit for a half sack. Stewart gets the primary tackle, Jimmy the assist.

Eight weeks later as we bared our souls to the NBA in Phoenix, the Cake Man disappeared with some money from ticket orders and most of the money in his girlfriend-partner's checking account. Sylvia Wellman was the victim of this melodrama. She had taken the Cake Man into her life, given him a piece of her heart and her telephone-cake business — Birthday Cakes, Unlimited — and the scoundrel hit the pavement with everything he could stuff in his ascot.

Back from Phoenix, we worried how bad the damage might be. Stew: "He left with some deposits and some paperwork. To heck with the money. I'd sure like to get that paperwork back." We were happy to give up the $100 deposits just to have the names and addresses of those who trusted that their ticket priorities had been recorded properly.

We discovered the Cake Man had some applicants make checks directly to him. He cashed the checks and ditched the order forms. Some even paid cash, leaving us with a fearsome fantasy. We could see a line of Cake Man victims stretching for miles, fists clenched, angrily demanding tickets. The vision fast focusing was an enormous public relations nightmare that might have scuttled the entire effort.

Thankfully, Stewart's final report from damage control suggested that the Cake Man's heist amounted to only about 100 tickets. We agreed to pay Sylvia Wellman $4,770 for her half of commissions we'd unwittingly paid directly to the Cake Man. She signed a release freeing

We used Kim Kopperud's phone banks (right) for three years after the Cake Man disappeared. Underneath Kim's beautiful face was a bulldog of a manager who continually pushed her dialers to produce more every day as the NBA deadline approached.

us from any liability. We made a police report only to discover several other warrants for his arrest on an assortment of charges.

I flashed back to the first time I encountered the Cake Man. Just after we set up in Robert Fraley's office, one of the radio stations ambushed me with a surprise kickoff celebration in Fraley's law library. Kazoos and streamers and balloons were provided by the radio station and a huge cake was provided by our benevolent friend and civic do-gooder, R.P. Moore himself. There stood the Cake Man, ironically framed by volume after volume on the American legal system. He had weasled his way into the Magic but he had to be nervous. The Cake Man in a law library is like Dom DeLuise in a health food store.

Fortunately, Jacob Stuart already had plugged us into a second tele-marketing operation headed by a woman named Kim Kopperud who divided her time between dialing numbers and the hair-removal business. We didn't miss a day of pounding the phone books. Kim and her callers were so effective that we used them most of the next three years. Had the Cake Man stuck around and played it straight he might now have the most impressive ascot collection in the land.

With the Cake Man fiasco settled, we turned to larger tasks — dealing with the NBA's concern over Jimmy's ownership group and girding for the new expansion committee's inspection tour. Larry Guest's col-

ON THE WAY TO THE N.B.A. WITH ORLANDO MAGIC '88

umn in the *Sentinel* the day after the Phoenix meeting shook us up. Some NBA owners confided to Larry their uneasiness about the size of Jimmy's Magic family. Orlando would be more acceptable, they told him, with that one heavy hitter. Larry framed the piece around a tongue-in-cheek premise that David Stern feared he might have to erect bleachers for the Orlando delegation at some future owners meeting.

It was a funny piece but there wasn't a lot of laughter that day in the SunBank conference room where Jimmy gathered his troops for a briefing on the Phoenix meeting. The mood was good news, great accomplishment, but how do we solve this one problem? At a chamber hobnob that evening, 2,500 people wanted to congratulate us. It was odd. On the surface there was euphoria. But out of sight, the problem bubbled.

Aside from the ownership burr, I felt let down. We'd been in a sprint and now the league was saying six more months. What to do for six months? I'm impatient. I decided the more aspects of a franchise we could complete, or at least get underway, the better we'd look to the NBA. We'd done the ticket bit (we thought) with more than 14,000 deposits. Now we focused on things like the arena, logo, mascot and team colors. At least the weather was great. It was 88 degrees on November

9. I flew back from several days in Philly, where everyone was bundled up, and drove through downtown Orlando as people water-skied on Lake Ivanhoe.

Dear Diary: I've been back to the big-time, but this weather is hard to beat.

On the Friday after Thanksgiving, I called Norm Sonju. He was on the new expansion committee which would meet for the first time the next week in Chicago. Usually a source of encouragement, Norm seemed distant and not particularly hopeful.

"Everything is up in the air," he said.

It was tough to live like this, day-to-day at the mercy of these men in the league office. I flashed back to something Chuck Daly told me. "This sport we're involved in," said the Pistons coach, "is a suffering business." And boy was I suffering.

At Chicago the committee decided to summon each candidate group to New York to meet with David Stern. Our appointment was December 18. Then we'd meet twice with the full expansion committee, once in New York on January 12 and later in Orlando when the committee made its tour.

Hairpin Turn No. 2,451: In a December 8 meeting of the Orlando City Council, councilwoman Pat Schwartz cast the decisive vote in a 3-2 decision to begin arena construction. She said she based her decision on advice from her son-in-law in Houston. Ten days earlier I addressed a dinner in Houston honoring Rockets Coach Bill Fitch. I ran into a guy named Vince Barresi, general manager of a television station, who said his mother-in-law was on the Orlando city council. I told him we desperately needed her help. He called Pat and told her how great pro basketball is and that she should support the effort.

She did.

The life-support system clanked along. If arena construction hadn't started, forget it. The expansion committee would arrive in three months to check our spit shines and military creases and if they didn't see a building sprouting, we were dead.

December 18 — All-time day. Up at 4:45 to jog, then a 6:50 flight to Newark with Jimmy and Bobby Hewitt. We cabbed to the NBA office

Robert Fraley made office space available even if nothing more than the end of a conference room table. I kiddingly tell Robert that he's the type lawyer who can look at any contract and immediately tell you whether it's oral or written.

for the 11 a.m. appointment with David Stern. To bowl over the commissioner with our proficiency I lugged a batch of drawings on early designs for our mascot, logo and uniform. It had to be a funny sight, us traipsing through the streets of New York, in and out of cabs in the ice and snow, carrying all this stuff. It had been 17 days since the expansion committee met in Chicago and we didn't know anything.

Waiting in an outer office, we were tense. We really didn't know what was going to happen, whether we were being eliminated or selected or what. There was some nervous laughter and small talk. We were ushered into David Stern's office, found seats and the commissioner began to talk. There was no mincing around.

"Two cities have been eliminated," he said. A tingle ran from my molars to my toenails. Surely he wouldn't call us all the way to New York to tell us we were out. He could have done that by phone, by Pony Express or by skywriting. Say it ain't so, David.

What he did say was that Toronto and Anaheim were eliminated. From six, we were down to the four — Orlando, Miami, Minneapolis and Charlotte — invited to New York that week, one at a time. Good news. We were in the finals. My molars applauded. My toenails tap danced. That was the great news. Now get a grip on your chair, Bubba, here comes the haymaker. We were told the price of cards had gone up to $32.5 million. Per franchise. All cash. No more five-year payout. A double whammy.

The owners saw the salivating at Phoenix and now $20 million had become $32.5 million. We argued about the new price. David was diplomatic, almost apologetic. Jimmy was sputtering. He'd have to rework the numbers with his investors. Bobby Hewitt became a little testy, asking how they could jump the price this much.

Coming home, the Hewitts were confused. They'd been hit with a bewildering right cross. Here were two Central Florida businessmen who hadn't experienced a lane this fast. The NBA had jacked the price by $12.5 million. The whole thing might be in jeopardy. "What have they done? Why did they do this to us?" Jimmy kept asking on the plane. Bubba was bruised.

"From October of '85 to December of '86," Jimmy said later, "you went from $20 million to $32.5 million and nothing else had really changed. Now I was saying, we've really got to look at this to see if we want to go forward. We called the investor group together the next day at the chamber to rework the numbers and take a hard look at it. The group voted to continue."

One of the investors asked a rhetorical question: If the price had gone from $20 million to $32.5 million, how could the new projections show a similar bottom-line return?

Michael Eisner. What a thrill to hear him say, 'meet me over in France' to talk basketball. I still find it hard to believe he was so enthusiastic about Orlando trying to get into the NBA.

"How could that happen?" he demanded.

Jimmy smiled, shuffled his feet and blurted: "I guess it's just magic."

Dear Diary: It's obvious now that we really need more than magic; we need that big hitter.

I called Russ Granik about our ownership. He said, "We're impressed with the Hewitts, wonderful people, and grateful for what they've done. But you need to think about a new investor in your group, maybe a big corporation. Just be aware that seems to be your most troublesome link."

There also were concerns over other cities. Was Charlotte large enough and could it fight through that area's infatuation with college basketball? Minneapolis had been in the league before but had competition from many other local sports teams. Miami was an enigma to everybody. Because of Orlando's problem, Tip Lifvendahl offered the possibility that Tribune Company might become involved. He always was there with a helping hand, a gentle prod to keep digging. Somewhere was a buried franchise. Tip: "Twenty years from now we'll write the history of Orlando's development and no one will believe it."

A month earlier he suggested wining and dining the NBA owners at the anticipated Penn State-Miami national title game if it had been held in Orlando's Citrus Bowl. After a spirited battle between several post-season datelines the big matchup slipped away to the Fiesta Bowl. Orlando felt jilted and betrayed. Was this an omen? Nah. Just football. I shrugged it off. *That* ball takes weird bounces.

I met Bruce Starling of Harcourt Brace Jovanovich to discuss hooking up with the giant publisher based in Orlando. And Bob Allen, the Disney World vice president, called about the possibility of Disney as a partner. He sent an accountant to look over our books. The notion of serious involvement by Disney soared after an odd, chance meeting with Disney's famed CEO, Michael Eisner, in the early fall prior to the Phoenix meetings. Jill and I were invited to Disney's 15th anniversary celebration and had the time of our lives. Our favorite country and western singer, Crystal Gayle, was there. We bumped into Buell Duncan, the SunBank chairman, who decided I should meet Eisner.

There was a small problem of protocol and logistics. Eisner was making a speech in front of the American pavilion. He was there with Chief Justice Warren Burger, Sen. Ted Kennedy and a cast of thousands. After the speech I swam through the throng, ducked in front of guards and introduced myself to Eisner. It was like getting to the President. He immediately knew who I was, stopped and animatedly said, "I want to talk to you. I'll meet you at 9 o'clock over in France." That's Epcot-ese for "see you at the French pavilion."

Jill and I wandered around for an hour and dutifully staked out a spot on a "Paris" street corner. Sure enough, here came the grand procession. Eisner saw me and came right over. We chattered like long-lost cousins. Turned out he was a rabid basketball fan. His kids went to school with Kareem's and Michael Cooper's children in Southern California. The Magic Johnson "I'm-going-to-Disney" commercials were his wife's idea. He wanted to know what Disney might do to help Orlando get into the league. "I know David Stern well," he said. "How can I help?"

I was uncomfortable because a big dinner for his VIPs was going on. I suggested that it might be a bad time to visit. He said, "Nah, nah, I'd rather be out here talking basketball. I've been entertaining Burger all night. I'd rather be here."

What a high. The guy at the top of the mouse-eared empire was aware of what we were trying to do. I figured we must have been doing

The late Bob Allen. Jimmy Hewitt and I met with him in July of '86 to share our dream with Disney. As we walked out of his office, the media was there waiting for a comment from Bob. One reporter asked Allen if he thought the NBA would go in Orlando. "It can't miss," he boomed. Jimmy and I floated home that day.

something right. I was encouraged.

The meeting touched off a serious study by Eisner and his aides to explore Disney involvement in Magic ownership. After several talks with Jimmy Hewitt, Eisner made a proposal on October 15, 1986: Disney would take 20 percent ownership but put up no money. In effect, the league would be asked to reduce the fee for an Orlando franchise by 20 percent, or $6.5 million. Disney would "pay" for its stake by sharing the Disney name and influence and all that entails. Eisner offered a list of 12 items:

1. A "sport" version of Goofy as a secondary permanent mascot.
2. Disney design for all logos and printed matter.
3. Use of characters for promotion at road games.
4. Transportation and wardrobe for team personnel.
5. Disney design for all uniforms and merchandise.
6. Creation of the team character and its promotional plan.
7. Production of halftime shows for home games.
8. A cheerleader group.
9. Disney as the Magic's advertising agency.
10. Promotion of Disney/Magic ticket packages, complete with ground transportation and promoted on the Disney Channel.
11. Help in producing a radio-TV package.
12. Handling the team's general marketing.

Jimmy passed the proposal to David Stern, who reviewed it with his staff and turned it down. Said Hewitt: "David felt it would be too difficult to sell to the owners particularly since it would mean one price for Orlando and another price for the other candidate cities. I think David was genuinely flattered that Disney was willing to link its name with the NBA. You have to understand that Disney has been wary about getting involved with professional sports because of the potential for drug scandal. This said a lot about the way the NBA had scrubbed up its drug image."

Eisner tracked our progress through the meeting in Phoenix. He called from a pay phone on the way to China the night before our presentation. He called again when he returned. But I never again heard directly from him. He subsequently has been on the cover of *Time* and on a *20/20* segment. In 1988 he earned $40 million in salary and stock options. He's become an absolute star in the business world. *Famous Men Who Have Known Me.* That'll be my autobiography.

Bob Allen, who died of a heart attack in November of 1987, also loved sports and had a great vision of Orlando as a sports town. From the first day he urged us to run with the dream. His loss was significant. I always was comfortable with Bob Allen, a down-to-earth guy, good family man, warm, kind and considerate.

Later I talked with Tom Elrod, Disney's marketing director, about a lesser level of joint promotion. Dealing with Disney is unusual because they are so selective with whom they get involved. People all over the world want a piece of them. Do a show here, join us in this or that project. With us they're supportive, they're interested and they like pro sports. We'd love for them to send visitors to our games through promotional activities. But their aim is to keep visitors there. People who came to see the Magic wouldn't be at Disney having dinner or buying mouse ears.

Disney became an ally, helping with creative support and other expertise, and signing on for a nice block of 43 season tickets. But like the other large, local corporations we pursued, ownership just wasn't in the mix.

As 1986 ended, our heavy hitter was sitting quietly among that bleacher crowd of Jimmy's 32 limited partners.

I met William du Pont III for the first time on January 6, a week before we flew to New York to face the expansion committee. On advice of someone in the league office, Jimmy Hewitt approached du Pont about moving from a limited to a general partner. Hewitt thought the owners might look more kindly upon our application with a man of Bill's financial clout higher in the batting order.

Bill: "Everything was pretty vague. Jimmy asked if I would increase my investment and move my interest into the general partnership instead of a limited, which I was happy to do."

Jimmy: "We wanted to consolidate the group and bring Bill up to 20 percent, same as me and my brother Bob. Bill owned one of the 25 units, or 4 percent. After consolidating, the group was reduced to 25 investors with none owning less than a half unit. We took that restructured plan to the league later that month."

Bill du Pont had not talked to anyone in the NBA. He said he didn't know how they picked him from Hewitt's investors. Let's just say they must have heard the name somewhere. That January day in the boardroom of the Swann and Haddock law office I thought Bill looked like

When the NBA asked for a big hitter, Bill du Pont III came to bat. Having brought the NBA to Orlando, Bill's next goal is to bring major league baseball to Central Florida. His mother is the former tennis great, Margaret Osborne du Pont. Bill played tennis at Davidson College before getting a master's at the University of Kentucky, where he became a big Wildcat booster.

most of the du Ponts I knew in high school. I grew up in Wilmington, Delaware, Du Pont Company headquarters. I went to Tower Hill prep school where there were du Ponts in every grade. My best friend was Ruly Carpenter, whose father owned the Phillies. Ruly's grandmother was a du Pont. Bill looked and acted like Ruly. He was quiet and listened more than he talked, choosing his words carefully.

A smallish man in wire-rim glasses. Very informal. He wore blue jeans and an open-necked sport shirt. That was his typical uniform when punching the clock at Pillar-Bryton Partners, the five-way equal partnership of du Pont, Paul Bryan, Peter Fox, Tom Peters and Richard Steets. Their development company primarily was into downtown Orlando real estate and highrises.

The company name came from the du Pont family crest, which has one pillar. Bryan came up with "Bryton" as a thoroughbred farm pseudonym when he joined Bill in the horse business. Bill's thoroughbred interests, from Kentucky to Australia, galloped under the banner of Pillar Farms. Bryan's steeds carried the colors of Bryton Farms. The ventures they share are Pillar-Bryton. Pillar-Bryton Partners. Pillar-Bryton Sports.

Jimmy laid out the terms. Bill reacted decisively. It wasn't a case of saying, "we'll get back to you in a week." At dinner that night, Jimmy was confident we'd taken the final step to bring the NBA owners to their senses.

January 12 — A harbinger of troubles for Eastern Airlines: Our flight to New York was marooned somewhere. We left two hours late after switching to a noon Delta flight. The group included the Hewitts, Stewart Crane, Bill du Pont and me. Bill and I sat together so I could bring him up to speed. I had two hours to condense the past seven months of mayhem. To show appreciation, he let me eat his baked potato. Bill has a kidding recollection: "I figured Pat and I would get along great if I could get him to eat out of my hand instead of out of my plate." Bill and I are thinking of co-authoring a new book, "How to Make Airline Food at Home."

We took a limo to the Olympic Towers and went to a dingy little diner nearby for a strategy session. Then it was up to the NBA offices at 4:30, a wait until 5, then into David Stern's office — the same office where, just four weeks earlier, that $32.5 million was tattooed on Jimmy's furrowed brow. The expansion committee was working through all four groups that day. We were last. Miami was coming out. We bumped into Zev Bufman, who was cordial. Through 90 minutes of grilling and probing the central theme was, were we still in at $32.5 million?

"Deal the cards," Bubba more or less said.

They wanted to know specifically who would be responsible for losses. We still were trying to sell the large partnership and could see the NBA was laboring with the concept. Jimmy explained how it worked with basically the same group in dozens of previous projects, though none as heavy as a $32.5 million basketball franchise.

I presented a little jar of dirt from the arena construction site and an arena seat provided by Gilbane Construction, the general contractor.

Because of the double Mickey Mouse ears coup six months earlier, I could tell David Stern was gun-shy about what I might do. He playfully mentioned it as I gave him the seat and the jar. Our people had to scramble to find the jar. It came from, of all places, Zev Bufman's office at nearby Carr Auditorium. Thank you, Miami Heat. We could tell the previous three teams had okayed the $32.5 million. The league seemed to like us. We made it four-for-four.

Bill modestly suggested that all he added that day was silence: "This was my first experience in this process and meeting all these people — owners on the expansion committee and members of the NBA staff —

and I was kind of overwhelmed. I tend not to have much to say when I don't know what I'm talking about. I don't just bubble on. I was impressed with David Stern. The NBA staff were all impeccably New York dressed and looked extremely professional. The owners in the room ranged from three-piece suits to sport coats and whatever. The way Pat had us psyched up, us vs. them, well, they all looked like real people to me. I remember passing the Miami group coming out as we were going in and they looked distraught.

"My reaction to the price was, 'Who's to say what the true value is?' If they say the price is $32.5 million, that's the price. I felt we were going to do it and so were the other applicants who were serious. Was the price a deal-killer? Absolutely not."

Back in Orlando I called George Shinn, the Charlotte owner, to compare notes. We often did that. We had good communications with the Charlotte group and, to a lesser degree, with the guys in Minneapolis. Conversation with Miami was limited. The Grapefruit Wall had gone up fast. I talked to Norm Sonju again at length. He said the New York meeting encouraged him, and he thought the addition of Bill du Pont was a solid stroke.

Dear Diary: Bill du Pont did a good job. He's bright. He's a plus. He adds real credibility to our group.

But two new developments were befuddling. One, St. Petersburg formally and belatedly applied to the league, though few onlookers could understand why. Second, Jill and I decided to adopt two Korean boys, though few onlookers could understand why. We already had six children. *"Are these Williamses masochists or something? If only they'd said something, we'd have given them OUR two kids."*

The next week Bill du Pont made a surprise visit to our office, which still was any vacant corner in Robert Fraley's law firm. Bill said he wanted to be involved. He was not going to be an invisible general partner.

Meanwhile, arena lease negotiations with the city slogged along at glacier speed, a danger sign as the expansion committee visit approached. Councilman Jeff Clark thought the city was giving too much. Jeff is a towering former football player and track man with brutal candor you appreciate and rarely find in a politician. In a three-hour meeting I stressed that the Minneapolis owners were building their own arena, meaning a lease was no factor; that Charlotte had a $1-a-year lease; and that Miami had a favorable lease. Sticking out as the one unfavorable lease among the four would be a negative.

We settled at $7,000 a night for 47 dates — 41 league games, two exhibitions and four other events at our discretion. This lease fell somewhere around the low third in the league in economy. Agreement on the 26 skyboxes was the final lease issue. The city, county and Magic each got a box. The other 23 were to be leased by the team with the city getting 25 percent of the revenue.

A lucky break on January 21. Herb Simon, the Indiana Pacers owner and member of the expansion committee, was in town on other business. I took him to the arena where construction was beginning. We also sneaked in a side door at the *Sentinel* where John Blexrud, the paper's marketing director, cranked up an impressive multi-projector slide show on Orlando. Herb seemed impressed. It was a great break to show one of the expansion committeemen around. Had David Stern and Russ Granik known, they'd have had to send for oxygen.

A terrible break on January 27. Jill and I attended *Cats* at Carr Auditorium with the Lifvendahls and the Hewitts. We discovered in shock that Joan Lifvendahl and Rosemary Hewitt had on identical dresses they had bought at the same store in London. Luckily for my high-fashion image, neither Jim nor Tip were wearing the same suit as me. Guess they just weren't around that day in my favorite haberdashery when the blue-light special went on.

We were anxious over the expansion committee's visit and the whole community wanted to help. I told an Omni Hotel luncheon of Orlando public relations people that the committee didn't want a dog-and-pony show. But I wondered offhand what would be wrong if it "just so happened" everybody's store window had a homemade sign or if everywhere we went with the owners, people yelled and waved. I was besieged by PR types who wanted to spearhead this "spontaneous" effort.

We found out the committee already had visited Minneapolis. Now we sat by the phone. On January 30, 1987, at 10:13 a.m., Eastern Standard, it rang. Russ Granik said the confidential visit would be Monday, March 2, from 2-6 p.m. Confidentially, the delegation would include him and three committeemen to be named later. Confidentially. Without a pause, he followed with the ground rules. They wanted to see the arena construction and downtown and have a private meeting with Jimmy Hewitt and Bill du Pont. Oh, and did I say *confidential?* No media, no brass bands, no Blue Angels flyover, no Spudettes.

Hey, Russ, babe, now would I do any of that schlocky stuff? *Me!?*

I called Jimmy and Bill. I called Tip, Mayor Frederick and Gilbane Construction to tell them to get ready. I felt a rush of adrenalin. It was coming to a head. I called Sonju. He told me to stay calm, be myself. I was calm. I was calm. I was calm. Say it 50 times, now. I was calm. Holy cow! Boy, was I calm!

Dear Diary: Why is my heart playing the William Tell Overture on my ear drums if I'm so calm?

We pored over plans for the precious four hours we would have with the committee. We wondered about a helicopter tour of downtown. Granik rejected the idea and again underscored one of the ground rules: No newspapers or TV. He threatened no franchise if media were there. It was my responsibility, he charged. But we had to compromise after the media learned of the visit. The league agreed to a press conference after the committee had gone but insisted on no reporters or camera crews shadowing the group.

Next day, a new idea. If we individually picked up committee members at the airport, the rides into town would give us an extra half-hour of schmoozing before the clock began our official four hours. We ran this one by the league. The league would check and call back. Bill du Pont said he'd pick up Richard Bloch, the Phoenix owner and expansion chairman, if Bloch came.

Bill: "Pat had some sort of almost paranoia about Richard Bloch. To him, Bloch was the hard guy on the committee. After meeting him in New York, I thought this was a guy I related to. I thought he was perfectly justified in asking the tough questions our guys were having trouble answering. He seemed like a nice, normal person to me. He was interested in horses and so there was a common thread there. Unfortunately, he sold the Phoenix Suns right after we were admitted so I never got to know him better."

It became moot, however, because the league ruled against individual welcoming committees, requiring the visitors to get to the Expo Centre on their own. The NBA was paranoid and so were we. We were afraid somebody else might pull some fast one to get an edge.

A Tampa writer called to say the proposed team in St. Pete would be called the Tampa Bay Thunderbolts, a name we had rejected. We didn't need that. We had enough intrigue without worrying about a possible fifth candidate, even though Tampa Bay seemed too little, too late. I was worried because two years earlier league officials targeted Tampa-St. Pete as the most likely Florida NBA city. The longshot that they might revert to their first impression was disconcerting.

Friday the 13th of February. An unlucky day for the air media of Central Florida. The *Sentinel's* Barry Cooper broke the story of Bill du Pont's increased role in the Magic ownership. Pat Clarke of Channel 9 was hot that he didn't get the story. I'd discovered the Orlando sports media to be fiercely competitive. The electronic media felt they had to keep up with the *Sentinel.* Ten days later the *Sentinel* scored again, breaking the story of the expansion committee visit. I frantically called Russ to tell him we hadn't leaked the story and there was nothing we could do about it. Please, Mr. Russ, don't boot us out. We appealed to the press not to trail us during the visit.

March 2 — The Big Visit. I had the same nervous feeling as in Phoenix. I bounded out to start the car and my battery was dead. What a start. The tour would begin on the second floor of the Expo Centre across from the arena site. The room was decorated with streamers and arena renderings and potential logos and uniforms on easels. We had a nice but simple buffet lunch, though the committee hadn't requested it. We anticipated they wouldn't have eaten lunch, so we scored one there. Remember, they had warned that, "Hey, Williams, you do anything that smacks of promotion and you lose the franchise." We gambled that a sandwich bar wouldn't be taps-on-rye for our application.

At 1:45, Bloch, Granik and Alan Cohen of the Celtics were first to arrive. Charlie Thomas, the Houston owner, was late. Jimmy Hewitt went down to the sidewalk to wait for Charlie's cab. We even had thought about how we could make sure the right cab drivers picked up these guys but realized that was out of our control. We were afraid they would get a negative cab driver and we'd be history. But Charlie Thomas' first words to Jimmy Hewitt: "Well, as far as I'm concerned we don't have to meet. This cab driver has already sold me on this

NBA expansion committee visits arena site. A taxi driver sold
Houston's Charlie Thomas (light coat, facing the camera) on Orlando.

place."

It was almost as if we had Jacob Stuart driving the cab. (We didn't.)
The cabbie, Ron Benson, tracked down by *Florida Today* sportswriter
Don Coble, was as effective with homespun candor as Stuart could
have been with color graphs and neon numbers. Unaware he was driving an NBA owner, Benson responded to Thomas' casual inquiries with
enthusiasm for Orlando as a sports-hungry town.

"This town is ready. We want the Magic," Benson declared, unknow-
ingly delivering his message to Very Important Ears.

John Christison and Bill Mack from the city and Bill Hodson from
Gilbane Construction did nice jobs explaining the arena schedule. Just
two months into construction, the only thing showing were two concrete pilings rising from a huge clearing. On an arena site tour after

lunch we encountered 17 construction pickets. How embarrassing. We were selling this great, friendly little city and here were scowling pickets.

As if that weren't bad enough, when we vanned the committee away several protesters jumped in a pickup truck and chased us, angrily shouting and gesturing. With prodding from Jimmy Hewitt to lose the hecklers, the van driver gunned it onto Colonial Drive, cutting across traffic with the pickup truck in pursuit.

Understand this scene: We had turned the expansion committee visit into the Cannonball Express, darting around corners practically on two wheels. We were chancing exposing them to three months in traction to spare exposing them to three minutes of protest placards.

"It got to be embarrassing," Jimmy Hewitt recounted with a chuckle. "We took off into the College Park section on Edgewater Drive and made a quick turn on Alba to lose them. I could see in the side mirror the pickup truck flying on past on Edgewater. Alan Cohen sort of facetiously laughed and said, 'Gosh, we've never seen picketers before in New York or Boston.' That put us at ease."

No media, right? Cameramen were shooting from the top of the Omni Hotel and from behind trucks and trees. At least the local media went halfway along with the program. We drove through town and disappeared through a back door of the *Sentinel.* Fortunately, Pat Clarke didn't witness this suspicious scene or the Orlando Regional Medical Center Emergency Room might have had to go on red alert.

We took the committee to the newspaper for that impressive multimedia extravaganza on Orlando and Central Florida. Granik: "That's the kind of thing, going in, you tend to moan a little and say, 'Oh, no, I gotta see another film.' But it was pretty good and helpful because our people didn't know much about Orlando, other than Disney World. Sitting us down and making us see that made an impression." Afterward, Tip Lifvendahl and Bob Allen deftly answered all the questions. Bob was a down-to-earth soul, with no airs. That came across as he spoke on that vital day at the *Sentinel,* and he was one of the reasons we were obviously swaying the committee.

As the tension faded we took the committee to Church Street Station for a walk-through and then around the corner to SunBank for the financial part of their probe. Bill Frederick popped in for a short presentation. "Just another chamber of commerce spiel," he modestly characterized it later. But it was more. Bill has a gift for that sort of thing. He comes off as polished, learned, gracious. Norm Sonju advised me to show our mayor off as much as possible. "He's an asset," Sonju said, noting that most mayors don't wear as well.

Dear Diary: "Even Dick Bloch seems to be warming up and looking halfway human."

Dick Bloch blurted out: "Mayor, we like your city." Underneath, I suspect he was saying, "Now let me get to your bankers." SunBank executives Buell Duncan and Jack Prevost obliged, then left the committee to huddle alone for an hour with the Hewitts and Bill du Pont. They lightly poked around the concerns with our ownership arrangement, but Jimmy came out of the meeting thinking everything was okay.

We took them to the Herndon Airport near downtown, which would have been nice except that the private plane waiting to whisk them to Miami was at Orlando International Airport, 10 miles away. The day started with my battery dead and ended with the committee at the wrong airport. This might have been a catastrophe except that things had gotten informal enough by then that they laughed it off.

My last words to Russ Granik as they left for South Florida: "You better not let the Miami people pick you guys up. You better take a cab." He laughed and nodded. We felt the NBA guys liked what they saw.

A MANHATTAN SPRINT INTO THE NBA

We learned some things from the expansion committee visit. No. 1, I *had* to stop mailing newspaper clippings to league headquarters and club owners. The league warned: Any more clippings, no franchise for Orlando. No. 2: A problem with the general manager — me — being part of the ownership. No. 3: Disagreement with our financial projections. Looming over all of this, however, was the NBA's apparent discomfort with our ownership arrangement. But they told us nothing directly.

Russ Granik called Jimmy Hewitt and was encouraging but casually wondered aloud if we had plans for Bill du Pont to become even more involved. Uh, no, uh, should he? Oh, that's up to you fellas, Granik said. He wanted more information on radio, TV, cable, the arena construction schedule and number of arena parking spaces to help the committee with its final recommendation March 23, two weeks later.

Still, I felt more and more confident Orlando would be one of their cities. But the feeling hardly was strong enough to order confetti and streamers. Tip Lifvendahl called and was thinking celebration. I loved his optimism, but I was thinking survival. I was thinking where I'd move if we didn't get a team.

There were two weeks until the final expansion committee meeting and we still didn't have an arena lease. No lease, no team. It was like studying for exams. Had we done enough? Had we done the right things? The jury was about to hand the verdict to the bailiff and the pressure seemed to be roughly whatever it is at 60 fathoms without a snorkel. I read in a book by Dr. Richard Strauss that "God already knows the future. It's a finished event for Him." I needed that. It was comforting to be reminded I just needed to relax — to have some peace of mind and realize I couldn't change anything.

Good news. The Korean government ruled against adoptions by families with four or more children. That's us. But they grandfathered in our adoption of the twin boys. Would we be as fortunate with the Magic?

Big news. Larry Guest broke the story of the higher $32.5 million for expansion teams. The league managed to keep the figure quiet for nearly three months, but Larry typically managed somehow to ferret it out. Now it was on the national news wires under an Orlando dateline. I was scared to death the league would read the phrase, "according to a report in *The Orlando Sentinel*" and link it to me. Stewart Crane blew two green eyeshades, fearful the NBA would blame the Magic just one week before the expansion committee meeting. Norm Sonju called, squirming. He felt he would get blamed because of his ties to me.

Sonju: "If I was a little jumpy it was because I didn't want to do anything to cause Orlando to lose the franchise. I didn't want the price to come from me. I really wanted to help Pat because he was like a brother. I was best man in his wedding. But I was torn between two roles — my thoughts about Pat and my role as a member of the expansion committee."

I was back on the phone with Russ Granik, frantic as usual, trying to make sure he understood that we were not the unnamed sources for the story. As I remember, he was understanding.

This close to the Decision Day, everyone seemed to have his own speculation and inside poop. Bob Ryan, respected basketball writer for the *Boston Globe,* wrote a column asserting Orlando as best of the batch. John Nash, who succeeded me as GM in Philly, said Harold Katz thought Miami was fourth and that the league would admit three teams. Roger Stanton did a hatchet job in *Basketball Weekly* on Miami as a league city. Jerry Colangelo, GM in Phoenix and a close friend of Lewis Schaffel, liked the Heat's chances. He told me what I didn't want to hear: "When the league owners sit down, anything can happen. Expect the unpredictable."

Peter Vecsey's speculative piece in the *New York Post* said Orlando, Miami and Minnesota would be admitted. At least the dateline wasn't "Orlando" this time. I couldn't be blamed for this one. These stories had one thing in common: Everyone thought three of the four cities would be named. I liked that. As least our odds had greatly improved from six months earlier when the party line was that the NBA would admit just one of the six candidates.

March 23 — The expansion committee was in final deliberation in New York. What a helpless feeling all day long. They were determining our fate and I was sweating bullets the size of bowling balls. There is a verse of scripture, Proverbs 21:1 — "The king's heart is in the hand of the Lord; as the rivers of water, he turneth it whithersoever he will." That was my thought for the day and I was holding onto it for dear life — that the owners' hearts were in the hand of the Lord and He could turn those hearts any way He wanted. I remember praying, "Lord, turn those guys' hearts our way." The tension was awesome. I went to bed that night knowing the fate of the Magic was resolved but that we wouldn't know it until the next morning.

The first hour in the office lasted only about a week. The next one seemed close to a month. I was sure the Fourth of July and Labor Day had passed before Russ Granik called. It was 11:24 a.m. I checked my watch to record history. Granik said, "We met yesterday and I want you to know" — my heart stopped — "we didn't make a decision. It was too hard. We'll call you April 2 or 3 and that'll be it."

We had a hung jury. Take the prisoners back to the holding cell. Another 10 days of agony. Can Chinese water torture be any worse?

Goldie Blumenstyk helped pass the time. She was the *Sentinel's* tenacious reporter-bulldog on the city hall beat. She seemed totally unsympathetic to all this squandering of public funds on something so frivolous as an arena and professional sports. Goldie wrote a story that the Magic was trying to strong-arm a giveaway lease and Councilman Clark was putting up a noble fight to protect the public coffers from this outrageous attack.

Jeff Clark was quoted throughout the story. I could see his intimidating, dark eyebrows hunched over every indignant comment. We decided to say nothing, not wanting to get into a fight with Jeff. But we were holding our breath that the lease difficulty wouldn't unduly sway the expansion committee at such a crucial point.

Thursday, April 2 — The committee was in final-final deliberation. I previously had agreed to speak to the Portland Trailblazers' end-of-season banquet. What a day to go. I got on a plane from Orlando to Denver not knowing. I had 10 minutes to get to a phone during a changeover in Denver. I called the NBA and Russ hit me with the thunderclap: Charlotte and Minneapolis were approved; Orlando and Miami were on hold until the next NBA Board of Governors meeting six months later. One of them would be selected then.

Granik told me to sit tight until the following Monday. Finally the truth began to emerge from the NBA office. They really didn't like our ownership structure. Months later, Granik explained why he and others in the commissioner's office could not be direct before this.

"David and I were in charge of managing the expansion but we weren't making the final decision. The owners would do that. We did indicate early on to Jim Hewitt there were some problems, although we didn't know how the owners ultimately would look at it. And it wasn't so much that Jim wasn't enough of a heavyweight; it was more that he and Bob Hewitt, out of a sense of loyalty to their usual investors, were tied to the kind of investment arrangement they had used in all their real estate dealings.

"Expansion is the one time our owners can be very picky about how they want a franchise set up. The model always has been not neccessarily how many owners or how deep the pockets are, but that somebody is pretty substantial and — this is the key — *has control.* If not one person, it could be brothers, or two lifelong partners as in the case of the new Minneapolis club. But there is some central control. A real estate-type arrangement has more disparate control. That gets us nervous and got the owners nervous. But we couldn't say much before the 11th hour because we didn't know how the owners would react.

"Jim said early on that he wanted to push ahead with it because he couldn't ask any of the investors to step aside. Our advice was, 'Maybe you could convince the owners and maybe not. We'll just have to go through the process with the committee and see what happens.' "

When the process reached the final hour, the two Florida cities were deadlocked.

Granik: "The committee started out with a mandate of one to three teams. They had pretty much decided to go for three but were split on the third team. Everybody agreed on a team in Florida. I think the Orlando-Miami vote was 2-2 with two guys on the fence. That's why the report came out like it did, taking Minneapolis and Charlotte and throwing Florida to the Board of Governors to decide."

I was stunned. I called Jill. She was double-stunned. I had a horrible flight to Portland. As the plane left Denver's Stapleton Airport I may have been directly overhead as Jimmy Hewitt heard the depressing news. Jimmy, on a Colorado skiing trip with his son to the Aspen area, received an urgent message to call Stewart Crane in Orlando. He stepped across the lobby of the Silver Tree Inn to a pay phone near the entrance to the grill.

"Great. We've gotten the word," Jimmy recalls thinking as he punched in Crane's office number.

As happy skiers clomped by in their boots and as waiters brushed past in and out of the grill, Jimmy got the word, all right. The sad word.

"I was just astounded," he recalled. "I promptly called Russ Granik, right there on the pay phone. Russ was great. He said, 'Well, Jim, so much is going on right now, let me work on it. We just needed to make an announcement and this doesn't mean they won't decide on the rest of it before six months. Just hold tight and I'll call you on Monday.' "

Perhaps Granik was vague because of another call moments earlier. At perhaps the same time I was taking off from Denver and Jimmy was picking up his messages at the ski resort front desk, Bill du Pont was in his Bay Hill villa with a TV set tuned to CNN Headline News. The twice-an-hour sports segment caught his attention and he looked up just in time to take in the grim news on NBA expansion. He promptly dialed Russ Granik.

"Russ, is it okay for you to tell me what the problem is here?" he asked.

"Well ... ," Granik began, followed by what they like to call a pregnant pause, "the problem is with the ownership structure. The hangup is no clear ownership control. The committee isn't comfortable with syndication-type ownership."

"Oh. What's the status of our application as it stands now?"

"As it stands now," said Granik, "you are 100 percent clinically dead."

"Okay," said Bill, putting in a pregnant pause of his own. "If the application were amended to some format where I had absolute control, is that worth me coming up to New York to talk to you about it?"

"I'll get back with you," said Granik, who called back and invited Bill to New York the following Thursday, April 9.

Monday, April 6 — The newspapers were ablaze with speculation in the days after the announcement that the Florida cities were on hold. Our office was swirling. To make matters worse in my life, my family was invited that Sunday to ride on the Sea World blimp, Jill's lifelong dream. But it was too windy and they canceled. Jill broke into tears. Our expansion effort was sinking and she couldn't even get her balloon up. She sobbed. She thought she was a loser. I ponied up all the words of assurance I could muster at a time I could have used a little assurance myself.

At least something was going right: The Orlando City Council finally approved our lease by the landslide margin of 4-3. Jeff Clark, Mabel Butler and Pat Schwartz voted no. Yesses were the mayor, Nap Ford, Glenda Hood and Mary Johnson. Hairpin turn No. 3,571. One vote the other way and the whole thing would have been history. If it wasn't already.

Credit large assists on the lease agreement to the work of attorney Lindsay Builder and John Christison, whom the city had just hired from the Portland arena. Lindsey has just one arm, the result of a water-skiing accident, but gets more done than a lawyer with three arms. Christison's experience in dealing with an NBA team was invaluable. Twenty years in the NBA have taught me that are-

The Orlando City Council declared Aug. 18, 1986 as Orlando Magic Day. Jimmy Hewitt and I happily accepted the proclamation. Looking on are council members Mable Butler and Jeff Clark who eight months later voted against us on the arena lease deal.

na managers typically are explosive and insecure. But John gracefully avoids the adversarial "us vs. them" syndrome and helped promote a cooperative spirit.

On that same Monday the lease was approved, Jimmy Hewitt, back from his ski trip, announced to his office staff he was expecting an important call from Russ Granik. When it came through he was to be notified promptly no matter where he was, no matter what meeting had to be interrupted. He was driving to lunch down Edgewater Drive when his car telephone rang. Jimmy's secretary told him Russ Granik had just called. He veered into the parking lot of The Sub Machine sandwich shop and drove to a quiet spot in the rear facing an old garage and a sprawling, friendly oak tree. He felt an anxiety attack coming on as he punched in the NBA's number.

"I was sitting there not knowing but feeling that everything we had worked on so long and so hard was about to come to a head with this one phone call," Jimmy remembers.

He was prepared for the worst when Russ Granik came on the

line. "He said, 'Jimmy, I just wanted to give you an update. Miami made some changes in their ownership. Ted Arison stepped in and agreed to take 51 percent of the team, and they condensed their group to five or six people. So they're right back in there. We've indicated what we'd like you to do with your group and I'm just wondering if there's more opportunity to do something in that area.'

"I said, 'Russ, we'll do anything we need to do. You tell us what you want and, within our power, we'll do anything. Bubba, the only thing that counts is getting this team for Orlando. Nothing will stand in the way. If it means condensing our group more, it would be tough on some of our partners to ask them to let go, but we'll do it. If we need to get the group down to 10, we'll do it. You just let us know.'

"He said, 'Jim, I really appreciate that you feel that way. I just wanted to know and talk to you first. We'll get back to you.' "

Jimmy Hewitt was perplexed. He was saying he would bow out if that's what they wanted. Just tell us something. Anything. You want Marvin Davis? Donald Trump? They never seemed to tell us anything directly. He began to think of what sleeker consolidation would please the NBA and there was an obvious answer: William du Pont III.

Thursday, April 9 — Bill flew to New York to lunch with Commissioner Stern and Alan Cohen, the Celtics' owner and expansion committeeman. They wouldn't commit outright on reviving Orlando's application under du Pont, but intimated that was the only chance. They invited him to meet with the expansion committee the night before the owners' meeting on April 21.

Bill returned to Orlando and called a meeting of the Hewitts, myself and other principals for the following morning in the Swann and Haddock board room. It's hard to say which of three dozen pivotal meetings or destiny-dripping developments were the most crucial crossroads in Orlando's wild ride into the NBA. But that somber gathering in the conference room of Swann and Haddock the next day certainly ranked in the top three of all major wire-service polls. It had a lock on a New Year's bowl bid.

Friday, April 10 — The Meeting. It was set for 9:30 then pushed to 10:15 to allow Bill and Jimmy to confer beforehand. Stewart

Crane and I walked the two blocks there, joining Bill, Paul Bryan, Jimmy Hewitt and Jimmy Caruso around the oval table. Bob Hewitt was out of town on business.

Bill spoke first. "This is the toughest day of my life," he began. He said the NBA told him he would have to take 13 of the 25 ownership units and be managing general partner. This meant Jimmy Hewitt, patriarch of the effort, was out except as a minority investor. And the NBA mandated no ownership slice for me. Even if we did this, Bill reported, the NBA expected only a 5 percent chance of Orlando being approved at the April 22 owners meeting. If we restructured they would recommend us in June for approval by the board in October.

"Guys, this is what it's going to take even to have a shot at anything," Bill said. "Look, today it's dead. It doesn't make any difference what Pat Williams has done in the community. It doesn't make any difference what all has been accomplished in anything. Today there is no franchise available to us the way things are. But they will reconsider the application under these circumstances."

It was emotional. There was pain and sympathy for Jimmy Hewitt. Here he was being told his deal would fly only if he was not The Man. All these guys were in the loop because of Jimmy. He invited Stewart Crane, invited Paul Bryan, invited Bill du Pont, and went out and hired me. Now on the half-yard line he was being yanked out of the game, banished to the bench. Tough stuff. Hard.

He responded beautifully. He held up and said, simply, "Well, let's do it." He was saying if he had to get out totally to make it happen, then he would get out.

"We have come too far and gotten too close. Whatever has to be done," Jimmy Hewitt said, swallowing hard. There also were lumps in every other throat in the room.

But there was relief that after all these months it was out in the open. Orlando had radically changed my professional life, which was flashing before my eyes. Jimmy Hewitt had plugged me into his dream. Now all of that was to change, presumably forever.

Looking back on that hour, Jimmy modestly says this: "Ownership wasn't the important thing to me at that time. We didn't want to lose the franchise. The hard part was that I had to go back to 15 individuals and tell them they couldn't be a part of it. They were the unsung heroes. They were such great people about it."

Bill du Pont: "Jimmy hit bottom so hard and was so distressed that he was open-minded to anything to get the franchise. He was a real trouper. He had put in a lot of time and effort. I was in an uncomfortable position. I didn't have a dream. I just stumbled into this. It had not mattered to me if it was Jimmy's deal. But he was willing to do anything to help get the team."

I reacted the same way about my ownership share. We were too far along for me to even raise the point, unimportant at that time. If this team didn't happen, we'd tied up a year and were all dead. In a daze, I went home to tell Jill. She was crying.

The Cranes threw their annual spring party that night at the Country Club of Orlando — a night you'd rather not show your face. But I was glad we went. Paul Bryan said Bill already had told Stern the ownership shift had gone smoothly because of how Jimmy responded. Now the owners could act on April 22. Little did David Stern realize he would be called an hour after we met. He probably thought it would take weeks. NBA heads are not used to dealing with cooperative, unselfish partnerships.

An Orlando radio station launched a petition drive and collected 30,000 signatures to ship to David Stern.

They also didn't realize that by creating the perception they were having trouble choosing between Orlando and Miami they unwittingly had intensified the rivalry between the two. The *Sentinel* unleashed a salvo of editorials and *The Miami Herald* countered with a few shots of its own. Chambers of commerce were slinging mud. Miami cab drivers were swapping snide remarks with Orlando cab drivers.

But the shot heard 'round the state came from Frank Kruppenbacher, a big, bombastic trial lawyer who loves his Central Florida and felt duty-bound as president of the Orlando chamber to speak up. "Orlando vs. Miami?" he echoed a reporter's question. "It's the difference between heaven and hell! And Orlando is heaven." The Grapefruit Wall was higher than ever.

Larry Guest's stirring column in the *Sentinel* imploring David Stern to choose Orlando produced 400 letters to the commissioner. A radio station said it was getting 30,000 signatures to be sent to New York. Suddenly, everybody was in the fight — letter writers, the radio stations. Adversity produces true beauty.

Dear Diary: "If this team is born the whole town will have been in the birthing room helping with the delivery."

April 14 is the day Abraham Lincoln was shot and the Titanic started sinking. Not a good day, I figured. But Bill du Pont walked in to assure me I would continue as GM and president. He sensed my concern. My original deal was for about 7 percent of the team. That had become a Richard Bloch issue. He didn't want a GM to have part ownership. Yet he later sold his team to his GM, Jerry Colangelo, and Jerry's investors. My ownership was deleted but I was promised a bonus to make it up.

Bill also confided that he was to go before the expansion committee at 2:30 p.m. on April 21.

We all hoped the NBA finally would make a decision one way or the other. Tell us something. We can live with a "no" but don't make us wait six more months. It's like the Jerry Clower yarn about one of his backwoods Mississippi buddies caught in a tree with a lynx. "Shoot up here amongst us," goes the punchline, "because one of us has *got* to have some relief!"

Two days before Bill's audience with the expansion committee in final-final-final deliberation, I stood in the cramped dining room at home, on the phone with Angelo Drossos of San Antonio. "If du Pont is the No. 1 investor," Angelo ventured, "Orlando is in, no doubt about it." I went to bed feeling we were going to do it.

The next day I spoke to GMs Stan Kasten of Atlanta and Bob Ferry of Washington. They felt the NBA was leaning toward taking all four teams. That was the first time I'd heard that leave anybody's lips.

April 21 — Du Pont Day before the NBA owners. Bill's solo approach was novel. "The previous time I appeared before the expansion committee was that day in January when I was silent and lost, just lending moral support to Jimmy and the others," he recounts. "Now for this second time before these gentlemen I decided to go by myself. Everybody wanted to go. I said, 'No way. You guys stay in Orlando and I'll go do the interview.' I did my homework on all the things I thought important. I visited the arena the day before I left so I could be specific about what was going on. I went over our budget and numbers thoroughly.

"I went to the meeting in the same conference room as in January with a good attitude. I had walked out of the January meeting perplexed. I walked out of this meeting feeling I had made an A-plus. I felt like I had scored 100. But when you're grading on a Bell Curve of just two, because they were intimating Orlando *or* Miami, you don't know if the other guy scored 101. I felt I had put the best possible foot forward for Orlando. But I wasn't about to hang around and make any assumptions."

Granik thought it worked: "They were impressed with Bill," he said. "I'd had more exposure to him than most of the others. That's one reason why I felt it was important for him to come to New York so he and David could sit for a while together."

Bill left the meeting and made the short drive to Yonkers where he and wife, Pam, spent the night with her parents, Ray and Ollie Darmstadt. Bill had dinner that evening with Pam and his in-laws at a suburban Italian restaurant rather than staying in Manhattan to lobby league officials.

"That's not me," he explains. "I didn't think that would break the case. We simply agreed that I would call them before noon the next

Scarlatti, the Italian restaurant in New York City where the big decision was made in a smoke-filled room after dinner in April of '87.

day to check in."

Back in the city, Stern, his aides and the NBA owners also were in an Italian restaurant. They informally convened in a little private dining room in the back of Scarlatti, two blocks from league head-quarters, for what has become a traditional, sounding-board dinner on the eve of their official meeting.

Only Stern and his top aides and just one owner from each team are permitted. Views on the next morning's agenda are aired openly, but no official tallies taken. The first decision after settling in at three circular tables was to choose between the veal and the chick-

NBA attorney Gary Bettman figured out how the league could work Orlando and Miami into the schedule. Orlando always will be grateful for the Bettman Plan.

en main course. Heavier matters could wait until after dinner.

Norm Sonju was outside in the cramped hallway, sitting on one of several discarded tables, feet dangling. In his unique role as the only non-owner on the expansion committee, he was on call for the after-dinner discussion on expansion. Awaiting his audience in the inner sanctum, he bided his time in small talk with a league security officer and with Nancy Hayward, an NBA secretary. Periodically he tucked his feet to accommodate an owner emerging from the dining room to squeeze past on the way to the men's room.

Finally he was summoned as Richard Bloch rose somewhere in the fog of cigar smoke. Bloch announced the expansion committee's surprising recommendation to take in all four teams, including Orlando *and* Miami. A lively discussion followed, a dozen owners anxious to comment. Sonju kept scribbling suggestions and passing them to his boss, Dallas owner Don Carter. "There must have been 300 of those little notes and alignment suggestions shuffled across the tables," Sonju said.

Granik recalled that "As they kicked it around you could feel the growing sentiment to take all four teams. But the biggest problem, as we still were meeting near midnight, was what to do about division alignment. The Atlantic Division, the short-handed division at the time, didn't want suddenly to take two teams and have seven or eight of 41 home games against expansion teams. That was a little scary in terms of competition and home draw. So we adjourned without reaching any conclusion. David told the owners we would work on it. But there was a sense the owners would go for all four if we could figure out realignment.

"I guess what people were saying around the room was that no one could find anything to dislike about Orlando or Miami. If you tried to punch holes in either, you couldn't. Both pretty much had met every requirement anyone could have set for them."

Granik, Stern and league counsel Gary Bettman went to Stern's hotel room, addressed an unrelated league issue, then honed in on the four-team expansion realignment. As they struggled, rumor has it that the very button-down and proper triumvirate removed their jackets and even — brace yourself — loosened their ties! At some golden moment near 3 a.m., Bettman came up with an acceptable alignment.

"I just kept scratching out different combinations on a legal pad," said Bettman. "Eastern Conference teams were concerned about having three expansion teams, so I hit upon the notion of rotating the three Eastern teams, Miami, Charlotte and Orlando, to different conferences and divisions during the first few years, even if it didn't make sense from a traveling standpoint. After that the teams could go into permanent division assignments that would make more sense from a travel standpoint."

Shortly after 9 o'clock that Wednesday morning, a slightly bleary-eyed David Stern unfurled The Bettman Plan and the owners, with little discussion, approved four expansion teams. I doubt we'll ever erect a statue of Gary Bettman in front of the Orlando Arena, but he'll have our eternal gratitude.

At about the same moment, Pam and Bill du Pont teed off at Winged Foot Golf Club, an hour north of the city, where Pam's father was club champion. Also where, three years earlier, Fuzzy Zoeller and Greg Norman went into their towel-waving antics of surrender before Zoeller won his U.S. Open title in an 18-hole play-off. Bill du Pont would need just nine holes before acquiring his newest title: NBA owner.

"At the turn I went to a pay phone and made my call to the NBA

Bill du Pont joined David Stern for the franchise announcement in New York. Bill speaks only when he has something to say.

office, saying I was just checking in," Bill remembered. A staffer told him he needed to be at the Helmsley Palace Hotel, in a suit and tie, in an hour. No further information. None was needed. Bill was confident they weren't summoning him to the city to tell him Manute Bol's shoe size. What he was not confident of was his ability to shower, dress and reach the Helmsley in an hour.

Within minutes, Pam chauffered Bill on a mad dash down the FDR Expressway. At 12:15 she veered onto an off-ramp and smack into midtown Manhattan traffic. They inched along, Bill nervously eyeing his watch, his 12:30 appointment approaching faster than the Helmsley. Would they start the 24-second clock if he wasn't there on time?

"Ladies and gentlemen of the media, we had called you here to announce that Orlando had been voted into the National Basketball Association. However, since there is no Orlando representative here . . . "

With but a minute or so to go, William du Pont III took drastic action. He wished Pam well, bolted from the car and dashed the last few blocks like a halfback, weaving through panhandlers and delivery boys and tourists from Iowa, his Countess Mara flapping in his wake. At precisely 12:30, our Marathon Man screeched to a halt at the revolving door of the Helmsley and took a deep breath to collect

himself. He strolled in with all the cool of a guy who had just come
from a casual manicure rather than the curling birdie putt he had
sunk on the ninth hole way up in Westchester County barely an
hour before.

The only preliminary was for Bill to agree that the Orlando franchise would start in the Central Division, go to the Midwest for a
year, then to the Atlantic as a permanent home. Is that okay?
"That's great," he said with a shrug. At that point the *Saturn* Division would have been just peachy.

Du Pont: "I had mixed emotions. Mixed in the sense I was happy
we had a successful conclusion to the franchise pursuit. And a sort
of a numb, stunned feeling. Never in my wildest imagination did I
have a clue that I would ever be in the basketball business. Boom!
You're in the basketball business."

Bill managed to enter the Helmsley hiding behind a facade of
poise, but the boys back home in Orlando were not so successful at
corralling their bare and pulsing nerve ends.

At 7:45 that morning I called Norm Sonju at the Helmsley. I
couldn't wait. He said Bill du Pont had done well before the committee. He said Miami's new majority owner, Ted Arison, was powerful and had resolved all the committee's reservations about
Miami. He said all four cities would be recommended but that there
had been argument over what years and what divisions.

Neither of us knew then about The Bettman Plan, but what he
was telling me was a gush of water to a thirsty man. Yet, there had
been so much us-or-them with Miami it would have been sweeter to
win an either-or situation. We wanted all of Florida and subcon-
sciously a little of that tugged at me as I learned both Miami and
Orlando probably would be anointed.

I felt uneasy all morning not knowing what was going on in New
York. It would have saved two years on my life had I known we
were approved in the first few minutes of the meeting. I tried to
stay busy in the office as the hours dragged by, but precious little
held my attention more than a few minutes. Finally at 1:15, Jimmy
Hewitt called. He had heard from Paul Bryan, who had heard from
Bill in New York. Bill has a knack for memorable quotes at memorable moments and was fully up to this one.

His first words to Paul were: "The bad news is we get in in '89.
You now know what the good news is."

WE'VE GOT IT. . . NOW WHAT?

Bill du Pont's historic bad-news-good-news bulletin from New York set off a flood of emotion in Orlando. Unabashed Joy swept down Orange Avenue in great waves, lapping at store fronts, startling women and children, and sweeping small cars into lamp posts. The awesome surge turned onto Church Street and crested so high at Cheyenne Saloon it rose to within three feet of one barmaid's hemline.

Bob Snow, ingenius founder of the Church Street Station complex, threw an instant celebration that was wild and noisy. Live TV and radio coverage. Reporters scribbling giddy comments. Bubba, Stew and I pulled on hastily arranged T-shirts that screamed: "WE BELIEVE IN MAGIC!" Men in conservative business suits pounded our backs, whooped like sophomores and exchanged high-fives. It was great to see how much this meant to people.

Behind the bedlam going on at Church Street Station, I was relieved it was over. I felt bad about not starting until '89. Charlotte and Miami would play a year earlier. Miami first? Though mostly a matter of whose arena was farther along, it was a

Whenever the Magic had a reason to celebrate we'd head to Church Street Station. This was special — the NBA had told us we were in.

huge disappointment. Still, there was a great sense of accomplishment. Also a let-down feeling I hadn't anticipated.

When you stretch for a goal and hit it, afterward it's like the old Peggy Lee song, *Is That All There Is?* She goes to the circus and there's a fire in her home. Is that all there is to the circus? Is that all there is to a fire? That's the feeling I had. Is that all there is? I ended this triumphant day by picking up two of the boys at baseball. I called my mother to share the news. Jill and I walked around the block to sift through it all. What now? An enormous task. We decided to get some sleep.

First item on the to-do list was to sort out the new ownership structure and owner-GM relationship that had sprouted in the madcap final two weeks of the expansion chase. The 32-investor syndicate that Jimmy and Bobby Hewitt had put together more than a year earlier had been supplanted by the tidy limited partnership with Bill du Pont in full control of eight minority investors.

Stewart Crane offered to bow out, but Bill, aware of his expertise and role in the adventure, encouraged him to stay. In the revised lineup, under Pillar-Bryton Sports, Bill and colleagues controlled fourteen units. The Hewitts had four units. The remaining seven were split among investment banker Toby Wagner, citrus man Steve Caruso and family, building supply magnate David Hughes and brothers, attorney Buck Bradford, businessmen-brothers Sid and John Cash, investment banker Loomis Leedy Jr. and Stew Crane.

Hewitt's original group had estimated the NBA franchise fee at $20-25 million on a relatively extended payout. Each unit represented an initial investment of $550,000. After the price of poker went to $32.5 million, due within the first year, each unit was $800,000. Among those who agreed to step out to make way for the du Pont restructuring were Robert Fraley, Don Dizney and, gulp, Patrick L. M. Williams, famed brown-bag luncher and general manager. The hollow-eyed Mr. Williams not only now had to deal with his new status outside of the ownership but also with a new boss.

Bill du Pont and I were thrown into an owner-general manager relationship not of our own making. Before leaving Philadelphia I painstakingly had sought to make sure Jimmy Hewitt was a guy in whom I wanted to entrust my future. Now with Bill — boom! — here's your new boss. Bill, here's your new general manager. And neither of us having a choice in the matter. Well, I suppose he did. But it wasn't like he interviewed 10 people and said, "I want this guy Williams."

Bill gets to the bottom line quickly. In a 30-minute meeting we'll cover as many as a dozen complex issues. Similar meetings with other owners have taken eight hours. Bill doesn't have eight hours to talk about 12 things. It's right to the business at hand. But unlike most wealthy men, he listens.

In an early session he told me, "Pat, I'm a reasonable guy. I've got some pretty strong thoughts about the way I do things. But I'm an eminently agreeable person. I know all of this comes as a great shock to you and maybe foiled what had been your expectations. But, believe me, if we can get through the honeymoon we may have a great marriage."

Bill and I hadn't been through any deals or survived any hailstorms together to find out how the other guy reacted in a storm.

But between his business trips I came to know and appreciate Bill du Pont — how he reacts to good or bad news, how he handles situations, his views, his style. Little things like how late in the night he would be comfortable taking a call. How early in the morning.

Some owners are early risers. Fitz Dixon, one of three I worked for in Philly, was up at 6 a.m. and functioning by 7. Then came Harold Katz, just the opposite. A noon flight is a red-eye for Harold. If he came to the Sixers office for an emergency at 8 a.m., the staff stopped for a lunch break. But he would work until 1 in the morning. You could call him at midnight, but never dare try to reach him before noon. Bill is middle of the road. Fairly early riser. Not particularly a night owl. You wouldn't want to call after 10 o'clock.

It was the same educational process for Bill. "I didn't know Pat from the man in the moon," he recalls. "I was committed to the concept that he had been retained by the ownership group — how-

After the NBA announced the Orlando franchise, congratulations poured in from all over the country.

ever reconstructed it was — and just because of this shift I wasn't going to put him out on the street. I grew to be satisfied with the relationship. As with anybody, there's the occasional little bump or bounce. But overall I think Pat and I have been a successful team."

During a one-on-one meeting more than six months after the shift, Bill suddenly asked, "Pat, how are you and I doing?" Blindsided, I stammered something like, "Very well. I think for two strangers thrown together, I feel good." I didn't know how deeply he wanted to go. I'd never had an owner ask that question. That he would ask, I thought, was a rare insight into the man. Of course, this is not to imply I'm a yes-man. When Bill says no, I'll say no, too.

Franchises for both Miami and Orlando lowered the Grapefruit Wall somewhat. But it neither wiped out the keen rivalry nor the half-kidding barbs that zinged up and down the turnpike. That summer I had a long talk with Billy Cunningham. A strain had developed between us because of the rivalry and the talk was good. Here's a guy I worked with for eight years in Philadelphia and, suddenly, we were thrown into opposite foxholes. It was nice to return to some semblance of a non-adversarial relationship, though the national media now was into the Miami vs. Orlando thing. *The Washington Post, Chicago Tribune* and others did analytical pieces on the rivalry.

My own low resistance to a waiting one-liner no doubt kept the coals smoldering. Each time the Heat had some problem, Williams was there to pounce on the new material. A shocking story revealed that rising Miami Arena had a severe shortage of restrooms. The flap came to be known as "Potty-gate." A vision formed of Heat fans dancing in the aisles, not over Miami victories but because they were stuck in long lines outside the restrooms. I regaled Kiwanians and Rotarians with the bulletin that Miami officials had adopted a new motto — "Plan-a-Head."

A month later the *Miami Herald* revealed that Heat season ticket sales were lagging. The league was on their case about parking. Even a Heat-sponsored clinic with Julius Erving disappointingly had drawn less than 300 youngsters. I announced the only difference between the Heat and the Titanic was the Titanic had a band.

It made Larry Guest's column in the *Sentinel* and our dear neighbors to the south got out their Pat Williams dolls and poked in another pin.

After Miami lost its first 17 games, I cracked that the Heat was losing so often their mascot should be a Democrat. This one got all the way to *Sports Illustrated* and *The Sporting News* for all my Dade County admirers to read and savor. Maybe I should have turned myself in to One-liners Anonymous.

Stew Crane, Bubba and me on the
Sentinel *front page after the NBA owners voted to include Orlando.*

Then the rivalry escalated beyond after-dinner speeches. In the '88 preseason the Heat played exhibition games in Daytona and Tampa over our objections to the league. We argued those were *our* strongholds. But the league ruled we didn't have a territory until we officially became a franchise the next season.

They did toss a few bones: We'd be given promotional public address announcements during the two games, be allowed to set up a table to sell our merchandise and be provided a room to entertain corporate types. Still, we weren't happy campers. The feud simmered.

The *Sentinel's* Barry Cooper called to say he had a story from Lewis Schaffel ripping the Magic. Barry asked if I thought we had a rivalry going. I gave him Bill Veeck's great quote: "If you're going to have a rivalry, don't have a secret one." Veeck said if it's secret, it's bad for your bank account and your ulcers. "If you're going to hate the other city," Veeck was known to say, "hate everything about them, even their park benches."

It was all kind of fun for me. Cooper said Ronnie Rothstein, the Heat coach, was under orders to win the two Miami-Orlando games during the Magic's first season. I planted a tongue firmly in one cheek and told Cooper that was the first thing we would tell our coach, too. We don't want to intimidate Matty Guokas, but when we play Miami we're going to put his name on the coach's door in chalk.

How did I have time for such foolishness? Almost immediately after getting the franchise I was out of Robert Fraley's hair and began staffing up in a suite Bill du Pont had on Pine Street. It's on the second floor of a disjointed old building with swaying floors. It was to be a stopgap until Bill's magnificent DuPont Plaza was complete. DuPont Plaza would serve as Stopgap II until our permanent offices in the arena were ready in early '89. I had rattled around to different places in Fraley's offices, so I could live with swaying floors for 90 days, right? Hey, chin up, Williams.

May, 1987, was National Magic Hiring Month. It was dizzy. By early June our Pine Street crew included:

■ Office manager Marlin Ferrell, a grandmotherly bundle of efficiency I pirated away from the chamber;

■ Ticket manager Ashleigh Bizzelle, once a schoolgirl ticket seller for the Florida State League Miami Marlins;

■ Bob Poe, a radio executive who would head our broadcast operations and sponsorship sales;

■ Jack Swope, who left the Sixers to become assistant general manager and marketing director;

■ Danny Durso, a Sixers refugee who took over the green eyeshade department from relieved investor-volunteer Stewart Crane;

■ John Gabriel, another Philly defector, as director of scouting.

Remarkably, we virtually completed our front-office staff in burp-gun fashion, which was exactly what Harold Katz was ready to aim at me now that the Sixers-to-Magic migration had reached four. Harold is not as vocal and visible as George Steinbrenner but in his own way is probably tougher. After a while, people working for him decide they want to stay in the big leagues but feel there has to be a *little* fun somewhere in it.

Katz called, upset. The gist of it was that in the NBA we don't do these things, don't hire people away from other franchises. Funny, I must have read right over that in the manual. My reaction was that if you want to keep people, you sign them to a contract. I told Harold it was nothing personal. We weren't trying to get him or get his organization. It was simply that these were the best I knew of for our jobs. I made offers and they accepted. Actually, there's a good

Ronnie Rothstein, coach of the Miami Heat, will be in the middle of the Miami-Orlando rivalry. I truly believe that this intrastate rivalry will be the most intense that Florida has ever seen at any level of sports.

bit of jumping around in the league. When it's time to move on, people move on.

In this case they were wondering just what they had moved to. The Pine Street building had walls the telephone company couldn't penetrate and the jury-rigged phone system was by Slapstick Bell. We'd go some days with no phones, then have a siege of multiple conversations somehow connecting on the same line. The next day we might be able to make outgoing calls but not receive any. I'd make a call, leave the number of a company across the hall and ask the secretaries to come fetch us if the calls were returned.

Most of the staff was bunched into one big room. The chairs were like a bad bed; you'd sink all the way down and they would go all the way back and flip over if you weren't careful. There were no inside walls, just partitions. I had a separate office and Jack Swope was in a little anteroom leading into my office. Poor Jack had no privacy. Anyone going in or out of my office had to almost climb over him, often when he was trying to have a high-level meeting with someone.

The previous tenant was a tailor. Gabe's partioned-off cubicle had been a fitting room. Mirrors were all around with a little platform in the middle. Gabe: "It was disconcerting each time I looked up and saw eight of me. And other staffers kept coming in, stepping on the platform wanting their pants hemmed."

Ashleigh Bizzelle went bonkers after a visit by Stetson's Glen Wilkes and freaked out after a visit by a mouse. We 'stole' Ashleigh from Zev Bufman's theatrical operation at Bob Carr Auditorium.

Staffers came to John Gabriel's cubicle, a former fitting room, requesting to have their trousers hemmed. An eight-sided mirror made the room even more fascinating. Gabe is one of the brightest young coaching and scouting stars in the NBA.

The only parking was a small, booked-up private lot next door. Even if we pulled in just for a moment to run in and out, the owner charged across the lot flapping his arms and taking David Stern's name in vain. One day I was on my way to a press conference to announce the hiring of Gabe and Poe. I stopped by the office just long enough to hustle in and pick up something. I looked out my office window to discover my car about to be hauled off by a tow truck. Welcome to the big leagues, staff.

In a way the Pine Street experience was positive. Being tossed together in close, trying quarters produced great camaraderie. Everyone's business was everyone else's business. The staff nostalgically looks back on Pine Street much as one clings to spartan experiences like Army barracks or college dorms.

Gabe and I still kid Ashleigh Bizzelle about the time Glen Wilkes, the Stetson basketball coach, dropped in. Glen is Mr. Southern Cornpone, a big lovable character who I'm sure was only trying to extend a compliment when he met Ashleigh, the epitome of the independent businesswoman. Wilkes took one look at her and in his deep Dixie drawl declared, "Y'all shore gonna succeed with a pretty little filly like this workin' for ya!" Ashleigh smiled politely until Wilkes was out of sight, then went bonkers. Gabe and I still jab Ashleigh with an occasional "filly" line. But we smile when we do it.

Ashleigh is an upbeat soul always in the middle of office high jinks, planned and otherwise. After her beloved Miami Hurricanes destroyed Cari Haught's beloved Florida State Seminoles, Ashleigh spent all that Sunday afternoon decorating Cari's work area with black crepe paper and black balloons. Cari took it in good humor. Not so funny, however, was the day a mouse ran across Ashleigh's desk.

Ashleigh: "We started getting glimpses of mice scurrying or we'd hear them. We had rat poison put behind the desks. One day I reached to turn my computer on and this little mouse sat inches away from my hand. I was totally freaked out. He was really cute and it was like he didn't see me. Now, I'm not afraid of a mouse, but I do have this vision of how horrible it would be for one to crawl up my leg."

She issued a casual announcement that possibly was heard in Leesburg. "THERE'S A MOUSE ON MY DEEEEEEESK!!!" she screamed.

The mouse escaped holding its ears and Ashleigh worked the rest of the day in the reception area. For days afterward she showed up for work wearing slacks with the hems tucked into knee-length University of Miami socks. No mouse was going to act out her worst nightmare.

Ever wonder what a big-time, major league sports team's front office staff does to earn their keep? We spent a large part of one of those early days in heavy meetings — Gabe, Marlin, Ashleigh, Doug Minear and I — to fine-tune our letterhead. Does the phone number go over here or down there? How far from the top should the logo be? How much wording at the bottom? That was the issue of the day.

Another Pine Street day was spent balancing chairs on short stacks of phone books. Chairs on phone books. Didn't you know that's the secret of how the Celtics became a dynasty? Red Auerbach took these old wooden folding chairs and Bob Cousy arranged Boston phone books in a neat, little parquet pattern and . . .

Seriously, we were trying to figure the slope of temporary seating that would rise beyond the ends of the arena floor. The question was how many rows with good sightlines we could put on the floor without blocking the front row of permanent seats. We put one chair behind another with a staffer in each chair, then adjusted the height of the back chair by adding or subtracting phone books until the staffer in the back could see over the head of the staffer in the front.

Alas, the chairs kept sliding off the phone books. It was an incredible scene. Somebody walking in might have put out an emergency call for nets and straitjackets. We finally decided we couldn't solve this riddle until the building was finished.

But there was plenty of serious business. Jack Swope began work to open our souvenir store, The Magic FanAttic, and hired Kathy Farkas to run it. He also began selection and negotiation for the arena scoreboard. Ashleigh had to make sense of the 14,000 ticket pledges and gear up for scaling the house and processing priorities and first-time seat selection. Gabe began the scouting effort so vital to our first expansion and college drafts still two years off. Bob Poe began a study of NBA cable and TV deals in preparation for negotiations for our local broadcast packages.

I was left with the truly important things. Like the time I dressed as a waiter for a charity luncheon at Church Street Station with most of our staff at the table I served. I ended up atop the table singing *"I Heard It Through The Grapevine"* with a flamenco dancer in my face. Well, somebody had to tackle the difficult stuff.

Dear Diary: The things you do to build a basketball team. Will it stop at nothing?

What Bill du Pont had been given in New York in April was not really a franchise but rather a conditional franchise agreement, one that was exactly 4 and 3/16ths inches thick. (Yes, we measured it. No, we didn't balance a chair on it). And to think attorneys call some documents legal *briefs!* The agreement detailed the four main requirements for having our franchise validated: (1) the $32.5 million franchise fee, (2) completion of the arena to NBA standards, (3) local radio-TV rights contracts with minimum $1.5 million net revenue for the first season and (4) 10,000 season tickets sold for the '89-'90 season by December 31, 1988.

There also were countless items on an approval checklist — size of locker rooms, practice facility, parking, arena lease, minimum arena dates, location of press row, uniform design, on and on, ad infinitum.

League officials were going to be tough on every item. They were like bloodhounds. Tough, unbending, sitting right on your head. Even at the end of our ticket drive they were no more conciliatory than at the start. There were no nice little words from the league until we became card-carrying members of the club. Until then, they were the Kremlin and we were Afghanistan.

Two young NBA attorneys, Bill Jemas and Joel Litvin, were like pit bulls unleashed on the four expansion franchises. I suspected their marching orders were to sharpen their fangs every morning and see what they could do to harass the new teams. They reminded me of something Celtics announcer Johnny Most used to say about Jeff Ruland and Rick Mahorn who played so aggressively for Washington. Johnny tagged them "McFilthy" and "McNasty." At times, that's how we felt about Jemas and Litvin. But after we were admitted they became the most delightful and courteous people in the league office to deal with.

Robert Fraley tried to gain a little leverage by trying to band together the four new teams to seek changes in some of the stipulations hanging over our battered little peasant heads. Fraley and representatives from the other three franchises met non-stop for two days in New York, poring over every word in the franchise agreement. But the "expansion union" dissolved.

"It became obvious that Lewis Schaffel was going to go along with anything the league wanted," says Fraley, "and once one team caved in, we were dead." The league didn't want our challenge. About all we accomplished was additional information on players who would be unprotected and available in the expansion pool. Under the original agreement we would not have been handed the names until just before the expansion draft. The amendment also permitted us to get copies of those players' contracts.

As the arena took shape on the Orlando skyline in the summer of 1987, selecting a name for it became a perplexing issue. This was the city's province, but our staff became involved because the building would be our home. We realized an esoteric name — if just the right one — could be a good identity hook. Even the casual sports fan can locate The Forum, The Summit, The Omni. Now ask for directions to Arco Arena. The search deservedly could have ended by naming it after Bill Frederick, the bulldog believer in the project who pushed it past every political logjam. However, he vetoed Frederick Arena as a moniker for The House That Bill Built.

Everything from Alpha to Omega was suggested. I asked Dr. Renald Showers, a friend and professor at Philadelphia College of Bible, if either Alpha or Omega could be offensive to the Christian community. His advice was to stay away from those, but he offered a suggestion: The Ultra. I threw that at the mayor's people, but it didn't hit. Too bad. We could have sold some golf ball advertising on the scoreboard.

Or, how about some Magic spin on the name? Magic Palace? Magicore? The Cauldron? I was reading a book at the beach one weekend in August and the word "quest" jumped at me. I called city hall. That didn't make it either.

Sentinel columnist Bob Morris playfully suggested things like Frederick's of Orlando. That got everybody scared that if we came up with a name that became a source of ridicule, it would be a negative. The name Orlando Arena evolved as others fell away for one reason or another. Mayor Frederick has a framed airline napkin

Bob Fillpot's design created unobstructed viewing. The weight of the building hangs from two giant steel girders.

Bob Fillpot looked at his creation and said it gave him goose bumps. But I saw tears in his eyes.

keepsake on which he and an aide reviewed the best names during a 1987 trip.

In addition to my "Quest," proposals scribbled on the napkin are Centro, The Grove, Podium, The Orlandome, Orbit, Signature and Centrum — the latter was the building's working name when it was proposed as a 7,000-seat facility in the mid-'60s.

When it finally evolved into a 15,000-seat, state-of-the art showpiece, enraptured visitors picked out another word for the structure: beautiful.

In time I suspect someone, despite the mayor's objections, will tack Frederick Arena up in letters.

"It isn't a monument to one person," Mr. Mayor argues. "And I don't say that in any self-deprecating terms. I'm very proud of my involvement in this project. It's certainly one of the most important things I've done and gratifying to me to see the building actually be delivered at the quality level we had hoped."

Two men responsible for that were Bill Hodson, project manager for Gilbane Construction, and chief architect Bob Fillpot. Hodson is a leathery, unflappable man who brought the building along under enormous time pressure. He humored my constant pleas for pesky tours for media and ticket prospects when he would have preferred an electric construction fence around the whole place. Fillpot, a colorful, pear-shaped Texan, designed Reunion Arena at Dallas, The Summit at Houston and the Miami Arena. But he viewed this as his lifetime monument, clucking and fretting over it like a hen.

At the grand opening I saw tears in his eyes as he stepped back, soaked in the sight and declared in that dusty Texas drawl: "This here's the only building ah've done that gives me goose bumps."

The arena grand opening. "Spectacular" was the word most people used to describe it when they saw it for the first time. One unsung hero in assuring a downtown location for the building was Orlando attorney Hal Kantor who expedited the development of regional impact.

WE'VE GOT IT . . . NOW WHAT?

Buell Duncan was a great friend from the beginning. SunBank helped with our early financing, bought 100 tickets plus a skybox and helped launch the Orlando All-Star Classic.

The 25,000 who flowed through the arena that day seemed to agree. A great feeling of pride was confirmed by a little old lady who caught my eye. Strolling in a throng of gawkers in the outer concourse, she spotted a tissue on the patterned terrazzo floor. She took it to a trash receptacle. Nobody wanted to get the place dirty.

I'd been disappointed over not playing until '89 but began to realize that the extra year would be an asset. We had time to do things right. Well, almost right.

I had a lunch meeting with Buell Duncan, the proper and proud chairman of SunBank, trying to persuade him to chair a founders group of 32 to underwrite our inaugural Orlando All-Star Classic for $5,000 each. The Classic is a week of practices and games two months before the draft in which many of the top college seniors undergo a final, intensive study by NBA coaches and scouts.

Buell liked the idea of the group and seemed to be leaning toward accepting. While delivering my knockout arguments I pulled out a pen to list the amenities and privileges for each founder. But on the pen in large green letters was "Barnett Bank." He noticed. Suddenly, you could have hung hindquarters in the room.

Buell somehow forgave me and agreed to chair the founders. Pat Williams exited, face poached, soft-boiled and over-easy.

Footnote: I later met with John North of Barnett Bank to pitch a skybox and Classic founder package. I did a strip-search to make sure no SunBank pen fiendishly lurked on my person. I was learning.

Dear Diary: I've always been amused by banks that advertise "We're a bank you can trust," then put their pens on chains.

The All-Star Classic previously was in Hawaii. During the closing months of our franchise campaign we heard the NBA wanted to move the event to the mainland. We got encouragement that Orlando would be a popular alternative and thought it would be just the sort of project to get us into gear during the two years before beginning play. Sort of an exhibition season for our staff.

So it was off to the '87 NBA fall meetings outside LA, armed with a whole new campaign to foist on the league. Doug Minear designed

A staff meeting in the new du Pont Center, our third office location. Jack Swope presides. From his left, Bob Poe, Dan Durso, Cari Haught, Betty Johnson, Marlin Ferrell and Scott Herring.

The most creative resume was sent by Gary Eslinger of Orlando. Unfortunately we didn't have a spot for him.

buttons as part of the pitch. "Take your spring break in Orlando," they implored. We had just finished the lobbying and Barnum and bull of the expansion chase and here we were at it again like we were running for sophomore class president. David Stern just shook his head.

Dear Diary: By now the NBA thinks we're nuts.

A month later Rod Thorn, league operations director, was in town to announce the tournament was moving to Orlando. More dramatic was what Rod said privately. He told me Miami was having trouble converting its pledges to season tickets. That was the word in the NBA office three months ahead of Miami's 10,000-ticket deadline. I wondered what that meant to us, a year and three months out. Twelve months later it was, as Yogi Berra would say, *deja vu* all over again.

I discovered that all of my new town picks up and moves 60 miles to the beach every summer weekend. The Williams family bought an oceanfront condo at New Smyrna Beach and joined the migration. One story: It's Labor Day weekend, 1987. The kids and I had gotten into net fishing with a friend, Seymour Lenz. You wade out

The Magic FanAttic started out in cramped quarters on Pine Street but moved to these spacious quarters at I-4 and Colonial.

Gilbane Construction's
Bill Hodson would rather have
put a fence around the arena
site but graciously allowed
tour groups.

neck-deep in the pounding surf then drag that baby in fast as you can. You have to be careful not to fall or you're down there tangled in the net just like the fish fighting to get out.

On this day, only three of us manned the nets and had to enlist someone off the beach to help. A friendly old guy happened by and obliged. As a big wave came along I quickly surveyed the troops just in time to see our volunteer making a frantic lunge with one hand into the foam. The wave had hit him smack in the mouth and knocked out his false teeth. The lunge failed. Bad teeth, bad hands. But he was a game old cuss and stayed with it. The surf was so bad, however, we had to drop the poles and swim for our lives.

We ended up with a four-pound sea bass tangled in the net — the biggest fish we caught all summer. The main course was grand at the Lenz's condo that night. But the poor guy whose teeth probably are drawing curious looks from passing manta rays and dolphin somewhere off the Bahamas couldn't join the feast. He probably was sipping Campbell's soup that night.

Another sudden and surprising catch would come soon — a head coach.

SHAKESPEARE AND GUOKAS, MIAs

In February of '88 the Philadelphia 76ers were delighted the NBA season had reached the All-Star weekend. The Sixers needed a break. Two starters were hurt much of the first half and trade rumors nibbled at the team's concentration. They limped home from Washington with three straight defeats.

Instead of traveling to the All-Star game, Coach Matty Guokas stayed home to try to find a remedy. The All-Star telecast from Chicago had just finished on the big set in his den when the phone rang that Sunday afternoon. It was Harold Katz, who asked Guokas to drive to his house for a talk.

Katz normally handled by phone whatever he had to tell his coach. Something heavy was up and Matty, hometown hero in the Delaware Valley as a college star, Sixers player and now head coach, reviewed a dozen possible scenarios during the hour drive — including the obvious.

"When I got there, Harold didn't waste any time," Matty said. "He said he had decided to make a change. So I said, 'Fine.' We were 20-23, which is not acceptable in Philadelphia. But if you examined it, believe me, we were overachieving."

Complicating this dark moment in Matty's career was that when

Katz called, Matty was home alone with his 8-year-old daughter, Robyn. He was forced to take her on this visit to the gallows. While Katz was firing him, Robyn was in the next room playing with Harold's daughter.

On the ride home, Matty figured it was as good a time as any to begin discussing this setback with his family. He told Robyn he no longer would coach the Sixers. The child didn't have a total perception of what he did for a living but knew he was away for days, even weeks at a time.

"Daddy, does this mean you'll be home more?" she asked.

Matty coached Julius Erving at the end of the Doctor's career in 1987.

Matty smiled at the child's perspective. "Definitely," he announced.

"Oh, good!" she said, beaming.

But Matty felt frustrated and rejected. Should he get back into coaching right away? Just get away for a while? Get out completely?

"Finally I decided I wasn't going to leap into anything," he remembers. "I decided to develop a feel for what I wanted to do with the rest of my life. I had more than a year on my contract, so that meant some time without the urgency of jumping right back out and earning a paycheck."

The news of Matty's firing cast a pall that Monday morning over the Orlando Magic offices — by then located in Du Pont Plaza. Four of us were on the Sixers' staff during many of Matty's years as a player and coach. He was a friend. Because we had done so much raiding of the Sixers it was natural to assume we might consider Matty as Magic coach.

Even Bill du Pont poked his head in my office and playfully posed this ironic question: "You're not going to tell me you're gonna hire Matty Guokas now that he's been fired by Philadelphia, are you?"

We had a little chuckle. I was glad to see Bill hadn't become so uptight over the Philly thing that he couldn't joke about it. Each time I hired somebody off their staff, Katz blew up and howled to David Stern, who called Bill. Which is not a pleasant way for a new owner to get started. It could have become a sore subject with him. But hire Matty Guokas? Wouldn't that be the capper? Ha, ha, ha, ha ... hmmmmmmm ...

Initially, John Gabriel told me Matty wanted to pursue a broadcasting career. He'd been a play-by-play and color commentator some years earlier. But now it was time to refresh and recharge. So Matty sacked up his golf clubs and headed to Florida for some time with his sister and brother-in-law at Palm Beach.

He stopped in Orlando. Gabriel got him a room at the Stouffer Resort, where they visited over Sunday lunch just a few blocks from the final round of the Bay Hill Classic. With our first game still nearly two years off they didn't talk about the Magic coaching situation. They kibitzed about the NBA and Matty told Gabriel to keep him in mind if anything in broadcasting came up.

Matty drove to Palm Beach and watched on TV with his brother-in-law as Paul Azinger wrapped up the Bay Hill title.

"Hey! I was just there!" Matty announced. "I didn't realize the tournament was going on."

Before leaving his sister's home, he got a message to call the Charlotte Hornets, who had launched a coaching search for their first season just seven months off. Still stinging from his firing less than two months earlier, Matty thought it was too soon to talk about coaching again.

"But I didn't want to rule anything out," he said, accepting an invitation to visit Charlotte in April. Before going, he dialed an old friend and colleague, Mr. P. Williams, to talk about the Hornets.

I told him George Shinn, the Charlotte owner, had great character and would run a pure and proper organization. One with discipline. Charlotte is in a conservative area and I thought they'd be looking for good citizens who wouldn't embarrass them. I suggested that in a small city making its first foray into big league sports, the first coach would become an absolute father figure. But I reminded him that expansion takes time and that he shouldn't promise quick results. I wished him well and told him to keep in touch.

At the time there was no serious notion of pursuing Matty or anyone else as Magic coach. It was all "a year from now." However, I already was thinking about any number of coaching possibilities likely available the next year. I developed a growing dossier of opinions from general managers, coaches, scouts, player agents, sportswriters and broadcasters. I had even had casual discussions with a few long-range prospects.

After being fired in Phoenix a year earlier, John MacLeod told me he'd be interested in an expansion team. In September of '87 I met with Dave Twardzik, a Jack Ramsay assistant at Indiana with spunk but limited experience. Norm Sonju had impressed upon me the one overriding coaching qualification necessary in an expansion setting. Experience. The really, really Big E. That stuck in my mind like a peanut butter and glue sandwich.

On December 7, TV commentator Rick Barry called from a pay phone somewhere after working a game on TBS. He wanted me to consider him. Did it mean anything that he called on Pearl Harbor Day? I figured I needed an even-keeled guy through the rough expansion period. I thought that Rick or any other rookie coach could go down like the USS Arizona by Christmas.

During this time I developed an empathy for coaches because of an experience at the Downtown YMCA where sons Jimmy and Bobby were playing in a basketball league. The regular coach didn't show one day and I was drafted. Wild. I'd never last in the NBA. I'd have no voice left. That's the only time I've coached but it was enough to make me realize the daze that comes over you when you sit in that seat. I'd be Arizona material by Thanksgiving.

My early research typically honed in on NBA assistant coaches. Others who got high marks included Boston's Jimmy Rodgers (who moved up to replace retiring K.C. Jones), Philly's Jimmy Lynam (who took over for Matty), the Lakers' Randy Pfund, Atlanta's Brian Hill, Milwaukee's Mike Dunleavey, Ronnie Rothstein (who got the Miami head job) and Chicago's Phil Jackson (who would replace Doug Collins).

Why overlook the college ranks? It had been 15 years since a college coach without previous pro experience stepped into an NBA head-coaching position. After John MacLeod vaulted from Oklahoma to the Phoenix Suns in '73 there was a steady stream of hirings off the benches of the NBA.

During the '87 All-Star weekend in Chicago, Phoenix columnist Joe Gilmartin suggested early NBA teams often turned to campuses for their sideline geniuses only because as late as the end of the '60s there were few assistant coaches in the league. Once teams started adding assistants and a pool of NBA-experienced candidates began to build, college coaches disappeared from the mix.

Was this a mistake? Was some guy out there on some campus ready to go right onto an NBA sideline? I added that question to my coaching queries and the result was eye-opening.

Cleveland GM Wayne Embry: "The Duke guy. Mike Krzyzewski. He's the one guy with the necessary people skills."

Agent Ron Grinker: "Coach Krzyzewski of Duke."

Commentator Billy Packer, my old college chum, put Krzyzewski and UNC-Charlotte's Jeff Mullins at the top of his list. Mullins, another old friend, made it clear he had no interest in pro coaching but was quick to add to my survey: "Mike Krzyzewski."

The Lakers' Jerry West: "One man. Mike Krzyzewski of Duke, whom I have never met."

I asked agent Herb Rudoy, NBA exec Rod Thorn, Philly basketball writer Dickie Weiss, the Mavericks' Rick Sund, TV announcer

Bill Raftery, Phoenix general manager Jerry Colangelo, Bulls coach Doug Collins, Denver president Pete Babcock, Nets scout Al Menendez, Knicks GM Al Bianchi, Boston writer Bob Ryan, Pistons GM Jack McCloskey.

The chorus came back in harmony: "Krzyzewski."

Scary.

In all, I must have asked 25 knowledgeable basketball people, a veritable basketball Who's Who. Every one, without a hint from me — not even a multiple-choice list of suggestions — said Mike Krzyzewski. What a tribute. You can't get that many basketball guys to agree on which horizon that large yellow ball will rise from tomorrow morning. I was amazed. I tossed out the question, sat on the other end of the phone waiting for the name to come back, and sure enough here it came. I'd shake my head. To get that kind of endorsement was awesome.

So my next call was to the Cameron Athletic Center in Durham, North Carolina. The next day, March 1, 1988, Coach Krzyzewski called back. We had a nice talk. I'd never met him and was just tickled to death to talk to him. The question was, simply, do you think at some point in time you'd want to be an NBA coach? He had not been offered the job. If he said yes, we'd proceed — along with about 15 other NBA teams. He said he thought the pros would never enter into his thinking, but enough people had been telling him it was the ultimate in coaching basketball.

"Maybe if the situation is right," he said, "maybe it would be something to think about."

A crack in the door. He said the NCAA tournament, about to begin, was the only thing he was thinking about right then. He said he'd think more about his future afterward.

April 11 — A week after the tournament, in which Duke went to the Final Four, I picked up my usual stack of phone messages one morning and the top one jolted me to a stop. Mike Krzyzewski had called. I felt a rush. My legs went limp. I plopped down behind my desk and excitedly began making notes of things I cleverly could ad-lib over the phone. It was like calling for your first date. My hands were sweaty. I dialed three numbers and aborted. I wasn't ready. What would we do on Mike's visit? Would he bring his wife down? I rehearsed my ad-libs again, took a deep breath, and began dialing, this time making it all the way through.

Best college coach for an NBA head job? Look no farther than Duke's Coach K.

"I've thought through my life," Mike said, "sifted through it, and right now the pros are just not part of it. Duke is my life. Pat, I'm genuinely flattered by your interest, but I'm not considering anything else at all right now."

That was that. But it turned out Charlotte also made an inquiry, Miami asked about him, and he had other NBA feelers. As my little survey indicated, Mike Krzyzewski's name may be hard to spell, but he was no secret. Everybody down to the bag boy at Publix seemed to know about "Coach K" as a hot property. I shrugged and went back to mascot designs and Miami Heat barbs and tabletop warbling — you know, the important stuff — knowing the coaching situation had more than a year to sort itself out.

Or so I thought. Three weeks later the Boston Celtics announced a move that had no direct bearing on our search. But it touched off the events that ended with the selection of our man before the month was over — a year sooner than we intended. Boston announced that K.C. Jones would semi-retire into a part-time, front-office role and that respected assistant Jimmy Rodgers would take over. This allowed me to scratch one assistant from my list.

But it set John Gabriel in motion. He poked his head in my office and asked whether we should be talking to Matty Guokas now.

Gabe: "I just brought it up and headed out the door. Pat let me go at least two steps and shouted, 'Hey, Gabe! Come back. Do you think?' It was like a light went on."

Gabe closed the door and we began to think out loud. What if Charlotte decided they wanted him? How many viable candidates would there be a year later? Jimmy Lynam and Jimmy Rodgers had been snatched from the picture and Mike Krzyzewski said he wanted to stay in college. Gabe was jittery. He reasoned that we knew Matty and knew what he could do. We knew all too well his situation at Philadelphia. We liked him and were comfortable with him. He obviously was a strong candidate. But do you pay a coach a year in advance when he's not even coaching? Matty had the year-plus remaining on his Sixers contract. Could that be worked out? Our brains were churning.

"Do you really think?" I said again, a little smile forming beneath my moustache.

"Yeah," said Gabe, "and we'd better move quickly because Charlotte has not chosen their coach yet."

The next morning Matty told me he'd done the Charlotte interview and was waiting to hear from Hornets GM Carl Scheer. I posed a hypothetical question: "If you had your choice — and I'm not saying you would have your choice — of coaching Charlotte in '88 or Orlando in '89, what would it be?"

He answered without hesitation. "Orlando in '89."

"It was early in the morning when Pat called," Matty would recall during the All-Star Classic week. "I was in bed watching a game I taped the night before. Old habits are hard to break. I answered that question the way I did because of Pat and Gabe and Jack and Danny — people I had worked with before.

"Also, I liked the city and I liked Florida. Why? Right up there," he said, pointing to a brilliant sun suspended over the Hotel Royal Palace pool deck. "I lived in Florida for one year when I played at the University of Miami, so I already had a little feel for it.

"But the biggest factor was whether I wanted to go back into coaching. Did I want to do this to my family again? It's painful for them at times. On the other hand, they like all the things that go with it. My son gets all caught up in it.

"Yet the negatives are there as well. So I thought if I coached again the best situation would be where the sun shines and it's new and fresh and not jaded by other sports teams. Even if it meant an expansion team."

He struggled with that one last item. Expansion teams have been known to lose a game or two and Matty has no great fondness for losing.

"Never did, never will. Never will accept it," he says. "On the other hand, this is different in that it's a challenge with a new team in a new city that doesn't have pro sports. The opportunity to build something in two, three, four, five years is something I thought might be fun."

Suddenly and unexpectedly, we wrestled with the question of hiring now or waiting. Might the pickings be so slim next year there wouldn't be anybody we'd really want? Might somebody be available better than Matty, who we probably could nail right then?

I flew to Chicago that afternoon for a speaking engagement and couldn't wait to return the next morning to get back into this Matty Guokas matter. I called Jimmy Lynam who remained high on Matty and reinforced our thinking that his personality would be perfect in an expansion setting. Matty is a composed man with enough self-control and realism to cope. No Arizona man here.

I'd heard enough. That Saturday morning — Kentucky Derby Saturday — I called and asked Matty to fly down Tuesday evening. The conversation was short. I was excited this was tracking faster than anyone had thought. I felt satisfied when I hung up.

Matty had a different feeling. "It was hush-hush, very secret," he recalled. "Pat didn't want me to stay at a hotel and told me I would be staying at Danny Durso's house. My first thought was they just didn't want to spend the money for a hotel. That scared me a little."

But Matty discovered it was only Pat Williams' mild paranoia over the aggressive Orlando media, a condition that would shade Matty's official interview visit with tints of Inspector Clouseau and Andy Hardy because Jack Swope — bless him — took my concern a little too much to heart. I called Matty again on Monday to confirm the arrangements — who would meet him and where.

We resolved one immensely important part of the strategy: Whether to pick him up at the gate or whether he should board the

Jack Swope started with the 76ers in 1977 at age 22, selling tickets. He's one of the top promotions and marketing people in the NBA.

tram from the airside hub and rendezvous with Jack at baggage claim. Obviously the whole future of our franchise — maybe even the eventual sports future of Orlando — might be in the balance had Jack and Matty frantically kept waving to one another from trams going in opposite directions. I learned that the hard way.

May 10 — *Ladies and gentlemen, we interrupt this program for a special bulletin: The Orlando Magic has conquered the airport tram. Film at 11.*

Jack hooked up with Matty and was supposed to show him around and entertain him that night with Danny Durso so the two of them could give me their interpretation of Matty's thinking. They would pass him to me the next morning and I would lateral him to Bill du Pont after lunch. Jack began the grand tour at the University of Central Florida, which we considered as a practice site until arranging to renovate a city recreation gym across the arena parking lot.

Chuckling as he looked back on the clandestine mission, Matty recalled they "kinda slithered into a hallway at UCF for Jack to show me the gym, all the time trying not to make eye contact with anyone. They were really into that not-being-seen thing."

Red alert! Red alert!

One step through the door, Jack was jolted by the sight of UCF assistant coach Eric Dennis shooting baskets. Swope's face suddenly ashen, he wheeled and poked one hand in Matty's chest, shoving him, startled and blinking, back into the hallway. "We can't go in there! We can't go in there!" Jack stammered. "There's a guy in there who would recognize you!" Amused, Matty felt like he was in a slapstick spy film, half expecting Maxwell Smart to pop from behind the next potted palm, speaking into his shoe.

Back at the office, Danny played out the intrigue to its fullest. On the way from the airport Jack called in on his car phone to report he had met the flight and was driving "the subject" to UCF. Danny scurried across the hall to Pillar-Bryton and stuck his head in Bill du Pont's office. Struggling to keep a straight face, Danny advised in hushed and dramatic tones: "The Eagle has landed." Bill du Pont knowingly grinned and winked.

The secret cargo wound up in Jack's home in Seminole County that evening, visiting with Jack and Danny and Jack's wife and

Danny Durso helped escort "the subject" around town without being noticed. I first hired him with the 76ers in '75. He's overseen the finances for me ever since.

kids. But a huge dilemma remained. Matty might be recognized in a restaurant, yet it was doubtful he wanted to wait until he got back to Philadelphia for his next meal. During a lull in the conversation, Matty asked, "Can we go eat somewhere?"

Panic set in. Jack and Danny hastily reviewed the nearby possibilities, ruled out the Burger King drive-through window and brazenly escorted Matty "By-gosh" Guokas right through the front door of Enzo's Italian Restuarant. And without even so much as a fake nose and glasses.

However, Jack does recall one last-instant chill about Enzo's, a quaint little converted stucco residence featuring several low arches. If Matty, all 6-foot-6 of him, were to split open his head on one of the arches it might have attracted undue attention before Jack could get the tourniquet cranked down. I mean, some nosy paramedic might have asked for the identity of the deceased and the *Sentinel* would've had a special edition out within the hour.

Matty luckily managed to duck the arches. The trio returned to Durso's and watched the Lakers vs. Utah until about midnight, Jack and Danny pretending to be interested, but thankful "the subject" was safely out of public view.

They delivered Matty to me the next morning, a rainy one. I took him to the arena, then three months into construction.

Matty: "I put on the hard hat and Pat gave me the tour of the site which at that time was a few concrete pilings and dirt. I slushed through the mud and Pat was going, 'There's the locker room over there and the center circle is here.' Of course it was all dirt and building materials."

I took him to Chamberlin's for lunch.

Matty: "That was so typical of Pat and in keeping with his health-food craziness. He still brown-bags it at the office just like he did in Philly with natural peanut butter and some crazy fruit like a kiwi or something. At Charlotte they took me to a fancy dinner club at the top of some bank building with an elegant dining room with a sweeping view of the city. But I'm not into all of that kind of thing, anyway. "In Orlando it was a corner table at Chamberlin's for turkey and bean sprouts on pita bread. But that's Pat. The conversation was all low-key, about the area and things back at Philly, and preparing me for what to expect with Mr. du Pont."

I took Matty back to our office and stashed him in a side room until time came to walk him across the hall to Bill du Pont. Matty strolled in unfazed that here was a young multimillionaire business-man in jeans and golf shirt.

Matty: "Pat had told me Bill was not into trying to impress peo-ple with his wealth. He was very laid back and relaxed. I liked that. We talked for a half-hour, some about basketball philosophy. He seemed interested in how I would handle not winning in the early part of a franchise. That's what I asked *him* — 'How are *you* going to deal with that?' We kind of reached a happy meeting ground of patience. We decided we would all be patient."

Bill: "My first impression was, this guy is a class act. He was well-spoken, presented an impeccable appearance and he humored me on my questions about basketball. I got a good, comfortable feeling about Matty."

Bill understates his basketball savvy, but suffice it to say he didn't ask Matty about the Ted Williams Shift or what sort of goal line defense he planned. Bill did ask how he handled star players who were difficult to manage because of ego or whatever. Matty explained, "Sometimes you have to close practice. Sometimes you just have to sit on them. And sometimes you just have to ignore the antics."

There was a comfortable atmosphere right from the nostalgic opening when Bill recounted that Matty had been a boyhood hero of his. Bill attended prep school in Philadelphia when Matty was an All-American at St. Joseph's College and idol of every schoolboy in the city. As the meeting ended we all felt this would work. At the airport, Matty and I sat in my car at the curb for about 20 minutes and talked as a heavy rain pounded. We agreed to sleep on it. No timetable.

Dear Diary: Matty has all the qualities we want and I think he is our man.

May 12 — I solicited reactions from Bill, Jack, Gabe, and Danny. I also bounced the Matty Guokas concept off NBA chief scout Marty Blake, Bulls GM Jerry Krause and the now-deceased War-riors scout Jack McMahon. The reaction was the same: A good fit.

I called Matty to tell him he was our man. His reaction was good. Matty is never going to jump through the telephone at you. That steady nature is invaluable. If we upset the Bulls one day and have to fly to Atlanta the next day, Matty understands the reality of it all. So he will not be atop the Du Pont Center cheering after each victory or having to be talked in off the ledge after defeats.

Matty: "I never say yes immediately. I wanted to talk to my wife and John Langel, my friend and lawyer. John has the ability to stand back, have a good perspective on things and keep emotion out of it. Pat and I had not even talked about basic terms, not during the two-day visit or on the phone when Pat offered the job. Basically he just said that if I wanted the job, we'd hammer all the rest out.

"I talked it over with my wife and son and that was a mistake. They were already into things like how big the pool would be and how many orange trees would be in the back yard. I said, 'Uh-oh, forget getting an objective response here.' "

So he turned to Langel, a former small-college point guard turned attorney. Now we get to eavesdrop on the heavy opening dialogue touched off when a big league head coach discusses a job overture with his legal confidant.

"John, Pat has offered me the job in Orlando," Guokas announced.

"Good," said Langel.

"Well . . . good what?" pressed Guokas.

"It's good to be offered jobs," said Langel. "Do you want to do it?"

"I don't know. What do you think?"

"Matty, you've got to make that decision."

"Oh."

Hey, this is big-time legal stuff, folks.

Langel then began to list the pluses and minuses. The pluses controlled the opening tip, scored on a 10-foot jumper, made a couple of quick steals, scored on a fast break, hit a three-pointer and had the minuses down by 12 at the quarter.

Langel later said he thought the decision was a "no-brainer. I thought it was a wonderful opportunity and he should do it. When you get to know Matty you find that he makes a decision and then thinks about all the reasons to stick to that decision. I think he decided early on, between Charlotte or Orlando, that it would be Orlando. But he had to think about moving his son, Chris, just as he was about to go to high school. And he had to think about curtailing his work in broadcasting, something he likes."

Matty called back and accepted, provided we could reach agreement on contract terms.

Matty: "Pat is a tough negotiator. Very tough. Always has been. We've negotiated many times over the years. And the one thing we agreed on the phone when I took the job was that he and John would work out the years and the money and I wouldn't get directly involved in that."

John Langel's law firm represented the 76ers before Harold Katz bought the club from Fitz Dixon in 1981. So John and I have sat on the same side of the bargaining table many times. To say he knows my negotiating M.O. is like saying the Titanic had a small leak.

Langel: "Pat has a certain negotiating style. He gives you a figure, gives you the benefits, he gives you this and that. You say no. Then Pat starts talking about travels, old friends, what's going on with the Phillies, what's going on with Fitz Dixon, and he'll talk about those things for 45 minutes. 'Life is still pretty much the same in Philadelphia. Now, why won't you take the deal?' he'll say. It's effective and congenial.

"He gets everything out on the table before he agrees to anything. And he leads you to believe he has agreed to several items without ever saying it. Then he takes the position that he never agreed. And you know he didn't. He keeps talking without saying a whole lot in terms of commitment, just trying to get a read on the reaction.

"He reminds me of the shy suitor who wants to get a date with the campus queen without taking a chance on rejection. So he sets it up, 'Well, if this guy made this offer to you and wanted to take you to dinner, would you say yes?' If she agrees, then he says, 'Okay, then, I'll pick you up at eight.' That's what dealing with Pat is like. The Magic really is a great name for a team headed by Pat because he really is the ultimate magician. But you come away feeling you have been treated fairly."

Langel began by asking for five years. We insisted on holding firm at three years. The negotiations went smoothly. Langel agrees.

Langel: "There was a lot of give and take. The interesting things

Barry Cooper, the Sentinel's *pro basketball writer. He's always digging around our office for news, which led to him breaking the Guokas story.*

were radio and TV revenue for Matty, which was left somewhat open-ended. There was a lot of trust in this deal. From both ends. For example, they wanted Matty to be in Orlando during the first year for a minimum of six dates, but we didn't want to commit to a given number. Yet, Matty's appearances far surpassed the six they had in mind. He must have gone down there a dozen times. It's that kind of good-faith relationship."

Nevertheless, Langel and Robert Fraley needed extra time to conclude the contract, partially because we were not actually hiring Matty until after his Sixer contract expired more than a year later. Obviously Katz hoped someone would hire Matty in 1988 and take him off the Sixers' payroll. When we threw him a curve, Harold sent up a mushroom cloud.

Barry Cooper sniffed out the story and splattered Matty Guokas across the front of the *Sentinel.* I went into my best Fred Astaire act, tap-dancing around a confirmation. I've learned the hard way you don't announce these things until the paperwork is done and autographed. Too many bad things can happen. We convened the staff in emergency session to discuss the dilemma and decided to bob and weave and hope the lawyers got their whereases into over-drive. Langel is tough. If we'd put out a story that it was a done deal, we'd have given him all the leverage. So we announced noth-ing and hunkered down for the media siege.

The contract was ready May 31, nearly a week after the story was out. A press conference was called for the next day with one slight oversight: Forgetting to make sure Matty could be there. He had said he would attend his nephew's high school graduation that day and he's not the type to break that sort of commitment even for a huge development in his own life. But we already had called the press conference. So we pressed on.

The Cheyenne Saloon at Church Street Station, a three-story, spectacularly ornate replica of an old Western dance hall, is great for celebrations but not press conferences. As I announced one of the most meaningful early steps in the franchise, curious tourists

I faced the media alone at Church Street Station. Where, oh, where was Matty? Fortunately he arrived the next day.

from Iowa and Michigan milled around at the foot of the stage, cameras hanging around their necks, ice cream dripping on their sandals and argyle socks. They'd listen for a moment then squeeze past irritated reporters for a closer look at the stuffed bear menacingly rearing on its hind legs by the front door. When I threw it open to questions about Matty, some vacationer in shorts and T-shirt asked about our scouting department.

The media was less than enthusiastic that Matty was not there. We announced Press Conference II would be the next day featuring a live, personal appearance by the new coach. Come back tomorrow and you can actually hear our new coach speak live words, maybe even touch his clothing. The next morning, Larry Guest stung us in his column for the unique, coachless press conference:

"Rumors and sketchy eyewitness accounts continue to circulate that there actually exists this Matty Guokas person who has agreed to coach the early editions of the Orlando Magic. However, we must continue to trust the likes of Pat Williams, an honorable enough man, who could not produce the guest of honor at a Cheyenne Saloon press conference called Wednesday to officially introduce Guokas as his man . . .

"The assembled media had foolishly assumed that some tangible link with Guokas might be provided. Alas, no coach, no telephone hookup, no prepared statement, no black-and-white glossy. Not even a thumbprint, verified by the MBI. Just a shock of hair might have been nice. Could this be a sequel to El Cid? Remember Charlton Heston playing the cadaver strapped in the saddle, in serious need of Right Guard, leading his troops into battle? See you back at the saloon today for 'Cheyenne II: Matty Appears!' Well, maybe. I'm checking with my doctor first to see if my heart can stand it."

In the Magic office you couldn't tell the red faces for all the red faces. To make matters worse, I made a glib remark that set off Harold Katz again. A reporter asked what differences Matty could

John Langel. Matty's attorney drove a hard bargain but wanted his client in Orlando.

expect in his new coach-owner relationship with Bill du Pont. "Fewer gold chains, no cigar smoke and no satellite dish reports on games in Peoria," I said. I intended it only as a funny, throwaway line, but it didn't come across so funny in Harold's *Philadelphia Inquirer* the next morning. He yelled to David Stern, who called Bill du Pont, who called me. I tucked my tail between my legs and wrote Harold a letter of apology. I heard he was so happy to get this apology from his properly contrite former general manager that he showed it off all around the office.

The irony of the awkward double press conference was that we had delayed to make sure we could sign the contracts at the same time we made the announcement. But even after two days of press conferences we were able to initial only an informal agreement because Katz brought the commissioner into the squabble over the Sixers' remaining obligation to Matty.

Langel wisely refused to allow Matty to sign a regular contract until the conflict could be settled. I think Harold's position was, "They really don't want Matty. They just signed him to aggravate me. It's a shot at me. And they think I'm gonna pay him?"

David Stern ordered a compromise: The Magic would pick up the last four of 14 remaining months on Matty's Philadelphia contract, a solution that cost us about $75,000 in salary, plus benefits. Matty was bothered by the outcome. But David was not going to have two clubs in a visible, hostile position. So he just said this is what it will be, gentlemen. He made a ruling he deemed the fair way to handle it and that was it. Period.

After Matty made his belated media appearance, Katz called, cooing paternal sweetness. Said Matty: "Harold said, 'I'm happy for you if that's what you want to do. Good luck. Anything I can do to help.' Meanwhile, his lawyers were out there trying to unhelp. I knew it wasn't a pleasant situation. Particularly for Bill. But the way it came down, I felt it was a definite commitment to me on Bill's part."

At least we kept the tourists out of the media's hair at Matty II. A bit of humor may have helped disarm the awkward situation. I told the reporters I could understand their frustration the previous day because I once took "Introduction to Shakespeare" in college and the guy never showed up the whole semester.

10,000 OR BUST

"Until we sell the 10,000th ticket, the value of the franchise is zero." — *Bill du Pont, July, 1987, when asked if he thought the value of the $32.5 million expansion club had appreciated.*

Of the four requirements for a franchise, three were gimmies for us. The arena would be completed before the '89 season, the $32.5 million franchise fee would be paid and we could meet the league's minimum local broadcast revenue. But the fourth was the killer — the requirement that we sell 10,000 season tickets for the first season with at least 50 percent of the money in hand by December 31, 1988. Less than a third of the established NBA clubs had season ticket sales that high, and it seemed unreasonable for an expansion team.

However, so many cities wanting franchises allowed the league to set standards so high that even Kareem would have to stand on his tiptoes. The league figured a new team selling 10,000 season tickets would have a better chance of living to tell about its formative years when the won-lost record would not be boffo at the box office.

When the league approved our application the ticket goal didn't appear that tough. In the first four months we'd hurriedly corralled $100 deposits for more than 14,000 tickets. Okay, there might be some attrition after applying the full price to the tickets, but 4,000 defectors? C'mon, be real. Besides, there were more than 20 months left to satisfy the 10,000. Time and numbers seemed to be a break-away layup.

Reality took months to set in. Because arena construction had just started, a seating chart wouldn't be available from the city until the end of that summer of '87. Until we had the chart we couldn't set prices for various sections or begin allowing the 14,000 pledges to choose their price ranges and seating preferences.

The delay gave us a chance to research ticket prices around the league. Denver consultant Paul Bortz, the NBA's expert on such matters, recommended locking prices in for the first three years to help build a more favorable relationship with fans. We wouldn't have to fight the negative public relations of annual price jumps. We agreed, though we'd be guessing, in '87, prices for the '91-'92 season, our third in the league.

Prices also had to be determined for the 23 skyboxes. The Magic would lease the boxes with 25 percent of the money going to the city. The high prices we initially considered reflect our early over-confidence in this whole ticket-selling matter.

Ashleigh Bizzelle surveyed NBA skybox prices. But every situation is different because some teams tie skybox leases with other events in the buildings. The highest number anyone dared say out loud for a Magic skybox was $125,000 per season. We went 'round and 'round and the spinning at last slowed at $80,000, though most of the staff seemed skeptical. Some of our owners tossed out that number to a few corporate captains around town, stepped back and waited to see if the captains clutched their hearts. An epidemic of palpitations sent us back to the pricing board.

Ashleigh: "Even Bill du Pont cringed, so we kicked it around some more." We settled on five-year leases at $45,000 for each of the first three years, going to $50,000 for years four and five.

The stock market took a sharp dip in October. What did that mean to us? Jimmy Hewitt, nervous, suggested holding the ticket price announcement until the market recovered. But what if it didn't? We could have been waiting for months. On the same day, Ashleigh completed the first of many drafts of a ticket price letter.

More energy was put into writing that letter than was expended on writing the Constitution. It had to be perfect. We spent time on it every day for the next two weeks.

Miami was having trouble converting pledges into season tickets. Because the Heat would take the floor a year earlier, their 10,000 ticket deadline also was a year earlier — December 31, 1987. With just two months left, their situation was whispered to be grim.

Russ Granik called, worried. He asked if we had done our pricing. I said yes. He said, "Well, you know Orlando and we trust you." He saw what was happening in Miami and he was saying "Is this going to happen in Orlando? Is this going to happen in Minneapolis?"

The Miami problem burst into headlines. A huge story ran in the *Sentinel* under the banner, "Heat Coming Up Short in Ticket Conversions." It revealed Miami was 2,500 short of 10,000 with only eight weeks until the deadline.

Quote from Lewis Schaffel: "Orlando will find out how hard it is. They're lucky to have the extra year." What terrific timing for us — just two days before the announcement of our prices.

While newspaper presses churned the news out of Miami, our computers cranked out 4,000 personalized letters to pledged ticket accounts. Getting them mailed on time was a miracle; the accompanying color brochures took extra time to dry because of unexpected November rain. A problem you'd never think of.

The day before announcing the ticket prices we met with key members of the *Sentinel* sports staff. They had obtained a copy of the prices and were poised to run with it. We agreed to help explain the numbers if they would delay breaking the story until the morning of our public announcement. We knew that would anger the television people. But if the *Sentinel* were going to break the story we wanted them to write it from an educated viewpoint. We wanted the public to know some of the reasoning that went into those prices.

November 6 — The *Sentinel* unfurled the prices, which ranged from $8, or $344 per season, for roosts in the upper ends, to $45, or $1,935 per season, for the "super star" seats in the first several rows off courtside. Because we had "given" the story to the *Sentinel* the other media outlets fired off protests to me, to the NBA office, to Ralph Nader, to Dear Abby and to just about anyone else who would listen.

Cari Haught impressed me with her work on the chamber ticket drive, then steered me to Doug Minear. I finally just hired her full-time.

Cari Haught, in only her third day as director of communications, bore the brunt. In her previous positions with the chamber and a local public relations firm, Cari had been a great help in the early days of the franchise bid. She was bright and tough and I was glad she joined us. Especially on this week. Welcome to the bunker, Cari. Grab a helmet.

Jill and I finally got to take some time away for a weekend cruise to Nassau. It was a good time to escape. On our first day in Nassau, a little street urchin bugged me to buy a local paper. In it was a UPI wire story about the Orlando Magic ticket prices.

Back in Orlando the next week there was clamor over the prices. Radio talk shows churned with opinion. The theme seemed to be, "I'll buy even though the prices seem high." A *Sentinel* story showed that our prices, if in force that season, would average highest in the league. Celtics $19.64, Lakers $19.92 and Magic $21.41. The catch was that we would not play for two years and were guaranteeing the prices would remain fixed for our first three seasons. The $21.41 was high in 1987, but how about five years later?

In the *Sentinel* story an associate in Paul Bortz' firm predicted our tickets would be comparable with the rest of the league during our first three years. Said league publicist Brian McIntyre: "In five years, that $21.41 is going to be right about the average. Pat knows his way around the block. He's no dummy."

Thanks, Brian. I needed that.

Most of the lower level seats were at $28 and $23. Most of the upper level were $23 and $17. This in a city where 10 bucks typically had gotten you not only into most sports events but on the 50-yard line. As season ticket applicants began multiplying those numbers times 43 games (including two exhibitions), the exercise for many was not to figure out what section they wanted but to figure out how to get their $100 deposits back.

We debated refunds to defectors. The original understanding was that fans were committing the $100 for a seating priority and that we would refund the deposits only if we didn't get the franchise. I favored keeping the deposits. We had kept our end of the bargain. Jack Swope and Danny Durso spoke for refunds. They thought the relatively small amount wasn't worth the public relations blight of little old ladies and schoolteachers calling us ugly names.

We decided to refund, but not readily. We asked fans to write letters explaining why they couldn't keep their commitment. Many excuses were legit: moved away, lost job, divorce, illness, etc. Best of the bunch, though, was an explanation that arrived about a month after the ticket prices were announced.

Mr. Williams:

It all started a couple of months ago when my house was swallowed by a sinkhole. Unfortunately, I did not have sinkhole insurance. Not long after this, I was conned out of $80 million by a local farmer who claimed to be on the verge of the first breed of kosher pigs.

I am currently being sued by a woman who claims the second-hand smoke from my cigarette caused her to lose all interest in sex and start following the Grateful Dead. My bank informed me last week that a man who robbed them asked specifically for my funds. I was told by my doctor four days ago I suffer from a condition that will cause me to vote for Max Headroom in the next election.

I hope to catch a couple of games, but as you can tell, I'm in no position to order season tickets.

Sincerely,

Edward Caron

We granted Edward's refund on grounds of originality. But not so amusing were defections from what we called our Golden 100s. Jimmy Hewitt had commanded that project, rounding up 36 individuals and corporations willing to buy blocks of 100 tickets. The *Sentinel's* Tip Lifvendahl had committed to 100 at that opening press conference. Now, as some companies were down-sizing orders, he went to bat for us again.

"We are not going to back down," he was quoted in a *Sentinel* ticket story, "and I would hope those other corporations that pledged to purchase 100 tickets would honor their commitments. This is not time for the faint-of-heart. We ought to stretch and go all out to see that this first opportunity for big league professional sports in Orlando is a success."

There weren't enough Tip Lifvendahls out there. Only eight of the 36 took 100 tickets. The rest trimmed orders by a combined total of about 2,000 tickets. Losing that many pledges was the biggest blow to our struggle throughout 1988 to reach 10,000.

Once prices were announced, the plan was this: Those with season ticket deposits paid were asked only to look over the seating diagram and prices, then respond with their preferences. Payments would come due in 25 percent increments starting in the spring of 1988. Though we weren't asking for money with those initial responses, we regarded them as gold. These people knew our prices and our deal. Except for the $100 deposits, we didn't have their checks yet, but we assumed they were with us. That turned out to be too large an assumption. A new adventure awaited the following spring when the first large installment came due.

By the end of 1987 only 200 people formally had canceled. But there was no word from others representing 4,500 pledges who had not selected prices or preferred location. They were just sitting out there, silent, threatening me with one of those Katz-size ulcers. It was like staring from a foxhole into the black of night. What was the enemy up to out there?

I began 1988 with a phone blitz to chase the silent 4,500. This would be my 1988. Our ticket people gave me 50 names at a time on yellow sheets and I'd curl up with the phone. I heard every cock-and-bull story ever invented. After two weeks I figured there had to be a better way. I called Norm Sonju. He was not comforting. "There's only one way to get them," he said. "One at a time."

I spoke again in Apopka, where the economy is anchored by fern nurseries. A man had an idea how the Magic could impact Apopka: Sign Larry Bird and have him live in Apopka. I told him, "Larry Bird might *buy* Apopka." I humored the guy. "Who knows?" I said, "with Larry's bad wheels and his $2 million salary, maybe we could do it. The Celtics might stick him out there in the expansion draft and Apopka could underwrite the whole deal." But that's a lot of Apopka ferns.

We slogged along throughout winter and early spring, getting agreements to buy in telephone spurts of 12 now, 15 this afternoon, 10 more in the morning. By late March we reached 8,000 responses — still no additional money, remember — with 1,500 MIA's still out there somewhere. We needed those names on the dotted line. We couldn't operate like the burglar who broke into the church and stole $100,000 in pledges. We'd squeezed all those deposits to get the 8,000 confirmations. Now there might be no juice left. We quickly had to mine a new market.

May 24 was the most significant day yet in this Pat Williams Year of the Tickets. A mailing was going out with seat assignments. Eight thousand people had dreamed of sitting center-jump circle, row three, but many of those dreams were about to end. The letters set off fires all across Central Florida. The next day the phones danced and Ashleigh Bizelle was swamped. It was hard just to get through. To get to me, one joker claimed to be Jerry West. It worked. He acted as if his seat were *in* Los Angeles.

With the seat assignments was a bill for the first 25 percent installment, due three weeks later on June 14. By mid-July, only 5,300 of the 8,000 had paid the first installment.

Enough progress had been made in 18 months of arena construction to take people inside to where their seats would be. We took groups of eight to 12, put hard hats on them and ran them in there and hoped a girder would drop off and hit them in the head. Just kidding, folks.

These tours, more frequent as the building progressed, were the single-best thing we did to shore up relationships with ticket buyers. Gathering in the parking lot in groups of eight to 12, they were sullen, put-upon, antagonistic — feeling they'd been dealt a bad hand. Inside, it was fun to watch their faces when they saw that the ceiling and back walls were not *that* far away. I'd point to where the center circle and baskets would be. Until then, these people had only a seating chart to go on. They had imagined sitting seven miles from anything with people pointing to them and smirking.

Some tried bribes to improve seat locations. One guy in the home security business offered Ashleigh an alarm system for her house. He wanted the green seats right behind the team, so he'd send her gourmet candy and cookies wrapped in green foil with notes saying, "Think green." Another guy twice enclosed $100 bills with his regular check payments, wanting to be moved to a better location. Each time, Ashleigh credited his account with an extra $100. He didn't get better seats, but at least his final payment was $200 lighter.

At the end of the summer of '88 there was even deeper concern over ticket sales. Moving from 6,400 to 10,000 would be an absolute grind. I kept wanting to believe that through providence or statistical happenstance or whatever, we would come in one morning and 1,000 orders would be in the day's mail. Dream on, pal.

Dear Diary: We've got a problem with these tickets.

Something dramatic had to get a fall campaign moving. Enter Joe White, a New York ad man specializing in political TV spots on an emergency basis. Let's say the candidate is running behind in Seattle. Joe rushes in, studies the campaign and gets spots on a specific issue taped and on the air in 24 hours. Salvages the campaign. The Red Adair of advertising.

White came to town in mid-September. The taping consisted of me talking under a tree and my son Bobby played basketball on a backyard court. White taped for three hours one Saturday morning, rushed back to New York that night, spent all day Sunday editing and had two awesome 30-second spots ready on Monday. That's the kind of turnaround stuff he does. He's not a low-budget guy. We poured some major dollars into the campaign.

Bobby's part was father-and-son backyard basketball with an actor as his "father." It was tedious for an 11-year-old, but I assured him he was part of Magic history. Said Bobby: "It's tough being a son when it's not your real father."

The first TV showing was during an Olympics telecast from Seoul. At home we all gathered to watch. It was touching, but Bobby was unhappy. "I did all that work for three hours," he said, shaking his head, "and they only used *three seconds* of it?" I think he envisioned an hour special.

The second 25 percent installment on season tickets was due in September, adding to the burden. The league wanted half the money for 10,000 tickets by December 31. But with just three-plus months to go we were up to only 7,000 with just one 25 percent installment collected. Suddenly we had to hit new prospects for 50 percent of their orders and hold our breath on attrition among people we already had.

A terrific new idea — weekly lunch tours of the arena for prospects. Curly Neal was enlisted to help dazzle them. A small, decorated banquet room was set up. I figured this would knock their socks off and optimistically bounced into the first lunch. Of the 25 people invited, just one showed. One. Uno. A guy from Cocoa, Keith Pendergrass. A 6-foot-8 former Virginia Tech player, Keith was manager of a plant that manufactured combat vehicles.

With our hearts cracking we put on the full show for him — a catered lunch, my oratorical brilliance, Curly's charm and the tour. Keith recalled looking around the room at all the vacant place settings with one recurring thought: "Boy, what a waste of money."

We sent him on his way with a Magic mug and bumper sticker. He didn't buy any tickets, so all we accomplished was to interrupt construction. Ten workers stopped to line up for Curly's autograph. I left thinking, "This is hopeless." I was really down. Fortunately, 20 or so typically showed up for subsequent lunches and most bought tickets.

September 12 — Monday morning worry from my kids and from Russ Granik. I'd explained many times to the kids the importance of 10,000 tickets. At breakfast they seemed upset. Questions like: "What if we don't make it? Will we have to move?" It scared them. I put up a brave front. "Kids, we're gonna make it," I said confidently. Inwardly I was petrified, and perhaps even more petrified after Russ called to check on ticket sales and other progress by the expansion clubs. "I just want to remind you that the 10,000-ticket issue is David Stern's hot button," he said.

Dear Diary: Obviously there will be no mercy.

Getting the public to believe that Stern actually would kill the franchise if the minimum wasn't met was another matter. The attitude was: "Oh, if you get to such-and-such number, the NBA doesn't care. They don't really mean they'd abort the franchise over a few tickets, do they? Aw, c'mon. Be serious. You've got this arena, you've paid the fee." David Stern underscored his stance at an NBA meeting in Palm Beach: "Orlando gets to the 10,000 or there will be no team." Any more questions, gentlemen?

Robert Fraley: "Not knowing if we could reach 10,000 and not knowing what the NBA would do if we didn't was one of the great dramas of this whole process. At least in my mind it was clear what the NBA was going to do. They were not going to grant the franchise. By this time the owners knew it was worth more than $32.5 million."

Nearly a year later Granik would hedge only slightly. "David was absolutely insistent on the 10,000. If a team had 9,500, I don't know. But if it had been 8,500, I think David absolutely would have gone to the wall with the owners and said, 'We don't want to admit this city.' "

We cranked up Kim Kopperud's phone bank again. We gave the 17 phone solicitors an arena tour, hoping that might motivate them to do something special. We led them from the second floor of the little building at Robinson and Palmetto, past the Dukakis campaign headquarters on the first floor and, blinking like moles, into the sunlight.

Phoner Angelo Mazza took me to heart and called Bob Colbert, Jack Nicholson's agent in LA, to try to sell Jack a Jack Nicholson seat. Give Angelo an A for ingenuity, but no sale. Will Jack be disappointed one day when he can't get in? He'll have to sit in the cuckoo's nest.

There was one brief Phonebank Phlap. Someone indignantly discovered we were using the same phones as Democratic campaign workers. They used the phone bank upstairs by night to sell Michael Dukakis. We used it by day to sell Michael Jordan. They'd take down the Magic

posters in the evenings and put up Dukakis posters to juice their workers, then we'd switch back the next morning. We got a few irate calls
about that from Republican basketball fans. The irony was that Oscar
Juarez, one of the leading Republicans in Central Florida, owns the
building.

Dear Diary: Did the Lakers run into these things getting started?

October 11 — Good news: We reached 7,500. Bad news: We have to
average 50 tickets every working day to reach 10,000 by the deadline.
Awesome task. The drive at least was starting to capture everyone's
attention. At an expressway toll booth the attendant recognized me and
as I pulled away, shouted, "Have you got the 10,000 yet?" I'll never tip
that toll-booth attendant again.

I was willing to do anything. Bob Poe's wife, Virginia, set up a session for me to pitch the employees at Vaughan Printing. Picture the
scene: A bunch of guys standing around with ink all over their blue
overalls listening to me hawk tickets. I got up at 5:15 the morning of
our 16th wedding anniversary and celebrated by trying to recruit truck
drivers for Wayne Densch's beverage distributorship as basketball ticket salesmen on their routes. Tried the same thing with the Pepsi drivers. All the time I was thinking, "Why are we doing this?"

Dear Diary: Stop thinking. Just keep going.

There were three Sunday afternoon public arena tours. At the first
one, 104 people bought tickets on the spot. Many saw the arena and
gasped, "Why did I wait so long?" One guy I recognized came up in a
Knicks cap. I'd taken him through the shell of the arena months before
and he had done nothing but grouse. He felt ripped off. Had a terrible
seat location. But now here he was, proudly pointing to his seats and
saying, "You were right. You were right. Terrific seats. I'd rather be up
there than down here on the floor. I can see the scoreboard better.
Terrific. You were right." I wasn't sure whether to kiss him or strangle
him.

While I kept comparing our progress to Miami's, the basketball world began measuring us against Minneapolis. Miami already was on the floor while Minneapolis was on our timetable. As we went public, revealing our sales almost daily, the Timberwolves were only slightly less guarded than Jim and Tammy's accountants. Our philosophy made us look weak and struggling.

The Timberwolves played it cool, creating an appearance that 10,000 was in the bag, no problem. They said only that they would cut off sales at 15,000, the implication being they had long since passed 10,000 and that those who dragged their feet might get shut out.

A Minneapolis TV station sent a crew to report on the relative progress of the two franchises. "It appears Minneapolis is doing better," the reporter said, "because you're having so much trouble getting your tickets sold while Minneapolis is having no trouble at all." We later learned that behind that facade the Timberwolves were paddling like crazy, just like we were. Two different schools of thought. If we had said all along that everything was just great, would we have reached the minimum easier? We'll never know.

Robert McAllan of Channel 68 bought a block of 100 to get us to 8,000 fully paid tickets. We were frantic to get to 10,000.

November 7 — We made a little noise by presenting local hero and Cy Young winner Frank Viola as our 8,000th season ticket holder. Time had come to consider desperate measures like reducing the prices of some sections. The 10,000 was looking pretty distant. Jack Swope and Ashleigh Bizzelle proposed converting four upper-bowl corner sections from $17 seats to $8 and $12 seats. Thanksgiving and Christmas were near and we feared the public would shove aside this ticket issue for more important things. We had kicked off the fall advertising campaign with Joe White ads, but that had run out. Now we had no advertising and were searching for any idea.

Ashleigh: "We had all but sold out the $8 and $12 seats — $344 and $516 for season tickets. We had 20 sections at the next price of $17 — for each season ticket. Jack and I wanted to convert four of the $17 sections to lower prices. One, we needed to get to the 10,000 — that was getting scary — and, two, it would be a good public relations move."

Good points, but to switch those four sections would've reduced our annual potential by $250,000. It was a calculated risk, but I took an adamant position that we couldn't change. I argued that we had established the prices and we had to stick to them. If we didn't reach the 10,000, so be it. But we couldn't back up any farther. We were at 8,167. That's 82 percent of the way there or 18 percent to go, whichever made you feel better.

November 21 — Another huge problem no longer could be ignored. About 1,000 buyers had paid the first 25 percent payment and were counted in our total of 8,490. But they were late making the second installment. At the December 31 deadline, a mere six weeks away, the NBA would count only those who had paid 50 percent. Without these the Orlando Magic would need more than magic. We could be Dead City.

The staff huddled on this newest crisis. You could hear the nerve ends jangling. One suggestion: Send telegrams to the delinquents. Then we realized the cost of sending telegrams. Nerve gas was ruled out. How could we inspire those 1,000 people to take out their checkbooks and keep us alive? We tried a letter, which made only a small dent.

December 12 — Nearly 900 second installments still were in a four-corner offense. We divided them into 10 pages of names and numbers. Each staffer took a page, attempting to charm these wonderful and loving patrons into realizing they were a distinct threat to the international balance of trade and might intensify famine in India and unrest in Central America if they didn't get off their dead duffs and pay the bloody second installment on their Magic tickets. Some responded, but most apparently had little concern for famine in India. But none were bailing out. It was, "Well, when my December paycheck comes, I'll get it to you." Or, "You mean Shirley didn't pay that? Oh, we'll get right on it." Every one of them had an excuse.

By now our ticket count appeared in huge numbers on a sheet hanging from the side of the DuPont Plaza. Motorists on I-4 saw an encouraging 9,581 on this day. But those lagging 25 percenters were hidden in there. Without them we were short of 9,000. With just two weeks to go.

It was time to get serious. Cari Haught drafted what came to be known around the office as Cari's Nasty-Gram, a final effort to get the remaining 780 foot-draggers up to 50 percent. Jack Swope, who tends to be our Nice Monitor, blinked at the terse copy in the Nasty-Gram and wondered aloud if we should at least insert the word "please" somewhere. The staff hooted him down and decided time had come to belt the laggards between the eyes. The catchy little opening line of Cari's love letter does just that:

> Dear Orlando Magic Season Ticket Holder:
> We regret to inform you that we have canceled your Orlando Magic season ticket order.
> We have repeatedly tried to contact you in regard to your outstanding 50 percent payment. To date, we have not received your payment. This lack of response has forced us to release your seats, as we have many people waiting in line to purchase your locations. We have run out of time!
> As you know, the NBA is requiring that we have 50 percent payment on 10,000 season tickets by December 31 of this year or they could pull the franchise. We must sell your seats in order to meet this requirement.
> We honestly regret your decision not to be a part of the Magic, but you leave us no choice.

If you have made your payment, please call our box of-
fice at (407) 89- MAGIC immediately!
Sincerely,
Pat Williams
President / General Manager

The Nasty-Gram brought quick results. Our switchboard stood
up, rolled over and performed six of the major movements in Swan
Lake. The 25 percenters couldn't dial the phone fast enough. They
promised to race in, not run, with missing payments. Virtually all
paid within the next few days, keeping Pat and Jill Williams' kids
from having to pack.

Former Channel 9 general manager Cliff Conley said he was going to present the check for his station's 16-seat skybox at the pre-
cise time we reached 9,983. Channel 9 could proudly announce it
had taken us to 9,999. Channel 9 — 9,999. Get it? Maybe a little

*Greg Wallace gulped, pulled out his American Express card and
became the 10,000th season ticket holder.*

hokey, but, listen, for 16 seats, I was ready to tattoo 9s on my ear lobes. There was a hitch. At the close of business on December 21 we reached 9,974. Cliff decided go ahead with the 16, in living color. So Channel 9 pushed us to 9,990. Well, three 9s are the next best thing to four 9s, right?

December 22 — Ten tickets to go. We'd honor the 10,000th ticket buyer but had declared only those who came to our office would be eligible. No mail or phone orders. "This Could Be the Magic Day," a *Sentinel* headline trumpeted. We opened at 9 and promptly sold a pair. That was 9,992. Eight to go. The whole organization was nervous. Television crews were poised. Twenty minutes passed. Nothing. What was going on here?

At 9:25, in walked a guy in T-shirt and blue jeans.

"How many to go?" he asked.

"Eight," said Rich Cramer, one of Ashleigh's ticket assistants.

The guy pondered a moment, obviously multiplying eight times $731. That's $5,848 and at least half had to be paid on the spot. Nearly $3,000. He swallowed hard and announced: "I want to do it." He pulled out an American Express card. New tension. Would his card clear? It did. And amid an eruption of hoots and cheers, Greg Wallace of the Bug Hut, an auto repair shop specializing in Volkswagens, became the 10,000th ticket buyer, nine days ahead of the NBA guillotine.

The rest of the morning we popped buttons off our chests, then whipped up an afternoon celebration at Church Street Station. I ran by the phone bank to thank everyone for all they'd done. They were the real heroes. I called Jill at home. "Yeah, I know," she said. "I just saw it in the sky." Joe Kittinger, Church Street Station's famed skywriter and ocean-hopping balloonist, etched a basketball in the clear blue sky along with the message: "10,000 YEA!"

Yea, indeed.

Atop the downtown Howard Johnson's for a magazine photograph showing off two of my passions — basketball and Orlando.

Bill Frederick (No. 1) had a grand time at the uniform unveiling with Curly, Matty (14) and me.

Tramping through the arena construction on a daily basis for two years ruined at least a half-dozen pairs of my shoes. But after it was finished, Russ Granik said, "There's nothing like this arena anywhere in the country."

*10,000 reasons to celebrate —
the day we sold the 10,000th
ticket, just before Christmas
of '88. From left are Mayor
Frederick, Greg Wallace (who
bought No. 10,000), Jack Swope,
carney barker Williams and
Orange County Commissioner
Tom Dorman. Without the
cooperation between Frederick
and Dorman, the Magic never
would have happened.*

*Jill and I with our tribe of 12 in front of the arena. We were
hosting fans who were touring the building for the first time
to select their season ticket locations.*

The dream finally became real when we hired Matty Guokas (below) and began adding players. Reggie Theus (above with Stuff) arrived from the Atlanta Hawks to give us a top-notch scorer. Nick Anderson was our No. 1 college pick in '89. We couldn't believe he was still there when it was our turn to pick.

The Magic hosted the first basketball game at the arena in February of '89 — a doubleheader with Florida-Stanford and Central Florida-Rollins. Seeing the packed building and getting a taste of what would come when the NBA arrived are among my most vivid memories of that afternoon.

The Magic girls. We debated long and hard whether or not to have a dance team. But Cari Haught convinced us we could put a team together to challenge the Laker Girls as the best in the NBA. The girls entertain at all home games as well as at a variety of community events. The first Magic Girl dance camp for youngsters in the summer of '89 was an enormous hit.

STUFF,
THE DROWNING DRAGON

Flashback to January, 1982, at Philadelphia's Spectrum. The Sixers are playing the Seattle Supersonics. Cavorting here and there, mugging with kids, swiping dangling shoes off women's feet, mocking referees and leading cheers is an experimental Sesame Street-type character named "Hoops."

During a timeout, the little furry thing flops on its belly and crawls combat-style ever closer to the Seattle huddle, playfully cupping one ear as if trying to eavesdrop. Sonics Coach Lenny Wilkens is in no mood to go along with the gag. Wilkens curtly shoos away the mascot. He doesn't know or care who's in the suit.

When he reads this, Lenny will find out for the first time the pesky clown in the silly suit was the dignified general manager of the Sixers, Pat Williams.

Crawling into the Hoops costume was part of my fascination with sports team mascots. Philadelphia is one of the mascot capitals of sports and the Phillie Phanatic, with gifted Dave Raymond inside, is one of the most successful and beloved in the business. I was determined to add that "smile" element to the

Sixers.

In the late '70s a Sixers mascot called Big Shot died a horrible death. Fans were more than just indifferent, they booed. Enter Hoops, who also fell flat. Undaunted, I secretly hired Dave Raymond to put on the Hoops costume one night — strictly a one-shot deal — to see whether the secret is the suit or the guy inside. It took only minutes to realize it ain't the suit; it's the guy inside. Dave breathed life into Hoops during the next two and a half hours, piping energy into every timeout and lull.

Our problem was finding another Dave Raymond. A guy named Joe Kempo came close. Thinking the first costume was the better of the two, Big Shot was resurrected with Kempo inside. Bingo. The combination has been a huge success.

With that background it was a given that I'd want a Magic mascot. Dave put us onto a friend who plays Dunkin' for the New Jersey Nets. The guy owns the costume himself and was willing to move to Orlando, lock, stock and feathers, and become the Magic's Dunkin'. But we wanted our own, fresh character.

Disney World PR man Ralph Kline and artist Tom Tripodi helped

Mascot suggestions included a magic bean, at left, that did not live up to Doug Minear's expectations.

start the project with suggested designs. Doug Minear and Cari Haught got involved, and the mascot search was off and flapping. In January, 1988, we called costume designers around the country including the people I thought were the best, Harrison-Erickson of New York. They produced the Phillie Phanatic, Big Shot and the mascots for the Expos and White Sox.

Bonnie Erickson was a member of Jim Henson's Muppets empire before branching off with Wade Harrison. She submitted three designs, including two Muppets-type possibilities we liked. We scratched the third, a tourist-looking character with stars for eyes. Many proposals from other designers were sorcerer-related.

We were anxious to see the design from a certain highly touted New York woman. Doug Minear installed her as the 4-to-5 favorite in the morning line. Cari: "We waited and waited. When her design finally arrived I excitedly tore it open only to discover a 'magic bean.' Just a big bean with eyes and legs. I shrieked: 'A *bean!*? Give me a break!' Even Doug had to admit it was pretty bad." It quickly became a has-bean.

By midsummer 1988 we honed in on Bonnie Erickson's surviving

two designs, leaning toward the one she named "Magic Dragon." Drawings bounced back and forth between New York and Orlando, each time with slight modifications. By August we had a deal with Bonnie to buy the mascot outright rather than rent or lease the design. She built two uniforms for her standard fee of $75,000. In Philly we had leased Big Shot for $10,000 a year.

One reason for two suits is to let one air out from the last performance while using the fresh one. There's nothing quite so enjoyable as crawling into that wet, clammy suit reeking of last night's perspiration.

Tossing Robert Fraley into the negotiating pen with these creative types was a test of his patience. Fraley: "Of all the documents needed to get the Magic up and running, the costume contract was the most bizarre. We were dealing with artistic people in a small business and it was almost impossible. They had a high level of trust with Pat. But they didn't want to do anything any lawyer would ever advise any client to do. We probably spent as much time trying to get the contract on those silly costumes as we did on some of the major sponsorship agreements.

Even more mascot suggestions.

"It dawned on us they were going to make this very expensive costume that might or might not fit the person best suited to be inside. They wanted just to make the costume and leave it to us to go find a guy that size. They finally agreed to build in adjustments ranging from 5-foot-8 to 6-foot-1. But it must have taken a week to get them to do that.

"Then we asked them to indemnify us from any breach of copyright or trademark the costume might create. As creators they were selling it to us as a free and clear original. They said, 'No, you've seen the costume. You ought to be able to know that yourself.' So we ended up having to go through the trouble and expense of doing a trademark search."

Robert wanted to protect us in case the character already existed or there was one too close for legal comfort. We brushed with just such a problem. Bonnie originally designed the dragon with a purple body. Doug Minear noted that Disney had a similar purple character — Figment, star of the Imagination Plaza at Epcot. Cari thought Doug was overreacting. Then she went to Disney's Lake Buena Vista Shopping Village and bought two stuffed Figment

How much purple is too much purple? In deference to Disney's Figment, we opted for a green Stuff.

dolls, plus hats, T-shirts and posters with Figment in all his purple majesty.

We decided Disney probably would never press the issue and, besides, Bill du Pont was the last guy who would be aware of some character at Disney World, right? Just to play it safe, Cari kept one of the Figment dolls handy as we prepared to run the dragon past Bill in a late-August meeting covering a number of items. Bill hadn't seen any of the designs and was just back from overseas. When the agenda rolled around to mascot time, Bonnie's full-color rendering of the dragon was unfurled. The first words out of Bill's mouth: "Isn't that Disney character out at Epcot also a purple color?"

"Interesting you should say that," Cari replied. "Just in case it came up, we happen to have a doll of the Disney character right here." From under the table she produced a miniature version of Figment. Bill, who developed an appreciation for Figment while taking his son to Disney, was impressed.

What are the odds that the owner of an NBA club would have a working knowledge of Disney's mascot characters? We were constantly amazed at Bill's awareness. Just like that, he recognized that the color of our mascot was similar to a character at Epcot.

We ditched the purple in favor of Kermit the Frog green. Bonnie designed Kermit when she worked with Henson. Later we were accused of copying the color of the Phillie Phanatic. Not true, but better to have a conflict with the Phanatic than with Figment.

Now came naming the dragon. Bill was sensitive to the obvious — Puff the Magic Dragon of Peter, Paul and Mary fame was a drug symbol of the '60s and we weren't anxious to invite that connection. When Doug showed the costume rendering to Wayne Jackson, a radio ad salesman passing through the office, he shrugged and said, "You ought to call him 'Stuff the Magic Dragon.' " It was like a light went on. "Stuff" was a hit.

Stuff was introduced to his public on Halloween night. Wade Harrison and Bonnie agreed to build the costume by then and I lined up Dave Raymond to come from Philadelphia to perform Stuff's debut. A campaign leading to the big night included strange footprints leading from a huge, broken eggshell near the arena, along with supposed "sightings" around town. We were amazed how the local media picked up on it. The *Sentinel's* Bob Morris had fun with the whole schtick. TV stations ran footage of the eggshell. Morning disc jockeys batted it around like crazy. The eggcitement mounted for the eggceptional eggstravaganza.

A huge broken egg, a smashed basketball, strange footprints — the stuff from which Stuff was made.

Stuff the Magic Dragon had a spectacular debut at Church Street Station.

October 31 — Halloween. In the top corner of the *USA TODAY* sports front, one of the two daily notes proclaimed to the nation that the Orlando Magic mascot would be introduced that night at Church Street Station. Dave Raymond went to New York the previous afternoon to get the costume, then grabbed a late-night flight to Orlando. I couldn't wait to see what he'd brought. At eight in the morning I knocked on the door of room 1416 at the downtown Radisson. "Sorry to wake you up, Dave," I said, feeling like a child on Christmas morning. "I've got to see it. You've got to open the box. You don't have to put it on. Just pull the head out so I can see it." I was amazed, delighted and broke into a huge smile. The color was terrific.

That night was fabulous. Two local magicians, Giovanni and Tim, plotted the whole show. Curly Neal warmed up the crowd jamming the street through Church Street Station. The magicians crammed Curly in a huge box that rose slowly up a pole. When the box re-opened — *voila!* — in Curly's place was Stuff, who slid down the pole to the cheers of the crowd. Inside the suit, Dave Raymond was psyched out of his gills. As the lively song, *Shout!* blared throughout the complex, David just took off, diving over people, darting here, darting there. He's so good and this was his element.

Along with the foolishness was great pressure. If you launch the mascot to yawns and guffaws, he's doomed forever. But David hit it big. The place was crazy, a wild scene. Our staff was absolutely giddy.

November 1 — I was up early and off to Gainesville to pitch ticket sales for the Florida-Stanford and Rollins-Central Florida basketball doubleheader the next February, the arena's first sports event. I still was pumped from the night before. Turning onto the Florida Turnpike I called Bonnie Erickson in New York on the car phone to tell her how thrilled we were. Before I could get started, she said, "I'm just so sorry about the accident last night. I'm so sorry about what happened."

Huh? happened?

"Bonnie, it was one of the greatest nights of my life."

"Pat, I hate to be the one to tell you this, but my phone has been ringing all morning. Something dreadful happened late last night and we hope we can solve this problem."

"Bonnie, tell me what happened."

"Well, maybe you'd better talk to your own staff."

In a panic, I called Cari. She unfolded one of the most bizarre and slapstick tales imaginable. Dave Raymond returned to the Radisson about midnight, exhausted but elated. He hung the wet, heavy Stuff suit on a hook by the closet. But the suit fell from the hook and caught a fire alarm handle, setting off the sprinkler system for the entire 14th floor.

David suddenly found himself stark naked, water firing at him from all angles. He grabbed a robe and raced out the door, which locked behind him. The hall was full of people, water and the piercing sound of the fire alarm. David, unable to get back in his room, tried to calm everybody. "It's not a fire! It's not a fire!" he shouted. Just a drowning Stuff.

A recorded voice boomed down the hallway, a voice that didn't know the difference between a Stuff and a fire. "Stay calm!" it ordered. "There is a fire in the building! Stay calm and move quickly to the stairwells! Do not attempt to use the elevators!"

That had the expected soothing effect on the visitors who raced in all directions, screaming and crying. The hotel night clerk burst onto the floor and soon threatened David with arrest for setting off the alarm and sprinklers. But when order and low tide were restored, David ended up in the hotel laundry room at 5 a.m. drying his own clothes, trying to salvage something to wear to the airport. He had called Cari some time in the middle of the night, but her reaction was, "Dave, I'm sorry, but what can I do tonight?"

Dawn found our downtrodden waif scrambling to the airport, his clothes a mess, too late for the flight to Philadelphia. Spirits listing heavily to starboard, he staggered to a pay phone, desperately needing to hear a sympathetic voice. But the only voice he reached was the recorded one on the off-hours answering machine at the Magic office. Twice. Dave's pathetic call was captured by the machine:

> "Yeah, this is David Raymond calling. Uh, if anybody is there, could you pick up because I want to discuss, uh, ... we had a problem at the hotel last night which I described a little bit to Cari .... Haught. I'm at the airport now and I missed my flight. I'm at a pay phone which does not have, uh, well, it's got a number of 407-857-9799. I'll wait here until somebody gets in the office. I need to talk to Pat Williams or Cari Haught about the costume. Last night I had a problem where I accidentally set off the fire extinguisher system and the costume got wet and got some dirt that came through the pipes on it. And, uh, the head got out of it unscathed. But the body is very wet and it needs to have the feather boa replaced on the back and a few other things. So, I just want to discuss the situation with Pat or Cari. Uh, it's not quite as bad as I thought it was last night, but it's still not good. Uh, the costume is at the hotel and it's in the laundry area. And, uh, they're waiting there for, you know, one of your representatives to pick it up. Uh, but please call me here first before you go over there, if you can remember. Okay, I'm here at 407-857-9799. Uh, and I will wait for you to call. Bye."

> Beep.

> "Yes, this is David Raymond calling again. Uh, I had left a message earlier. I needed to talk to either Cari or

Pat Williams. It's extremely important. It's about the, uh, uh, the accident that happened at the hotel last night and the damage to the costume. (sigh) Uh, I missed my plane flight this morning, so I'm gonna be at the airport until one o'clock. The number I gave you is a wrong number. It was just a number that was posted on this telephone and it's not right. I'll keep calling. Uh, I hope someone will be in by nine. Uh, and, uh, I'll try to get ahold of Pat or Cari. Tell them the only way they're gonna find out, uh, well, I can talk to them about the costume, but the costume is over hanging up in the laundry at the hotel with the cases and everything. There were a lot of things destroyed. The head of the costume made it without any real damage. But the body got completely soaked with water. Uh, I'll keep calling until I get ya. Okay? Bye."

Is this a script for the Keystone Cops or what?

The next day, Bob Morris went wild in his column. He ran pictures of Stuff and the Phillie Phanatic along with gripes from a local Phillies fan who didn't like the similarities. Imagine if he'd known that inside the Stuff costume *was* the Phillie Phanatic. Morris also suggested lyrics for a parody on the song, *"Puff, the Magic Dragon"* . . .

> *Stuff, the Magic Dragon*
> *Lived by the court*
> *And frolicked as a PR tool*
> *For O-town's big league sport.*
> *Little Pattie Williams*
> *Loved that mascot, Stuff*
> *He made the 10,000 ticket goal*
> *A job not quite so tough.*
> *Together they would travel*
> *The rubber chicken trail*
> *Pat would trot out Stuff to help*
> *Him make a ticket sale.*
> *Fat cats and corporations*
> *Wrote checks wherever they came*
> *Yes, football-mad Floridians*
> *Paid to see a round-ball game!*

The DJs at Y-106 invited Bob and me to record the song. We were backed by a chorus of stagehands. The singing was atrocious but the whole bit was a gas.

Dear Diary: If David Stern could only see me now.

Stuff Debut Footnote: November 3 I spoke to a small business group at the Radisson, where a convention of Christian athletes, Professional Athletes' Outreach, was being held. I enjoyed an impromptu reunion with Ernie Harwell, the longtime Tigers announcer, and baseball players Tommy Herr, Tom Foley, Tim Burke and Alvin Davis. They told about an unusual experience during their first night in the hotel. Seems they were awakened when some kook running around half-nude on the 14th floor set off all the fire alarms.

Oh? Is that so?

The search was launched to find a permanent "Stuff." After Dave's Disaster we couldn't have lured him to Orlando even with the promise of a personal key to fire alarm boxes. Not that he ever indicated interest in ending his rule as the Phillie Phanatic. But his backup, Mike Stevens, was interested and highly recommended by Dave.

Nevertheless, we held a Stuff tryout in January, 1988, promising that the finalists could audition again at the college doubleheader in February. I was impressed by a group of mimes at Sea World and thought they'd be serious candidates. They were invited but failed to show for the tryout, leaving us with only five aspiring Stuffs. The five became four when one pulled on the suit and became claustrophobic. Cari was high on the guy because of his impressive credentials. He had done commercials, worked entertainment at Disney and was a graduate of the Ringling Brothers Clown College, sort of the Julliard School of Rubber Noses. When his turn came, Cari anticipated something unique. She got it.

Cari: "They put the Stuff head on him but within 30 seconds he freaked out. He ran for the exit in a panic, shouting, 'Get me out! Get me out!' They took the head off and the poor guy was a basket case."

During the doubleheader Stevens worked the nationally televised opener in which Stanford handily beat Florida. The two finalists from the tryouts each worked a half of the Rollins-Central Florida game. We named Stevens as permanent Stuff. I cautioned him about sneaking up on Lenny Wilkens' huddles.

Jeff Mullins of North Carolina-Charlotte said what makes it difficult to compete with an NBA team is not so much the quality of the basketball but the quality of the *show*. "It's the whole thing ... the uniforms, the laser lights, the music, the mascot, the dance team, the production," he said. "It becomes more than just a game; it's an event. We just can't compete with that."

A pro team *is* more than just players, and those extra trappings become all the more important to an expansion franchise. To create a personality during the two long years before we had a roster it was important to move ahead with the logo, Stuff, the uniform design, a floor design and the Magic Girls. Cari Haught or Doug Minear or both were involved in all of these.

CREATING A UNIFORM: Doug Minear presented a design in early 1987 that essentially didn't change for the nearly two years until we had a finished product. In that first presentation somebody wondered aloud how the design would look with pin stripes. The idea set off an exhaustive elimination process with the MacGregor company until we married the stripes with just the right colors and material. MacGregor is the sporting goods company that makes all NBA uniforms.

Doug thought pin stripes would be a perfect touch to create a special team identity. But sending his design to the MacGregor factory in Wisconsin was the first step in a uniform struggle that became a battle of attrition. About nine little things were wrong with MacGregor's first sample. We returned it, noting the changes. They'd send it back with the nine things corrected but with four new things wrong. The pin stripes would be too wide or the star on the side of the pants too big. Next time, the silver would be gray and not silver, the blue not really our blue, or the cut of the neck changed. That lasted for more than a year of trial and error.

At first we weren't worried because we were so far ahead of the game. But we became concerned as the uniform samples kept making the Wisconsin-Florida loop. Finally I told Doug to fly there and make sure, once and for all, they got it exactly like we wanted. On a balmy Florida day in February, Doug found himself blinking in the snowscape of Fond du Lac, Wisconsin. Doug: "It was minus 16. The people in the MacGregor factory were, like, working in a meat locker. I was encouraged when I saw a tiny bit of green peeking through the snow. Then I discovered it was the top of an evergreen tree."

Their main problem was getting our oddball blue right. Magic blue is a special creation, the bright, electric blue we invented after I was outvoted on my beloved Wake Forest black and gold. Magic blue is distinctive and I'm glad Doug came up with it. But it has been a nightmare for printers and clothiers to produce from the standard printing inks and dyes. Ironically, we had to go to the Du-Pont Chemical Corp. in Wilmington, Delaware, to have the dye custom-made. It cost about $2,000. Bill was not involved in pulling Du-Pont strings but was amused when Doug told him where we turned for the Magic blue.

The pin stripes created another problem. We wanted uniforms made from the light, "breathing" perforated nylon material so prevalent today. However, MacGregor said that they couldn't knit stripes and punch holes in the same material. It just didn't work on their machines. When Doug went to Wisconsin they were saying we either had to drop the stripes or use the heavier double-knit material. The solution was an accident when Doug and a MacGregor rep dug through a large box containing dozens of rejected sample uniforms from pro and college teams.

"The box was wonderful," recalls Doug. "It was full of the most bizarre uniforms ever created. I happened to pull out this one shirt that was a lightweight material with pin stripes. The guy told me it was made of something called Durene, a fabric they hadn't produced in years. It's cotton on the inside plated to nylon on the outside."

"Funny you should find that," the MacGregor man noted. "The trainer for the Cleveland Browns, a guy who's been with them for years, called not long ago and said, 'Remember that old material you used to make in the '60s? We're getting complaints about the double-knit being hot and scratchy.' So we're doing Cleveland Browns uniforms right now in this stuff."

Bingo. We were next in line on the Durene machine. In the blink of a mere seven more months, MacGregor rushed the finished product to Orlando. After a year-and-a-half of painstaking effort, Orlando Magic uniforms were different from anything in the NBA. But would the press and the public accept them?

October 21 — Dog-and-pony show to introduce the new threads with some season ticket holders and the media invited. Three TV crews were at the Omni Hotel to cover it live on noon newscasts. Matty, the mayor, Curly and I were the models, Bob Morris the emcee. The Dr. Phillips High School band and the Magic Girls were there. The mayor was a stitch, though he probably didn't want to do it. Bill Frederick can be staid and reserved. We made it easier by telling him he could keep on the warmup suit over his uniform.

But he ended up in the middle of the show, stripping off the warmup and cavorting around the stage shooting free throws at a little basket we set up. He was great, really putting some life into it. Loving it, the crowd gave an ovation to the mayor and, more important, to the uniforms.

DESIGNING A FLOOR: Unleashed to plan a home floor, things like the logo placement and color arrangement for the sidelines and free-throw lanes, Doug Minear produced a revolutionary design that spawned what may be known in the NBA as the Orlando Magic Rule. The feature of Doug's creation was a stunning trail of shooting stars and vapor in the lanes, stretching from the foul line through the lane and across the end line. Bill du Pont's reaction was one word: "Wow!" I think that meant good. Initial reaction in NBA headquarters was the same. Then it shifted to, "Let us think about this a bit." Finally: "Nix, nix."

The trail of stars was revolutionary, but the NBA was afraid we'd be opening Pandora's (or maybe Minear's) box. Before long on NBA floors, you wouldn't be able to find the lanes for all the artwork. The league declared that lanes must be a solid color. Doug was depressed. He loved the stars. They had been his inspiration. Sorry, Doug, but if the Magic is going to have shooting stars on the floor, they'll have to come from the NBA draft.

We managed to keep Doug's second color in the half-circle behind the foul line. The league insisted that part of the circle be the natural color of the floor — unpainted. But we pointed out that some arenas already had second colors in that area. They relented but declared that no future floors could have the second color there. So our lanes became black and the half-circle behind the foul line became Magic blue. The NBA emblem also was included on the floor

The NBA turned down Doug Minear's trail-of-stars design in the lanes.

design. That scored a point with the league. Nobody else had that.

We decided on a parquet floor that enhanced Doug's surviving design when it appeared for the first time at the college double-header. I didn't see Doug during the games but happened to pass him on I-4 the next morning. I waved and signaled him to roll down his window. At 60 m.p.h. we shouted back and forth between cars. "Your floor looked great! Congratulations!"

The league feared that other teams might copy the idea.

THE MAGIC GIRLS: A dance team concept was approached with one premise: You succeed only by producing a group close to the quality of the classy Laker Girls. Some teams' performers are girl-next-door types only if you live in Las Vegas. A dance team in Central Florida would need a certain wholesomeness yet be sufficiently appealing. Anything else might come off schlocky and detrimental to the festive, upbeat atmosphere we want. Done right, the girls become a positive extension into the community. One thing we established quickly was a rule forbidding dance team members to fraternize with players.

Cari Haught dipped into her beloved Florida State Seminole sphere and arranged for several of FSU's Golden Girls to perform at halftime of the first Orlando All-Star Classic in 1988. Jodie Penn-

The Magic Girls are so good that the Bullets and the Mavs called to see how we did it.

March 1, 1989

Sun Bank, National Association
200 South Orange Avenue
Orlando, Florida 32897

Orlando Magic, Ltd.
390 North Orange Avenue
Suite 275
Orlando, Florida 32801

Re: Expansion Agreement dated June 22, 1987
      between the 23 Entities that then constituted
      the National Basketball Association and the
      Orlando Magic, Ltd. (the "Expansion Agreement")

Dear Sir:

      In my capacity as commissioner of the National
Basketball Association (the "NBA"), I am writing to advise
you that the NBA has received the final payment (as defined
in the Expansion Agreement) and the closing documents
required under the Expansion Agreement. Consequently, the
franchise (as defined in the Expansion Agreement), has been
duly granted to the Orlando Magic, Ltd. in accordance with
the Expansion Agreement and the Constitution and By-Laws of
the NBA.

                              Very truly yours,

                              David J. Stern

Boy, were we glad to finally get this letter.

ington, their choreographer, expressed interest in joining us if we planned to have a dance troupe. That decision was at least a year away, but she'd be kept in mind. Three months later she was on board, organizing auditions for the Magic Girls. Cari noted that the decision was made earlier partially by our struggle to sell the 10,000 tickets.

Cari had been adamant on having the team, studied others around the league and ran some numbers on how to keep it from being a huge expense. She said it even could show a profit, especially if we obtained a corporate sponsor. The Gatorade Magic Girls? Magic L'eggs? We had to be careful, though. I didn't think the public would embrace, say, the John Deere Tractor Magic Girls. In addition to performing at games, the Magic Girls would be available for store openings, sales events, etc., for a fee, $40 per hour per girl, split between the girls and the club. The club's share would be applied to travel, makeup, hair-styling, uniforms, promotion and Jodie's salary.

Tryouts, scattered around Central Florida in the fall of '88, attracted overwhelming coverage and public attention. The *Sentinel* did a huge color spread and the TV stations were all over it. The finale at J.J. Whispers nightclub, where the final 16 Magic Girls were selected, drew 1,500. I was floored. In Philly this just hadn't worked.

The name Magic Girls seemed to fit. There were some other suggestions, but most, like Magic Makers, had a suggestive double-entendre we were careful to avoid. Magic Girls seemed the safest bet. We were only too happy that Matty Guokas likes an up-tempo, high-octane attack with players aggressively flying across the floor. But in the matter of a dance troupe I wanted to bring the ball up court very deliberately.

SEE YOUR MILLION, RAISE YOU TWO

Income from local radio and television and from corporate sponsors no longer is a luxury in pro sports. It's a life-giving necessity. For the Magic to compete on the floor, particularly with teams from bigger cities, this money became all the more important. Suddenly we'd be in the same lane with the Pistons and the Bulls and the Lakers. And the guy in the stands doesn't want to hear that your area has 7 million fewer people than Chicago or that your TV market ranks 14 spots behind Detroit's. Time comes quickly even for an expansion franchise when the only ranking that guy really cares about is the one in the newspaper with the W's and L's beside his team.

Part of our pitch to the NBA was that while Orlando was not large by league standards, Central Florida's growth eventually would take care of us. Still, some in the NBA were worried about our initial earning potential. Our optimistic claims materialized in spades thanks, in part, to some extraordinary timing and circumstance. Just as the Magic was starting:

— Two huge sports cable operations drew sabers over Florida;

— A new independent UHF TV station prepared to go on the air in Central Florida;

— And Coca-Cola and Pepsi chose the Orlando Arena as a major battleground in their ongoing wars.

We were happily in the middle of a money fight that more than satisfied league requirements for ancillary income. The NBA asked that local TV, cable and radio contracts guarantee at least $1.5 million the first season and our cable contract alone surpassed this. The cable deal became the focal point of a struggle between Sunshine Network and SportsChannel Florida for the Florida cable market. SportsChannel already had the Florida Gators and Miami Heat and viewed the Magic as a knockout punch.

Sunshine, an arm of Houston-based Home Sports Entertainment, was far ahead in distribution to Florida cable systems and viewed the Magic as important to holding that advantage. Our five-year contract with Sunshine Network has been widely estimated at $13.4 million. A league official congratulated us on what he said was the NBA's fifth most lucrative cable package.

The start-up of WKCF-TV, Channel 68, just as we were coming on line created credibility and cable distribution for the station and economical airtime with low-risk profit potential for us. We bought time for 25 games and would produce the telecasts and sell the commercials ourselves. While the established stations were talking in the $25,000 to $30,000 range per game, WKCF general manager Carlo Anneke revealed to the *Sentinel* that his station sold the time for $7,500 per game in the first year of a five-year contract.

"We made a deal I think is great for both of us," Carlo told the paper.

Coca-Cola wins most of the deals for exclusive soft-drink pouring, signs and promotions in the nation's arenas and ballparks. Orlando is one of the few places where the edge goes to Pepsi, which decided to make the Magic and Orlando Arena a beachhead.

Quoting the *Sentinel:* "Coke hooked up with the Miami Heat for roughly $100,000 per year for three years. But at the urging of local Pepsi officials, the parent company agreed to go to the wall to hold its Orlando turf. The result was a five-year deal for — brace yourself — $500,000 per year. The pact gives Pepsi exclusive signage and pouring in the arena, advertising on Magic broadcasts and joint promotion with the team."

Our largest sponsorship package went to Budweiser. Miller Lite won the beer contract with the Miami Heat, so Anheuser-Busch

Is the basketball stuffed or inflated? Bob Poe may not know for sure — but he sure knows broadcasting and the Orlando market.

reached a little deeper to keep Miller from cornering the Florida NBA market.

Even with the fortuitous timing, more than good fortune was involved in these deals. Central to all of them was the banjo-eyed radio executive who arguably bought the first pair of Magic season tickets at that opening press conference. Bob Poe, general manager of station WKIS and Florida News Network at the time, stopped by on the way to the airport for the big announcement.

Bob: "I never carry a check, but it so happened I did that day because my wife and I were leaving town right after the press conference on a Caribbean vacation. The possibility of an NBA team was exciting. I wrote a check for $200 as a reservation for two tickets and I told Pat and Jim Hewitt that the station would be willing to donate about $20,000 in air time for the season ticket drive. We were on the air that afternoon with spots promoting the $100 season ticket deposits. My motives were not altogether altruistic. I wanted our station to have an edge in getting the broadcast rights. I confessed that right up front."

That station did become the flagship for our radio network, but not before changing its call letters and losing Poe. An ownership change converted WKIS to WWNZ and a change of careers converted Poe to a Magic basketball executive. The irony is that I keep telling him he doesn't know whether the ball is stuffed or inflated. He became director of broadcasting and sponsorship sales in May, 1987. But long before that he was one of three broadcast people I leaned heavily on for advice and brainstorming about Central Florida — Bob in radio, Channel 35's Norris Reichel and Bill Brown of Cablevision of Central Florida.

Bob's jump from WKIS began during a hush-hush meeting early one morning at a Waffle House. He had decided to leave the station, and I was all too happy to talk to him — privately, he insisted — about coming with us. I still shared Robert Fraley's conference room so I suggested the rendezvous over pecan waffles. Funny. He seemed startled that I brought my own all-natural Vermont maple syrup in a little brown bag. Doesn't everybody do that?

THE CABLE TV DEAL: Before beginning serious negotiations with stations or sponsors, Bob Poe was sent darting around the country on an NBA cram course to adapt his broadcast expertise to pro basketball. It was another luxury we enjoyed by not playing the first year. Bob talked to the league's most respected broadcast executives. Most valuable, he said, was a long session with Jim Hunkins of the Lakers.

Poe: "Hunkins stressed how we should integrate everything — radio, television, merchandising, signage, program ads and promotions — to provide sponsors with one-stop shopping. He showed how to truly service those sponsors. The Lakers command top dollar and could be pretty arrogant about it. But they're not. I was impressed with how much attention they give to extra little things like providing autographed basketballs or VIP treatment as a favor for one of the sponsor's clients. It's a relationship business and we need to make sponsors feel part of the Magic family. The Lakers are great at that."

By the spring of '88 we were ready to negotiate. Marc Lustgarten of SportsChannel and Ed Frazier of Sunshine made it clear they would be aggressive in pitching for our rights. Florida is one of the nation's leaders in cable connections, and we knew the cable deal could be a revenue bonanza. After some preliminary telephone and mail posturing we met with Lustgarten and Frazier at the beginning of the summer.

Lustgarten jumped into a full-court press to make a deal in the first session, an offer similar to the reported five-year, $12 million package he gave the Miami Heat. He just wouldn't take no for an answer. A big, bearded man, Marc's sheer presence can be intimidating. He's New Yawk all the way, a bull-moose negotiator talking 90 m.p.h. with occasional gusts up to 100. I wanted just to show off Orlando and set the stage. He was there determined to close the deal. We explained how we had to negotiate in good faith with Sunshine.

Ed Frazier was a contrast. A Texas farm boy and Baptist deacon with a disarming good ol' boy demeanor, he seemed too nice to be a big-time cable magnate. But he, too, was insistent that Sunshine *had* to have the Magic. We were still in the study-and-observe mode, but one thing was clear: The league's $1.5 million first-year broadcast minimum was going to be a piece of peanut-butter and carob cake.

Paul Bortz outlined how to negotiate with the two companies. He said we should get all the small issues resolved first and hammer dollars last. Paul thinks people often make the mistake of getting the big items settled, leaving little things that foul a deal. It may have been the most valuable negotiating advice I've ever had. He recommended 40 games for the cable package, mostly home games, and 25 on the over-the-air telecasts, all road games. We informed the cable companies and waited.

July 22 — Sunshine and SportsChannel both made what they characterized as final offers, which were similar. Our strategy was to decide which company we preferred, lock them in a room and hammer a deal. We'd tell the chosen company, "This is what we want and if you'll do this, we have a deal." If they didn't, we would bring in the other guy and wrap him. The one major difference between the two was Sunshine's Florida distribution, something like 1.5 million Florida homes, at the time, compared with about 200,000 for SportsChannel.

The gamble with SportsChannel would be a presumption that all Central Florida cable systems would add SportsChannel if it had the Magic. But the Florida Gators had gone with SportsChannel with that assumption and it didn't happen. If the Gators couldn't do it, could we? What if no one could see our games? UF athletic official Jeremy Foley told us they were frustrated. He encouraged us to go with SportsChannel, hoping the Gators-Magic combination would force cable systems to fall in line. Still, it would be a calculated risk.

There were two other things. We had become friends with John McMullen, who has a home in Orlando and owns the Houston Astros and Home Sports Entertainment. He said HSE was about to link up with several other high-profile sports cable operations and advised Bill du Pont in Bill's pursuit of major league baseball for Orlando. McMullen is bullish on Orlando as *the* baseball city in Florida. Second, Sunshine did not already have an NBA team and SportsChannel had the Miami Heat. We thought we might be better off with our own company, so to speak. We decided to pitch Sunshine and invited Ed Frazier back to Orlando for our home run swing.

Dear Diary: This is an overwhelming experience — our first major deal.

August 9 — Frazier and Dave Almstead, general manager of Sunshine, met with Bob Poe and me in our offices in the Du Pont Plaza. Ed said, "This is stiff, but not as bad as I feared. I need your phone and your office a few minutes." He seemed relieved and he wanted to call the home office. I got the notion he seemed to feel he could make it happen, though the numbers were higher than he wanted. Bob and I excused ourselves, closing my office door and leaving Ed and Dave inside with all those commas and zeroes and the telephone. I assumed they were calling John McMullen.

Meanwhile, Bob Poe and Pat Williams began wearing little oval paths into the marble hallway floor outside our offices. There was great anxiety. This had been going on for a long time. If they took the deal we would have met the NBA's $1.5 million radio-TV requirement even before going to our over-the-air TV contract or peddling our radio rights.

Fifteen minutes oozed by. Thirty minutes. My toes were tingling, my mouth dry. Bob had a doctor's appointment. He left, saw the doctor, and came back. I was still pacing. Should we check on them?

What were the odds of a double coronary? Were they taking a nap? Had they escaped through a window?

After 45 minutes, Ed Frazier finally opened the door. He announced Sunshine would accept the deal. It was all I could do to keep from doing cartwheels, but I managed to play it cool, acting as though I did deals in the tens of millions of dollars every day. Inside, Ferris wheels and roman candles were going wild. We negotiated some of the payments, weighting them more toward the back years to help Ed's cash flow. That was really all he needed. We ended with a handshake and agreed to push the paperwork.

The usual post-deal remorse hit later. I asked Bob if we'd pitched too low. If Ed flatly had said he couldn't consider our offer, we'd have known we pitched high. But we sensed from his first reaction that he thought he could sell it to the boss.

We'd researched thoroughly, picking every good cable brain we could find. We gave it our best shot. There's always the tendency after negotiating a deal — whether buying a car or closing on a multimillion-dollar cable package — to ask "could I have done a little better?" Still, we'd struck a huge deal and were excited. We beat the Heat. That was important. And we wound up with the cable company that best fit our needs.

August 19 — Ed Frazier came back in town and signed the cable contract. He sent a giant potted plant as a gift to our office. I was glad we left *something* in their pockets.

I was left with one ugly assignment. An hour before announcing the Sunshine deal I had to call Marc Lustgarten at SportsChannel in New York. I had known Marc for a number of years, going back to deals in Philly. I hated making this call. They had been so aggressive and wanted us so badly. It was brief. Mark was nice about it, not screaming or cursing. But you could tell he was disappointed. Somewhat agitated, he said, "It's really gonna heat up down there now." One of these days I'll have to get around to asking Marc just what he meant by that.

THE OVER-THE-AIR TV DEAL: Rarely does a major league sports team do play-by-play business with a network affiliate. Pre-empting that much time from network programming typically creates too much grief from networks and viewers. Michael Jordan may be a nice guy and gravitational wonder, but put him in place of Cosby and the local stations have to put crocodiles in their moats.

Still, we thought we might have something when Cliff Conley of Channel 9 trotted out a radical, intriguing concept in May, 1988. He proposed the three network affiliates and Channel 35, the leading independent in town, share the over-the-air Magic TV package, each carrying six or seven games. It would get us on the major stations while reducing their pre-empted evenings to a tolerable level — roughly once a month per station.

Channel 35 dropped out immediately; Norris Reichel wanted the whole package or none of it. Bob Poe initially had warm receptions from the other two network stations, channels 2 and 6. But when we put a pencil to it, the Magic-VHS consortium fell apart. Channel 35 was the next alternative.

Poe: "The people at Channel 35 were in a tremendous market position and wouldn't sell us the time anywhere near the price we felt we needed. I started digging around and found that a company called Asbury Park Press in New Jersey had a construction permit to start a station in Orlando."

Poe set up a meeting and in walked this very funny fire hydrant named Carlo Anneke, already ticketed as general manager of the yet-to-air WKCF-TV, Channel 68. But Bob didn't know that Carlo and I were old friends from Philadelphia where he was GM of the station that carried the Sixers. Carlo does a wonderful impression of Gene Autry, for whom he once worked in California, and loves to tell a hilarious, ribald story about The Cowboy.

Poe: "That first meeting was to determine if WKCF was for real. There are a lot of construction permits around — licenses to build stations — but many don't get built. I thought Asbury Park Press was little more than a weekly shopper."

Bob and Jack Swope flew to the Neptune, New Jersey, headquarters for Asbury Park Press, and discovered a veritable corporate mother ship of publishing and broadcasting. Our enthusiasm for Carlo's yet-to-be WKCF-TV began to show a pulse.

Channel 35 was the established independent in the market, but we were reluctant to accept their numbers. The VHS stations had been talking about selling time for each game in the area of $30,000. Channel 35 was only about $5,000 under that. At the same time, Carlo and his people were aggressively courting us.

Around the league, broadcast eyebrows were reaching 39-inch vertical jumps. Here we were considering a station not even on the air and with no commitments from the neighborhood cable systems. My friend Norris Reichel said we were making a horrible mistake and doubted WKCF would go on the air.

But in June we decided the new station was our best bet. The deal began to come together a few nights later at a marathon, somewhat comical dinner at the elegant and private Citrus Club above downtown Orlando. The diners: Jack and Debbie Swope, Bob and Virginia Poe, Carlo Anneke, Asbury president Don Lass, vice president Bob McAllan and finance officer Al Colantoni.

Poe: "We had a big round table in one corner of the Citrus Club's main dining room. Carlo was supposed to be the scribe, to make notes on the proposals and counter-proposals. Carlo will say it was intentional, though it wasn't, that he was seated between Virginia and Debbie and often was distracted from the exchanges across the table between Lass and me or Jack and McAllan."

Carlo: "I missed a lot. I grabbed the last seat, between the ladies, and I loved it. We talked about my grandson, Mrs. Swope's children, and Mrs. Poe's printing business. Everything but basketball."

Meanwhile on the other side of the table, WKCF and the Magic were inching closer in the disjointed Poe-Lass and Swope-McAllan exchanges while Al Colantoni frantically tried to keep up with the numbers on a little computer on his wristwatch.

Poe: "The funny part is that Jack and McAllan would be having a side conversation hammering on some deal between themselves, only to discover that Lass, who had the final say, had already settled that issue a half-hour earlier in our own side conversation." Poor Carlo wasn't sure what had been settled, except maybe the sale price of some dress at Fashion Square Mall.

What started at 7 p.m. with cocktails, progressed to dinner and wine and rocked along through several rounds of coffee and nearly non-stop negotiations. The few other diners had gone by 10. The waiters were standing around looking at their watches, discreetly clinking glasses and clearing tables. Shortly after midnight the party broke up with a basic agreement, though it was hard to tell from the sketchy notes Carlo managed to scrawl.

Carlo: "What occurred that night began a real friendship and awareness of who we were and how dedicated we intended to be to the Mag ic. Up to that point it had been pretty much Poe, Swope and me. Now we had put together the moneybags from the North. It was a vitally beneficial evening."

Terms were completed that summer in New Jersey and involved the same cast as over dinner except for the two wives. The final detail was how the 25 telecast games would be selected. With that resolved, McAllan drove Bob and Jack to a train station for the ride back to New York.

McAllan is a great guy but always tries to capture one last bargaining coup. As the men stood on the train platform in the late-night chill, McAllan announced the deal was done as long as an agreement on game selection could be reached. Poe laughed and reminded him they had agreed on that during dessert. McAllan shrugged sheepishly. They all laughed. The Magic and WKCF were betrothed — an engagement that had a lot of NBA parents nervous.

With the paperwork done, this bold gamble was announced on November 3. It began paying off the next month when Channel 68 blinked to life. By early summer 1989 — five months before our first telecast — the station was plugged into more than 80 percent of Orlando-area cable homes. Carlo revealed to the *Sentinel* the five-year contract initially charging the Magic $7,500 for each game, escalating in annual increments to a high of $10,000 per game in the fifth year.

And with WKCF as the flagship, Poe went to work assembling a network of stations in St. Pete, Jacksonville, Tallahassee and Gainesville to carry the games. They would receive telecasts free in exchange for 12 minutes of advertising sold by the Magic. They would have an additional 12 minutes of their own to sell. On WKCF the Magic controls all 24 minutes of commercial time.

Carlo petitioned the Federal Communications Commission for a ruling that would allow him to swap numerical channel designations with Brevard Community College's Channel 18, WRES-TV. The lower number is considered more desirable. Brevard C.C. agreed, in return for financial considerations from WKCF.

More desirable to us, however, was finding the right play-by-play man to hire for the telecasts. There certainly was no shortage of prospects. Very quickly, Bob Poe was inundated by sample tapes from a wide spectrum of courtside talent. Some we sought, some sought us. We pored over the tapes of obscure guys doing small college games on 50-watt stations to some of the largest names in the business who, like so many of us, welcomed the chance to move to Central Florida.

As the calendar rounded the corner into 1989, there were no lights flashing on. Of the ones we thought capable, some were too old, some wanted too much money. Some wanted to commute from where they already were living. I was adamant about getting a guy who would move to Orlando, put his roots in, rub elbows with fans at the supermarket, coach a Little League team, become part of the community. I didn't want some stranger who just flew into town on game days or met us in Sacramento.

The first step toward getting this vital position filled, oddly enough, came in February at the All-Star game in Houston when I was in my hotel room, reading an *Inside Sports* feature story on Skip Caray, the droll star of WTBS Braves' and NBA telecasts and son of legendary Cubs play-by-play man, Harry Caray. A brief line in the story mentioned the third-generation Caray-caster, 24-year-old Chip Caray, a University of Georgia grad then working as a sports announcer at a Greensboro, North Carolina, television station. I closed the magazine and headed downstairs for an All-Star reception, where I promptly bumped into Bob Neal, an old friend and member of the WTBS team alongside Skip Caray.

I told Bob about our search for a play-by-play man and he suggested a couple of the usual names. Then, as an afterthought, he added: "But if you're interested in a new face, my favorite young guy coming along is Skip's son, Chip Caray." The irony jolted me.

It turned out that Neal had taken an interest in the kid as he grew up and became more of his mentor than Chip's own father or grandfather. Bob cautioned that Chip had never done a play-by-play in his life, but he had grown up around it and broadcasting was in his blood. I gave Chip a call and invited him to apply.

He began going to Charlotte Hornets' games with a tape recorder, doing mock "broadcasts" of the game. We brought him down in April to work a couple of games of the Orlando All-Star Classic on the Sunshine Network as sort of an audition, pairing him with veteran NBC color man Bucky Waters. After the barest of production meetings, Chip dove right in, calling the game with players he had never seen before. Under the most adverse of circumstances, I thought he did a fine job. I was sold on him. He was handsome, handled himself well and the bloodlines weren't bad.

Our staff was impressed, but scared to death. The thought of taking a multimillion-dollar TV package and turning it over to a 24-year-old kid who had never done play-by-play was just too big a gamble. So young he signed his autographs with a crayon. But I couldn't resist.

We formally announced Chip as our man on July 10 and Bucky Waters seconded the motion. Bucky had been skeptical about working with this raw neophyte on the Classic telecasts, but obviously was impressed. A few days after we hired Chip, Bucky tapped out this letter to his young partner:

> Dear Chip:
> Well, when you write your book, I expect at least a sentence about the guy who caddied for you on the big audition in your first ever play-by-play experience.
> I guess it's too late to buy stock in you?
> Every good wish for the fulfillment that should come from this marvelous opportunity. When you're settled in Orlando, let me know how to reach you as I do hope to catch up with you long before your Hall of Fame induction.
> Sincerely,
> R. C. Waters

Chip's "crutch" will be a veteran color man, former Kentucky and NBA player Jack Givens, 33, who has worked as an analyst on U.K. and national network telecasts for seven years. Givens' expertise will allow him to help Chip with the telecasts and Gabe with some spot scouting.

Earlier, I had made a kidding remark on the phone to Chip that I would consider him only if I got a free, autographed copy of his grandfather's new book, *Holy Cow!* I had forgotten about it until Chip arrived for the Classic and handed me a copy of the book. Sure enough, the flyleaf was personalized to me by Harry, a longtime friend who once gave me the thrill of my life by asking me to fill in as a guest announcer on a Cubs telecast during his 1988 illness. What Chip didn't realize, however, was that Harry also had poked a sealed letter to me inside the book. "My grandson is terrific," wrote Harry. "The third-generation Caray might be the best of all — 6-foot-5 and as you will see a handsome lad who might even attract many of the fairer sex, which won't hurt the box-office!"

Any dividends Chip represented as a handsome bachelor, however, were short-lived. Moments after the July 10 press conference to announce his hiring, Chip made an announcement of his own. He turned

The broadcasting Carays. From left, Harry, Skip and our man Chip. Harry and Skip were invited to Orlando when we introduced Chip. Both declined. Said Skip, "This is Chip's day in the sun and dad and I wouldn't want to take away from that." Chip is proud of the family name but determined to make it on his own ability.

to us and invited the entire staff to Charlotte in September.

For his wedding.

In the spring of '89, protracted negotiations were completed with WWNZ-AM, Bob Poe's old station, as the flagship of our radio network. The delay resulted from an ownership change at the station and all the legal machinations involved. David Steele, respected play-by-play voice of the Florida Gators for the past seven years, moved to Orlando to describe the Magic action on radio. A family man concerned about how pro sports travel would affect him at home, David is a perfect fit for Orlando. His statewide contacts were invaluable in setting up the network.

COLA WARS: The arena lease assured that either Pepsi or Coke would be exclusive in the building, but we didn't have much time. In addition to the arena deal, the chosen soft drink company as well as our beer sponsor would have scoreboard display, radio and TV spots, exclusive joint promotions with the team and a five-year commitment. We were pushed by the city's requirement that scoreboard and beverage equipment be in place for the arena opening in January, 1989, more than eight months ahead of our first game. The more we dragged out negotiations with the beverage and scoreboard companies, the greater the strain on John Christison.

In something of an upset, we ended up with Pepsi, which made a huge investment, as big as Pepsi has made anywhere in sports. They absolutely put blinders on and said, in effect, that they were to be in that building no matter what. The two top local Pepsi guys, Steve Albert and Ronaldo Swilley, are basketball fans, really into hoops. They saw what we could do for Pepsi in Central Florida. So they pushed the parent company and came up with a lot of creative ideas for billboards and other cross promotions.

Central Florida is unusual in the soft drink industry because Pepsi has a larger market share than Coke. They're proud of it and didn't want to lose the arena. The Coke people were interested but didn't have the same enthusiasm.

Coke executive Walter Dunn of Atlanta gave his company's final offer. I had to tell him that Pepsi's offer was significantly higher. Surprisingly, he said it was important that Pepsi occasionally wins one — that half the time his bosses didn't think there was any competition out

John Christison pushed us relentlessly to make a decision on the scoreboard. A visit to Indiana cinched the deal for the Sony Jumbo-tron.

there.

"This will help me convince them that Pepsi is alive," he said.

THE SCOREBOARD: John Christison was worried about our indecision. Jack Swope's 12 months of research came down to two manufacturers — the Sony Jumbo-tron with its four instant-replay panels, and a supposedly revolutionary new model by a California company called Multi-Image. The latter was to be installed later that fall in Market Square Arena in Indianapolis. It was said to be the board of the future. But in August of 1988 it wasn't operating yet. It was like an H-bomb in some mad scientist's laboratory.

Nervous because of the January debut, Christison pushed for a decision. We'd rather have waited until the summer of '89, stalling for any technological breakthrough. But Mayor Frederick was adamant that we install the main board for the arena opening. We could have put in a temporary board for the first few months, but that wasn't a negotiable item with hizzoner. The arena was his jewel. He wanted everything complete for the crowning moment of his administration.

Because no new technology was on the way during the first half of

The Jumbo-tron got rave reviews. The crowd cheered when Jack Swope and I (on the big screen) picked Nick Anderson.

the year it seemed better to go ahead with a permanent board anyway. Jack wanted to protect us to the latest possible day in case the Japanese developed some awesome new technique that would make all other boards a bunch of Edsels.

The city agreed for us to go see the Indiana board in mid-November before making a decision. Though cutting it close, that would still allow time to get the Sony board if we didn't like the other. In Indiana, Christison and Swope discovered problems getting that board working. We ordered the Jumbo-tron. John Christison breathed a jumbo sigh of relief.

Flanked by Virginia and Debbie at the negotiating (and dinner) table, Channel 68's Carlo Anneke missed a few things.

Ed Frazier seemed too nice to be a big-time cable magnate, but Sunshine Network got the contract in a wild negotiation against SportsChannel.

THE DAWK TALKS, SQUAWKS AND WALKS

With most of the trimmings in place, we'd finally get to the main course — a team of living, breathing basketball players. In truth, determining our first roster had begun while negotiating my own contract with Jimmy Hewitt back in 1986. I'd insisted on a satellite dish and big-screen TV at home to scout NBA and college games. I figured Harold Katz, the Sixers' owner, had one, so why shouldn't I?

Harold always would come in and talk about how some college kid from Fastbreak Tech looked great last night or what happened in the Sonics-Clippers game. He had a great advantage. So one of the rooms in our house in Winter Park was designed for a huge TV in the corner, enabling me to scout every college and pro player alive. Many nights I watch all or parts of seven or eight NBA games. It's a remarkable asset, better than flying to games. You cover way more ground with the dish.

Jill manages to control her enthusiasm for this. Pro sports is not conducive to marriage. I learned the hard way to temper the urge to sit in front of the TV six hours a night. In sports there's a great imagined danger, whether you're a coach or a sportswriter or an executive, that if you miss one game or are out of the office for one hour the competition is getting one-up on you and that the whole sports world will end up laughing at you.

The spadework for our first roster shifted into a higher gear in July, 1987, when John Gabriel came from Philadelphia. Even two years away he put into place the scouting structure that led to decisions in our first draft. He hit the road to build files on college players who would be rookies in 1989, the first Magic season.

Matty was scouting college and pro players from Philadelphia and

In '88 Classic action, Florida's Vernon Maxwell puts pressure on Anthony Mason (with the ball) of Tennessee State.

new assistant Bob Weiss was tracking the NBA from his post as color man for Dallas Mavs' telecasts.

Gabe was also the guy pushing the buttons on the Orlando All-Star Classic. This became a rehearsal for the regular season, exposed top players to the appeal of Central Florida in an upbeat setting and gave Gabe, as camp administrator, a relationship with players you don't get as just another scout in the stands.

With the Orlando Arena unfinished, the first Classic in 1988 was in the Lakeland Civic Center, 45 miles down I-4. Controversy dominated that one. First, the NCAA ruled we had not obtained proper sanctioning to use the college coaches hired to handle the four teams. There was a bylaw that the Extra Events Committee had to have applications by August for the coming school year. Impossible, since we weren't awarded the tournament until September. Also impossible was any chance the NCAA would apply any flexibility to these circumstances. That was the way the rule reads and that would be it. Period. So on the eve of the tournament we had to excuse Bradley's Stan Albeck, UNLV's Jerry Tarkanian, Alabama's Wimp Sanderson and Princeton's Pete Carril and replace them with an impressive lineup of volunteer NBA coaches and scouts — Cotton Fitzsimmons, Al Attles, Dave Wohl and Don Nelson.

With that settled, the dark story broke the next morning in the *Sentinel* that Florida star Vernon Maxwell, one of our Classic players, had failed drug tests during his senior season, including one before the Gators' early-round defeat in the NCAA tournament. With the controversy suddenly swirling around his head, Maxwell failed to show for the tipoff luncheon and engineered a rock-star escape from the media following his team's first game.

Maxwell jumped into Bob Poe's car and was whisked away into the night. It looked as if *we* were the ones trying to keep him from speaking to all the reporters salivating to talk to him. Oops. That's what dress rehearsals are for.

The second Classic in April, 1989, was larger, smoother (the NCAA sanctioned us this time) and more meaningful because it involved players who'd be available in our first draft two months later. It also moved into the new arena's magnificent stage and was supported by 36 area companies, each paying $5,000 to cover the expenses of the players. The crowds were larger — 8,100 one night — and the games terrific. The largest glitch was a leak in the roof,

We brought the top college players — and names — to Orlando for the All-Star Classic. The one on the right is a guy named Russell.

right over one baseline. Ball boys kept having to mop up little puddles every time the action moved to the other end of the court. I held my breath that we wouldn't have one of those marvelous young players at the brink of a lucrative pro career slip and puncture his pancreas or something.

Also during the second Classic we initiated a Pete Maravich Award to honor a college player for excellence both on and off the court. The first recipient will be hard to top — Jay Burson, the embraceable Ohio State guard who broke his neck a few months before in his senior season. Jay is a skinny little Ichabod Crane-looking kid whom everybody said couldn't play. But he just kept proving everybody wrong. He was confined to a halo neck brace for six months and was still wearing it for the Maravich presentation, which he handled in Midwestern gosh-golly-gee-whiz fashion, further branding himself as the kind of kid you really root for.

In March, approaching the '88 expansion draft, Bill du Pont asked what kind of team we could have expected had we been starting that season. Gabe and I conducted a little mock expansion draft of players expected available for Charlotte and Miami. The pickings weren't especially thrilling. However, this was the first of countless college and expansion "drafts" Gabe and I conducted over the next 15 months until we finally got to do the real thing. In the first expansion year, one of us would be Miami and the other Charlotte. (Neither of us picked Rony Seikaly or Rex Chapman, the actual first round picks by Miami and Charlotte, in any of those drafts).

For our real expansion draft we'd list the players we thought would be unprotected and Gabe would be Minneapolis and I would be Orlando. Next time, we'd switch. The frequency of these war games increased to weekly, then almost daily in the final month as we approached our inaugural drafts in 1989.

While watching the NFL draft in April, 1988, it occurred to me that few events in sports are more exciting than a draft. There's more drama and intrigue in a football or basketball draft than in the games. If you could just have drafts and no games, these would be wonderful sports, wouldn't they? Just like on a wedding day when there's no ugly bride, on draft days there are no bad players. Every club feels it has acquired just what it wanted and solved all of its problems.

August 3, 1988 — Darryl Dawkins, Orlando hometown hero out of Maynard Evans High School, now a 13-year NBA veteran and living cartoon character in residence on his imaginary planet, "Lovetron," announced his goal to play for the Magic. My last contact with this hulking man-child had come two years earlier when we were still an expansion applicant and desperately peddling season ticket pledges. We'd utilized willing local sports celebrities like Frank Viola, Tim Raines, Davey Johnson and Curly Neal to ceremoniously take us to new milestones — 5,000th pledge, 8,000th pledge, etc. We asked Darryl Dawkins to pledge two tickets. He said no. He said he had too many family members in the area and it would create chaos deciding whom to give them to.

When he called a press conference on that August day, Darryl had been in hiding for months. He surfaced to announce he was back in circulation, was ready to play for the Pistons that season and the next year would make the Magic an instant contender. He typically said all the wrong things. Happy to play at home close to family and friends? Anxious to help a new franchise get started in his hometown? Nahhh. Darryl announced he was interested in the Magic because of all the green he could pluck off this new money tree. He closed by mugging for one of the TV cameras and saying, as only Darryl can do, "Pat Williams, get my contract ready! And make it BIG!"

Dear Diary: "Double D is too much."

Darryl might have been the ultimate what-comes-around-goes-around saga. I flashed back to the madcap events in '75 when I shocked most of the basketball world by signing Darryl to a 76ers contract right out of high school. It was a revolutionary idea, but our scouts and coaches were convinced this 6-11, 250-pounder already was a man at 18. So I got veteran agent Herb Rudoy of Chicago to represent Darryl and we flew to Orlando that spring to cut a deal contingent on us drafting him that summer.

Here's how my book on the Sixers' '83 championship season, *We Owed You One*, written with outstanding Philadelphia columnist Bill Lyon, documented the development:

> "We meet in the law offices of Paul Perkins. With Perkins is the Reverend Mr. William Judge, Dawkins' minister. We take a lunch break, and Perkins departs with Darryl's mother. Upon their return, they pull the pin from the hand grenade and announce that the Reverend

Mr. Judge will act as Darryl Dawkins' financial adviser. Herb Rudoy, who has done all the work, sees that he is about to be niftily cut out of the deal. Goodbye to a hefty agent's percentage. And now it looks like goodbye Darryl for the Sixers. The deal, so close to consummation, is about to collapse. We frantically convince Herb to accept a smaller percentage. This mollifies Herb only slightly. He turns to the Reverend Mr. Judge and says: "This isn't right. You're a man of the cloth." And the Reverend Mr. Judge turns to Herb and replies: 'Mr. Rudoy, there are many kinds of reverends, and *I* is a financial reverend.'

"Incredibly, one other obstacle remains before we finally acquire Darryl. That is his high school coach, Fred Pennington. He had been very helpful to the Sixers. We'd used him to keep Darryl out of post-season all-star games and to fend off about 200 colleges that wanted to recruit Darryl, plus some pro bird dogs, and without his cooperation we might never have landed Darryl. Now Fred gets wind of the deal between the reverend and the lawyer and he thinks there should be something in it for him. So we make him the official Florida scout for the Philadelphia 76ers, at $5,000 a year for seven years. That wasn't bad for glorified baby-sitting.

"The final cost of acquiring a high school senior was $1.4 million over seven seasons, *plus* a hundred grand to get his signature, *plus* another 35 thou to appease his coach. And what we did, of course, had never been done before in the NBA — draft a kid from high school. But the Sixers' position at the time was, what might he develop into? Was he going to grow five more inches? Would we end up with a center who was 7-3 and 290 pounds? The prospects were intriguing. He certainly didn't lack for self-confidence. And in that regard, I got a preview of just what sort of flamboyance when Darryl moved to Philadelphia to play in the summer Baker League. I phoned his apartment and was greeted not by some shy, anxiety ridden high-school kid, but by this booming bass voice which cheerfully said: "Hello, this is the Dawk, and I'm ready to talk."

***Darryl Dawkins and Rev. Judge at the August, '88 press
conference to announce that The Dawk wanted to go Magic.***

Darryl came to be known more for his occasional glass-shattering
dunks and wild braggadocio than for being the dominant force we
envisioned. He oozed charisma. There was an appealing charm
about him. But the problems seemed to multiply as his playing time
faded to a trickle. He went back to Detroit for the start of the '88-
'89 season, his 14th in the NBA, but played little and was cut halfway through. It was the fourth consecutive season Darryl, due to
injury or personal problems, had played only in spots or not at all.
By now, nobody had seen the guy or knew what he could do. We
wanted to see him in action and Darryl had to answer the question
himself.

We expected that answer in our first free agent camp in May. We
had invited Darryl — through the Rev. Judge — but Darryl called
Barry Cooper at the *Sentinel* a few days before the camp to say he
might not participate without a guaranteed contract. Rev. Judge
quickly followed up and assured us Darryl would participate.

On the eve of the camp, The Dawk hit town and made a grand entrance into the Magic offices, the Rev. Judge in tow. I gave them a tour of the arena and when we got off alone on the floor, Darryl confronted me. He was not happy. He had to pay for the upgrade to first class on his flight from New Jersey. And he was being asked to slug it out with these unknowns in the tryout camp starting the next day. He could sustain a career-ending injury, he said, though in many minds his career already was over. Our view was this could be a career-resurrecting camp.

Darryl proposed coming to our pre-season camp in the fall to prove he could still play. I told him we would think about it and continued the arena tour. After discussion with our coaches, I told Darryl to show up at UCF the next morning at 8:30 for a final decision.

Darryl arrived in uniform, but after a 30-minute meeting with me and the coaches, refused to play. We had all ducked into a little coaches' annex just off the locker room. It was a small room and Darryl took up half of it. Maybe two-thirds, considering his unhap-

Dawkins later changed his mind, angrily stalking out of rookie camp at UCF in May of '89.

piness. He was upset, insulted, irritated. Not a happy camper.

We were saying, "Darryl, this is your opportunity. It'll help us make up our minds, give us some insight into your effectiveness." Matty calmly explained that we were interested and would love to see what he could do. *Earth to Darryl! Earth to Darryl!* But it was obvious our transmissions were not reaching Lovetron. Finally, a few minutes after nine, with the other players out on the floor shooting and waiting for the camp to begin, Darryl announced he would not be playing basketball on this day.

I suggested to Darryl that we discuss how we were going to handle this, with the media waiting outside. "I'm a 14-year veteran," he boomed. "I know how to handle the media!" With that he stormed out with his entourage.

After lunch, the Rev. Judge called and said he would have Darryl at the camp's second session that evening, but we'd have to provide an injury insurance policy. We thought that would be a dangerous precedent and politely declined.

On this same day, Rod Luck, the controversial Channel 6 sports commentator, pulled me aside and confided he would be leaving for a resort job in the Antilles. It became a day all the great characters were bailing out on us. Was life simply destined to become a bore?

The answer was no. There would be more to the Darryl Dawkins saga.

As we began to stuff our roster with expansion and college draft players and a key draft-day acquisition, Darryl apparently began to realize we were not quite so desperate for his services. The Rev. Judge dropped by my office in late June to advise that Darryl had recanted and would be willing to participate in our second camp, a July affair involving rookies and free agents in three days of workouts and four days of summer-league scrimmages with similar teams representing Miami, Charlotte and Atlanta. He apologized for Darryl's action at the May camp, but assured us that Darryl would be the best center in the NBA for the upcoming season and badly wanted to play for the Magic. He made an impassioned appeal for another chance. Somewhat against our better judgment, we caved in and extended Darryl an invitation to continue the tragicomedy.

In mid-July, Darryl was quoted in the *Sentinel* as anxious for the camp to start. A week later, a full-page ad depicting Darryl with the

Rev. Judge's full-page ad in the Orlando Times.

Bobby Weiss, Matty's No. 1 assistant. He is bright, witty and best of all for us, a top-notch amateur magician.

caption, "Have Shoes, Will Travel" ran in the *Orlando Times*, a neighborhood paper. Rev. Judge paid $1,140 for the ad, which he said was to assure the black community that Darryl was anxious to try out for the Magic.

So anxious, in fact, that Darryl informed Rev. Judge the very next day — on the eve of our camp — that he was staying in New Jersey. Rev. Judge was mortally wounded and embarrassed.

I said, "Rev. Judge, what are you going to tell the media?"

"I don't know."

I asked, "Rev. Judge, what do I tell the media?"

"You tell them, 'I don't know, either.'"

It was funny and it wasn't. We'd agreed to the second invitation because Rev. Judge was so relentless and earnest. I think it really stung him when Darryl let him down the second time, and my heart went out to him. He's a nice old gentleman and was trying so hard to spare Darryl from himself. I gathered that he washed his hands of Darryl with that one. I know we did. We kept hearing that Darryl was going to make one more run at us for a spot in the October pre-season camp, but that's not the time for experiments. It was over.

By that spring Bobby Weiss, Matty's top assistant, was on the job and headlong into evaluating prospective draftees. Getting Bobby was a real stroke. Matty and Bobby were teammates on the Bulls and fast friends. Ironically, Bobby called Matty a week or two after he had been named our coach to recommend another old Bulls teammate, Jimmy King, as Matty's assistant.

Matty: "Instead, I asked Bobby, who had just been fired as head coach at San Antonio, if he would be interested in joining me. He said, 'Oh, I'm not interested in getting involved with an expansion team.' Then in the next sentence, he said, 'I think I might get the Minneapolis job.' I said, 'Bob, am I missing something? Did I miss a sentence in there?' What he meant was he didn't want to get in as an assistant at the expansion level. He thought he had a shot at becoming head coach of the Timberwolves."

However, we went after Bobby when the Minnesota job went to Bill Musselman. He accepted with the understanding he would be released for another head coaching job if one came along before the Magic began play. Bobby and Matty mesh nicely. Bobby likes Matty's idea of playing an up-tempo game rather than a plodding, hold-the-ball-and-try-not-to-get-beat-by-20 philosophy. He's a good person with a quick, dry wit and had been through expansion as both a player and coach. Bobby is over-qualified for this job and it's just a matter of time before he's a head coach again. We couldn't have been more fortunate.

With the pressure on to make the right pick with our historic first draft choices in June, 1989, it was great to have another set of experienced eyes. At an overblown ceremony at the LA Airport Marriott on a Monday during the Lakers-Pistons finals, a coin flip would decide whether Minnesota or us would go first in the expansion draft.

I was really nervous about the flip because I've never fared too well in coin flips. In one amateur league I worked in, another executive would call on the phone to flip for our tournament matchups. He'd flip the coin, I'd call it, and he'd win every single time.

Bob Stein, president of the Timberwolves, and I had agreed to send our coaches to the flip. Matty and Minnestoa's Bill Musselman flew out on Sunday. Back in Orlando, we all were in our conference room as Commissioner Stern prepared to flip a coin with a Magic logo on one side and a Timberwolves logo on the other side. But an earthquake hit just as the coin was to be flipped, shaking the room in LA. The trembler must have created the horrible phone connection we were left with. We'd hoped for a nice, detailed account of the whole proceedings:

Commissioner Stern now has the coin in his hand ... he is prepared to flip ... the coaches are hovering over the spot ...

We heard none of that. All we heard was a faint voice through a crackling phone line: "Orlando won." I couldn't believe it. If only I could've called my old flipping buddy to tell him what had happened. The room erupted in shouts of joy. We had decided to go first in the expansion draft if we won the flip. This would allow Minnesota to pick No. 10 in the regular draft, one slot ahead of us. I went to the podium to explain this decision to the media. Before I could speak, another phone inadvertently placed on the podium began to ring. As the assembled masses waited for great pearls of truth, I did the natural thing. I picked up the podium phone, which I was about to discover somehow had been connected to the speaker system set up for the California call. Cameras and tape recorders were poised to record every word of this important moment in Magic history.

"Hello?" I said.

A woman's voice asked: "Is Betty Johnson there?"

Betty Johnson heads our speakers bureau, and this call probably was to see if the Magic Girls or somebody could come over to blow out the candles at some little girl's birthday party. Talk about breaking the tension! The whole place went wild with laughter, and at that point I needed a good laugh, too.

Betty Johnson was in the room, heard all this and, red-faced, scurried to her office to deal with this unexpectedly famous call.

Actually the tension for me had been broken earlier that morning. I got a call from Watson Spoelstra, an old friend in St. Petersburg, retired Detroit sportswriter and founder of Baseball Chapel. Said Waddy, "I know this is a big day for you what with the coin flip and all, so take a minute to look up Proverbs 16:33 in the *Living Bible.* That's a key verse for you today."

I hung up, found the verse, and read these timely words from

Solomon:

"We toss the coin but it is the Lord who controls its decision."

Long before the coin flip we sought insight from coaches who had worked with the Orlando Classic teams. Todd Lichti's name kept coming up. Stetson's Glen Wilkes, Florida Southern's George Scholz and Rollins' Tom Klusman all were high on the Stanford guard. So were NBA scout Marty Blake and Bucky Waters, the TV color man.

"Lichti is your player," Bucky said, flatly. So did Boston writer Bob Ryan. This was getting as scary as that Mike Krzyzewski survey two years earlier.

Our draft strategy would be shaped during the next few weeks as several key underclassmen began coming out early. On May 2, North Carolina Coach Dean Smith called to say his celebrated junior, J.R. Reid, was considering the jump. Dean wanted to know what interest there might be in Reid. I told him the same thing I

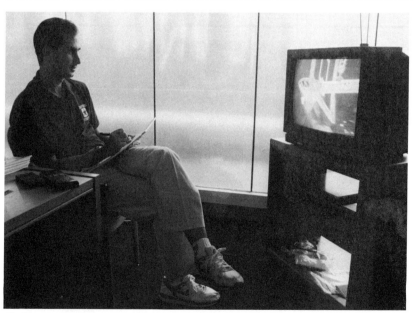

Gabe spent hours and hours and hours and even more hours watching video of college players.

tell all these coaches — players are better off spending their senior years in college. But if J.R. came out, I predicted he would be taken no later than ninth in the first round.

Reid's decision a week later to turn pro had a great impact on us. He filled a draft slot ahead of us, making possible a trade in which we acquired a veteran center and enabling us to draft the player we most wanted.

A few days later, May 13, our draft destiny fell into place. Our oldest son, Jimmy, was to receive his baseball letter during a sports banquet at the Orangewood Christian School where he was finishing ninth grade. We had kids' baseball games all afternoon with the younger boys and rushed to Orangewood a few minutes late. Entering the dining room I bumped into Sid Cash, a banker, superfan and Magic minority owner, who had just completed the season as volunteer baseball coach at Orangewood.

Sid and I began exchanging typical kidding remarks. He had repeatedly but facetiously vowed he would be the one to decide our first draft choice. I reminded him he had only a month left to give us the name. His response: "Did you hear about Nick Anderson?"

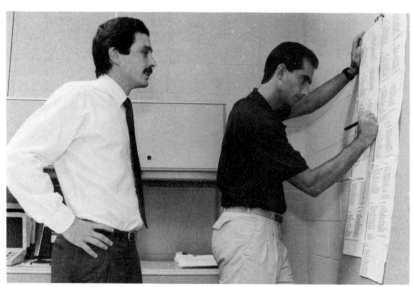

Jack Swope and Gabe study an extensive list of potential Magic players.

I recognized the name as the star University of Illinois player who had completed his junior season. My first thought, from the way Sid asked, was that the kid was dead or something.

"Anderson announced today he is coming out," said Sid.

This was the last day for underclassmen to declare. Intrigued, I invented a reason to slip out of the banquet and call John Gabriel, who hadn't heard about the Anderson development.

Back in the office on Monday, we went to work researching Anderson. Lou Henson, the Illinois coach, predicted Nick would have been a certain top-three pick in 1990 had he stayed in school. Tough, hard-nosed, better all-around, Lou assessed, than Michigan's celebrated Glen Rice. Can't shoot with Rice. But Rice can't play one-on-one with Anderson, he said.

Gene Keady, the Purdue coach, said Nick Anderson would be a sure-shot pro. Iowa Coach Tom Davis predicted the same, saying Nick "would have been the Big Ten Player of the Year in 1990, and I'm not so sure he wasn't this year." That honor went to Glen Rice. Michigan Coach Steve Fisher said Anderson is "special — Illinois' most dangerous player. We couldn't defend him. He was too quick for our big guys, too strong for our smaller guys. If I was a pro coach and could have him, I'd lick my chops."

San Antonio Spurs Coach Larry Brown later would confide: "If I had the guts I'd take Anderson with our third pick. That's how good I think he will be."

June 5 — Gabe, bleary-eyed from watching days of TV tapes, emerged focused on four guys: FSU bomber George McCloud, Georgia Tech forward Tom Hammonds, Anderson and Lichti. We tabled our study of college players to concentrate on the expansion draft.

Existing teams had to send expansion lists by overnight carrier, to be in our hands the morning of Wednesday, June 7. The two teams playing at that time in the finals, Detroit and LA, were excused until the day after the championship series ended. Denver's list arrived a day early. That left 20 envelopes to come piling in on the next day, containing untold treasures for new teams in Orlando and Minneapolis.

I spoke early that morning to the Orlando city recreation workers, then drove to the arena where I saw a Federal Express truck stopped in front of our office — knowing that in that truck were 20

An incredibly anxious general manager, just before opening packages from established NBA teams containing the names of expansion players.

vital envelopes from NBA teams. My stomach did a little flip. I'd agreed not to open the envelopes until the media had time to photograph the stack on my desk. It was the hardest thing I've ever had to do, like walking downstairs on Christmas morning and being told you couldn't open the presents until after breakfast. I had nearly an hour to kill looking at those treasures. And there's no way to peek inside a Federal Express package.

Actually, only 16 Fed Exxes were there as I arrived. The missing four, New Jersey, Seattle, Indiana and Dallas, would stagger in by other carriers. By 10:30, all had arrived and the TV and print photographers were there to shoot the scene.

That done, Danny Durso and Marlin Ferrell pulled my office door behind them and we began pulling drawstrings on the envelopes, in alphabetical order. Atlanta, Boston, Chicago, etc. Marlin was there to compile the list of exposed players and Danny was there to make notes in preparation for his trip to the league office to examine the available players' contracts. The coaching staff was in Chicago for the start of the NBA scouting camp. This reminded me of going down to The Smoke Shop as a kid in Wilmington, Delaware, to buy baseball card bubble-gum packages. Slowly and excitedly I'd peel that wrapper back, whiffing the aroma of the gum, then easing the first baseball card out to see what player I had gotten, praying that it would be Richie Ashburn or Robin Roberts.

It was the same peeling open these envelopes, slowly pulling out the roster and hoping a particular player would be among the unprotected. Each envelope contained a sheet showing which eight players had been protected. For each exposed player was an NBA contract transferral form, in triplicate. If you take a player you complete the form, transferring his contract to your club, and discard the other forms. Once a club loses a player in the expansion draft, that club is exempt from losing any more players.

Early the next day I flew to Chicago to join Matty, Bobby and Gabe. We fanned out among the NBA people at the camp to learn all we could about players on the expansion list. We'd have only a few days to research the players. Every morsel of information or opinion from their former coaches or teammates was golden. The first guy I ran into was a dear friend, Jack McMahon of the Warriors, a man with great player insights. Three days later, on the

The old gray Davis Armory, she ain't what she used to be. John Gabriel had the idea to convert the gym and the city's Bob Haven made it happen. Rex-Tibbs Construction Co. put in a beautiful new floor, locker rooms, lights and backboards.

final night of the camp, Jack died in his hotel bed.

At the Rosebud Cafe, a noisy Italian eatery, we attempted to con-
duct our most serious meeting on the expansion draft, but birthday
parties kept breaking out. Four of them in an hour. Waiters singing, Italian band playing. In the midst of all the revelry we came
away thinking that Sidney Green of the Knicks and Reggie Theus
of the Hawks were the two key players. One can get you 10 boards
a night; the other can get you 20 points a night. Picking first, we
felt we could get both of them, then fill in around them. The big
concern was that going first in expansion and being left to pick No.
11 in the college draft might make it impossible to get Nick Anderson. But as we stood out on the sidewalk after dinner, we all pretty
well agreed that if we won the flip we'd definitely take the first pick
in expansion, allowing Minnesota to have the better of the college
picks. I jotted down a note that night, about a week ahead of the
expansion draft: "Maybe we can't have it both ways." Spooky.

As the draft approached my phone began to jangle with attempts
by various clubs to shield specific players in the expansion disper-
sal. Jerry Colangelo of Phoenix offered two draft picks in exchange
for *not* selecting two certain players off his roster. Jack McCloskey,
Detroit GM, offered his 27th and last pick of the first round to lay
off Rick Mahorn, who had been added to the pool since our "Rosebud Summit." We rejected those and other similar deals. We decided we were going to take the best players, as opposed to future
draft choices and promising youngsters. We wanted to be good
right away.

With Mahorn suddenly in the mix — a significant player for the
newly crowned world champions — our debate became Mahorn vs.
Sidney Green. We were up and down. You could argue for Mahorn,
coming off a championship team. But he's had back surgery and is
older, 31. I decided to call NBA friends and ask that one question:
For Orlando, Mahorn or Green? I was on the phone until close to
midnight. When returns from all precincts were in, 20 respected
basketball people voted 10 for Mahorn and 10 for Green.

Our team doctor, Jim Barnett, tracked down the Pistons' doctor
for a read on Mahorn's back surgery. The medics agreed that Mahorn's career could be short-lived. So we decided to go the other
way. Green is in better health, is three years younger and publicly
has expressed a desire to come to Orlando. Mahorn, on the other

hand, was less than enthralled with the notion of showing off his new ring in an expansion city. "Bleep Minnesota, bleep Orlando," is the way he was charmingly quoted nationwide.

Whether Rick Mahorn liked it or not, the drafts were upon us.

The NBA created commemorative coins for the flip with Minnesota to determine who got the first pick in the expansion draft. We were all thrilled when we won and selected Sidney Green of the New York Knicks.

IS THERE A GRAIN ELEVATOR IN THE HOUSE?

D-Day ... the fifteenth of June, 1989. The expansion draft. Because the Pistons swept LA in four, the draft suddenly was upon us, moved up from June 22. Three long, tortuous years and boom! We'd be drafting a ballclub. Adrenalin attack!

An hour before the draft, Detroit's Jack McCloskey frantically called on a portable phone from a float in the middle of the championship celebration parade noisily making its way through downtown Detroit. Trying to talk over the screaming multitudes, Jack still was desperate to make any deal to protect Rick Mahorn. At Jack's elbows on the float were Pistons stars Isiah Thomas and Dennis Rodman.

"We don't want to lose him. I'll give you our first pick," Jack yelled over the bedlam.

Here they were, right in the middle of all this jubilation, the highlight of these players' lives. They'd won it all, swept the Lakers to end 30 years of frustration in Detroit. And in another hour, this kid was going to step down off the parade and be told he'd been banished to some expansion team.

Jack is a friend and I was having trouble telling him no. First, I had trouble hearing him and wasn't sure he could hear me. And he was limited in what he could say because of the players next to him. I felt

Jack McCloskey. Desperately tried to save Rick Mahorn from the expansion draft. Known for his sales ability, Jack could sell a Toyota to Lee Iacocca. But he couldn't sell Minnesota on not taking Mahorn.

sorry for Jack's dilemma, but we had to think about us.

At 1:50 we marched into the conference room for the draft. The NBA sent a security rep from Miami to make sure no one entered or left the room for the next four hours. The league didn't want someone stepping out and telling a secretary that Joe Blow had just been picked, have that leak to some radio reporter and have poor Joe hear he'd been tossed to the expansion wolves before his own team officials could give him the news. Theoretically we couldn't even go to the powder room. We firmly were told by the league to take care of those details before the draft started.

Around the conference table were the coaches, Bill du Pont, Danny, Jack, Robert Fraley, his assistant Rick Neal and our excellent young publicity guy, Alex Martins. There were two boards, one to keep track of the draft, the other to keep track of the contracts we were assuming. As an expansion team under the league's collective bargaining agreement, our first year's player payroll had to fall somewhere between about $5.2 million and $6 million, although those numbers would increase after the NBA salary cap was raised on August 1. Already in our hip pocket, by a matter of minutes, was an oral agreement with agent Warren LeGarie to sign Jeff Turner, a veteran 6-9 forward. Turner grew up in Central Florida, starred at Vanderbilt, played in the '84 Olympics and had three unproductive years with the Nets before resurrecting his career with two fine seasons in Italy.

At 2:02, the conference call came from a classic New York telephone operator. The tension was broken when she said, as only Lily Tomlin might have, "Please hoe-wwwwwald!" Everybody laughed. League counsel Gary Bettman came on, had us and Minnesota identify everyone sitting in our conference rooms, and it was jump ball.

"Orlando," Bettman said dramatically, "you have five minutes to make your first pick."

We'd already made the decision and didn't need five minutes. I immediately announced we were taking Sidney Green. Now came the fascinating part. For eight months we'd held those countless mock drafts. The war games had come and gone. Now we were firing real bullets.

As expected, the Timberwolves promptly took Mahorn. Without hesitation we countered with Reggie Theus. We'd rehearsed this so many times there wasn't even any discussion. They took small forward Tyrone Corbin of Phoenix, which we didn't mind. We were concerned whether he'd be able to score enough for an expansion team.

Now we faced the first real decision. Do we take Bullets power forward Terry Catledge, whom Matty liked when he had him in Philadelphia, or Portland's Steve Johnson, the best center in the expansion pool? Our information was that Minnesota liked Chicago point guard Sam Vincent and would take him among its top three picks.

Matty said adamantly, "I want Catledge."

We took him, gambling that Johnson, who has a history of injuries and is 31 years old, would still be there on the next round. But they took Johnson. Again we moved quickly and with no debate. We came back with Vincent. We were trying to put a starting team together and at this point had two big forwards in Green and Catledge, a scoring guard in Theus and a quarterback in Vincent.

The thing was just flying by. Seven selections had been made. Allotting five minutes per pick, that could have been as much as 35 minutes. But just eight minutes had elapsed. We were going to finish far short of the allotted four hours.

Minnesota completed the fourth round by taking seven-foot Brad Lohaus from Sacramento. The Celtics had given up on him earlier in the year and we couldn't figure out whether he was a player or not. We were kind of relieved Minnesota took him that early because that left

Otis Smith of the Warriors for our fifth pick. Smith is a capable backup big guard and comes from Jacksonville, which won't exactly hurt us in that nearby market.

Minnesota's fifth pick was Lakers point guard David Rivers, who never really established himself in his rookie year and remained a mystery. Our sixth pick was kamikaze point guard Scott Skiles of the Pacers. The *Sentinel's* Barry Cooper quipped that Skiles isn't happy unless he's bleeding. We were tempted to wait a little longer before taking Skiles, but Matty wouldn't hear of it.

"I want him on my team," he said, "so let's not gamble."

Minnesota countered with Mark Davis of Milwaukee and picked up the Bucks' second-round college choice in the process for passing up a couple of players the Bucks wanted to keep. Ironically, Davis would become a free agent two weeks later and ended up sparking our Summer League rookie team to a 4-0 record. He was the league's MVP and was rewarded with a lucrative contract with a Spanish team.

We took swingman Jerry Reynolds of Seattle seventh to fill that hole in our "complete team" concept. Then Minnesota took Scott Roth of San Antonio, a player Bill Musselman coached in the Continental Basketball Association.

Into the eighth round we had a problem. Still no grain elevator for the middle. We looked at each other with the same expressions on our faces. We had to get a center from somewhere. With no NBA-ready centers at Maynard Evans High this time, we settled on 6-11 Mark Acres from Boston. Then we held our breath that our sleeper from Dallas would still be there for the next round. The Timberwolves thankfully let him sleep; they took Shelton Jones from the Sixers, a player Matty had seen all winter and was not interested in.

Having done color commentary for the Mavericks the previous season, Bobby Weiss was high on rookie guard Morlon Wiley. He played only once a week, it seemed, but Bobby was intrigued with his tools. We gleefully pounced on him. I said, "Can you believe how deep this draft is? Minnesota's taking guys we're not interested in and we're still getting good players on the ninth round!"

We were intent on outdueling Minnesota. All winter long they were putting out stories about how many miles their scouts were logging, as if we weren't doing any work at all. We'll be compared with Minnesota in our early years and we wanted to get the jump on them quickly.

By the tenth round, Danny sent a warning from the salary board. We closed out the final three rounds by drafting away from contracts, taking restricted free agents Jim Farmer of Utah and Keith Lee of New Jersey whom we had little intention of keeping. Reynolds and Wiley fell into that same category, but we had word they were receptive to signing with us. Within days, they did. Our final pick was guard Frank Johnson of Houston who comes from Weirsdale, Florida, near Ocala.

The complete harvest, in order, looked like this:

Orlando Magic	Minnesota Timberwolves
Sidney Green, Knicks	Rick Mahorn, Pistons
Reggie Theus, Hawks	Tyrone Corbin, Suns
Terry Catledge, Bullets	Steve Johnson, Blazers
Sam Vincent, Bulls	Brad Lohaus, Kings
Otis Smith, Warriors	David Rivers, Lakers
Scott Skiles, Pacers	Mark Davis, Bucks
Jerry Reynolds, Sonics	Scott Roth, Spurs
Mark Acres, Celtics	Shelton Jones, Sixers
Morlon Wiley, Mavericks	Eric White, Clippers
Jim Farmer, Jazz	Maurice Martin, Nuggets
Keith Lee, Nets	Gunther Behnke, Cavaliers
Frank Johnson, Rockets	

The whole thing was over in 50 minutes. There we were at three o'clock, finished, but required to stay in the room for three more hours until the six o'clock announcement from New York. We spent part of the time evaluating what had just happened. All winter long, I'd been asked whether we'd build as Charlotte did, with veterans, or like Miami with rookies. My answer was a middle ground, and after this draft we felt we had accomplished that with a mix of established pros and young prospects. We also felt the pickings were better than the Miami-Charlotte draft a year earlier.

We were happy about our crop but unhappy about being held captive in the room. Finally, in the last hour, the NBA security man felt sorry for us and let us leave on the basis that we say nothing to anybody even if threatened by a Cyndi Lauper tape. At six, the arena press room was jammed with reporters from all over Florida.

The day ended with Channel 6 sportscaster Mike Storms doing a live remote from the Williams living room during the 11 o'clock news. Our Chihuahua, Magic, jumped in his lap and entertained throughout the telecast. Would not leave. There was Mike fighting to hold his information sheets with Magic poking his nose right into the copy. When Mike tried to report whether the Reds beat the Cubs, the dog was licking his neck.

Dear Diary: Pinch me. This is really happening. We have players. We're a real team. This is why I came to Orlando three years ago.

There were two pressing concerns as our final cramming began for the college draft. We might actually get Nick Anderson. But where, oh, where would we find a center? We hadn't gotten a starting center in the expansion draft and none were visible on the college draft horizon.

Three days before the draft, on a Saturday morning, Chicago Bulls GM Jerry Krause, called. He wanted two future second-round picks for his backup center, seven-foot veteran Dave Corzine. This was the first time we'd heard this. We agreed to give him an answer on Monday.

Sunday was beach day, and son Jimmy, who had just gotten his learner's permit, was driving. I was into Corzine research on the car phone, including a call that awakened Chuck Daly at home. I congratulated him on the championship and asked him about Corzine, since the Pistons had just beaten the Bulls in the Eastern Conference finals. Chuck said two things: "I liked it better for us when Corzine was on the bench. And, I wish we had him." His testimonial was interrupted by a piercing scream. Mine. I had looked up just in time to see Jimmy closing in fast on the car stopped in front of us at a traffic light.

"Stop the car!"

Jimmy slammed on the brakes, an inch short of the car ahead. I let out a thankful sigh and explained to a confused Chuck Daly what was happening. He cracked up.

Sunday night I talked again with Krause, who was not moving off his demand for two seconds. We were pushing for one second-round pick, this year's. He was insisting on two, though he wasn't adamant on the

Alex Martins, director of publicity. We had serious interviews with at least 10 other candidates. But basketball writers around the country kept calling and raving about this assistant sports information director at Georgetown University.

years at that point.

Monday, June 26 — Crazy day of rumors. Calls. Agents. More talks with Krause on Corzine. Downstairs in Gabe's office there was a long, final session with the coaches to discuss Corzine and finalize our game plan for our No. 11 pick. Each of us had done separate homework on Corzine, a fitness nut in great shape. The concensus was he could still play for at least three more years. The overriding factor was that we needed a center. Only two other names were available — Blair Rasmussen of Denver and Tim McCormick of Houston. Both were in their mid-to late 20s and a little above backup quality. But the price for either one was our No. 11 pick. Too high. Besides, what would we do at our public draft party at the arena the next night without a first-round pick? It would be Shakespeare all over again. We finally settled on a pecking order of Anderson, Hammonds, Lichti.

Throughout all of these machine-gun developments, Alex Martins was proving his mettle in almost-daily press conferences to introduce our expansion players, some as they signed Magic contracts. Alex, 25,

Travis Stanley, assistant director of publicity. Uniform-designer Doug Minear was concerned that sweaty players' bottoms would show through the clinging wet fabric. He had Travis work out with the Magic shorts on under a sweltering sun. After comically chasing him around at close range with a camera, Doug announced that the shorts were not too transparent. Travis then announced the end of his modeling career.

bright, wide-eyed, detail-oriented workaholic, had been assistant sports information director at Georgetown. The Central Florida media were glad Alex had forgotten all he learned from Coach John Thompson about media relations.

But being exposed to big John had not supressed his sense of humor. Taking a cue from a gag I pulled on Jack Swope years ago, Alex engineered a practical joke on his assistant, Travis Stanley, on the eve of our first draft. Travis was to fly to New York to sit with Danny Durso at our table during the nationally televised NBA draft. Alex, after setting up the gag with me, advised Travis that I wanted to inspect the outfit he would be wearing to represent us in New York. An hour before he was to catch his flight, Travis dutifully reported to my office, laid his garment bag across my desk and proudly displayed the classy new suit he'd just purchased.

"Oh, no!" I gasped, rolling my eyes in my best act of exasperation. "You can't wear this zoot suit on national TV! I don't know what you were thinking. You'll be representing the Orlando Magic in our first draft. What will people think of us? You're just going to have to get over to Kuppenheimer's as fast as you can. You'll have to get fitted and

I just don't know if you can get all that done today. When's your flight."

"An hour," Travis said, his spirits crushed, his reponse barely audible.

"Oh, no!" I gasped again, woefully shaking my head. "We might have to get someone else. This is the biggest moment in the franchise's history. I just don't understand it. I thought you had better judgment. We just can't send you up there like that."

I burst out the door, shouting for Alex as if I was going to commission Travis' pinch-hitter right there. Most of the office staff was waiting as Travis emerged, his face sagging to knee level. Everyone broke into laughter and the gag was over. Travis saw me laughing and joined in the fun. Fortunately he didn't have a gun in that garment bag or somebody might have been buttoning a dark suit on me.

Tuesday, June 27 — Draft day II. Moved to night and cablecast nationally by WTBS, the draft was now the biggest media event on the NBA calendar. On the phone all day with Krause. He's about 5-foot-6, 50 years old. As round as he is tall. Clips his toenails by memory. Has a total eclipse of the feet. Non-stop talker. Always looks as though he just finished eating a box of powdered doughnuts. Michael Jordan dubbed him "Crumbs."

Jerry scouted for me when I went to the Bulls in 1969. The most ferocious scout in history. Intense worker. Covers every detail. For years he scouted both baseball and basketball. The only guy in history to work for Jack Kent Cooke (basketball Lakers) and Charles O. Finley (baseball A's) in the same year. When White Sox owner Jerry Reinsdorf bought the Bulls in '85 he moved Krause from his scouting job with the White Sox to become GM of the Bulls. His nickname is "The Sleuth." Damon Runyon would have loved him. He always talks by putting a hand up to his mouth, whispering as if the KGB might be listening.

We accepted having to give up two seconds for Corzine, offering our second-round picks in '91 and '93. The Sleuth wouldn't budge. Because the Bulls had three first-round picks on this night, he was willing to let us keep our second-rounder. But he was adamant about getting our '90 and '92 second-rounders. No more negotiating. Either make the deal or don't make the deal. We took a deep breath and agreed to dance.

Jerry Krause. Hammered a hard bargain before we could get Dave Corzine. It was either grab Corzine and make sure we had a proven center for the early years or muddle through with any big bodies we could pick up off the street. I said to Matty, "If you picked up the paper tomorrow and read Corzine was dealt to the Nets, would you be unhappy?" He said, "Yes." I said, "Let's make the deal."

Jerry then introduced a new wrinkle. The Bulls' first pick that night would be No. 6. He said he would make the Corzine trade only if able to draft one of these four: Pervis Ellison, Danny Ferry, J.R. Reid or Stacey King. Moving Corzine would create playing time for the Bulls' young, third center, Will Perdue. But Jerry needed another big man as insurance in case Perdue fizzled as starter Bill Cartwright's understudy.

It seemed as though the day would never end. Lots of pacing. Nervous chatter. Sweaty palms. We wanted Anderson so bad we could taste it. There was a midday morsel from his agent, Bill Pollak, who was told by Minnesota Coach Bill Musselman that the Timberwolves would take a point guard. Could this be true? We didn't know what to believe. We had a press conference at noon with several of the expansion players in town to lend glitter to the arena draft party that night.

All the players were bubbling about the strength of their new team and how they thought we could win right away.

At last, the big event. Expansion players on the floor signing photos. Music pounding. Magic Girls prancing. We pushed tickets. Matty and I did a Q&A with the crowd, which numbered close to 7,000. Lots of excitement. Finally, 7:30 arrived and the draft was here. It felt like the start of the Indy 500. Gentlemen, start your engines!

Small Forwards:

1. ~~S. Elliott - Ariz.~~
2. ~~G. Rice - Mich.~~
3. ~~N. Anderson - Ill.~~
4. ~~K. Battle - Ill.~~
5. ~~J. Sanders - Ga. S.~~
6. ~~M. Ansley - Ala.~~
7. ~~K. Payne - Louis.~~
8. ~~S. Brundy - DePaul~~
9. ~~R. Blanton - LSU~~
10. ~~C. Brown - N C St.~~
11. ~~R. Turner - Ala. Birm.~~
(12) T. Dawson - FSU
13. ~~D. Nix - Tenn.~~
14. ~~B. Quinett - Wash. St.~~
15. ~~P. Durhan - Col. St.~~
(16) R. Henry - Mid. Tenn St.
17. P. Graham - Col. St.
18. H. Henderson - S W Missouri St.
(19) G. Church - Missouri
20. H. Hudson - S. Carol.
21. C. Thomas - N. Mex.

Centers

1. ~~S. King - Okla.~~
2. ~~V. Divac - Yugo.~~
3. ~~G. Leonard - Missouri~~
4. ~~D. Roth - Tenn.~~
5. M. McMullen - SanDiego
6. G. Mateen - Ohio St.
7. W. Tinkle - Montana St
8. J. Calavita - Vermont
9. R. Lokkel - New Mex.

Power Forwards

1. ~~D. Ferry - Duke~~
2. ~~P. Ellison - Louisville~~
3A. ~~R. White - La. Tech.~~
3B. ~~J.R. Reid - N.C.~~
4. ~~T. Hammond - Ga. Tech.~~
5. ~~M. Smith - BYU~~
6A. ~~A. Cook - Ariz.~~
6B. ~~C. Robinson - Conn.~~
7. ~~R. Turner - Ala. Birm.~~
8. ~~F. Kornet - Vander.~~
9. ~~R. Cross - Hawaii~~
(10) L. Taylor - Cal.
(11) R. Ramos - Seton Hall
12. ~~E. Horton - Iowa~~
13. ~~Sean Kemp - Under~~
(14) H. Wright - Stan.
15. M. McCounts - Purdue
    D. Gues... - C... Ill.

Points

1. ~~B.J. Armstrong - Iowa~~
2. ~~T. Hardaway - UTEP~~
3. ~~M. Blaylock - Okla.~~
4. ~~P. Richardson - UCLA~~
5. ~~D. Barros - Bos.~~
6. ~~H. Workman - ORU~~
(7) K. Armstrong - SMU
8. ~~J. Morton - Seton Hall~~
9. C. Smith - Georgetown
10. ~~S. Douglas - Syracuse~~
11. ~~J. Lewis - S. Ala.~~
12. ~~G. Grant - Trenton~~
(13) T. Jackson - Wiscon.
(14) G. Green - Seton Hall
15. B. Goheen - Vander.
16. M. McFadden - Clev. St.
17. C. Childs - Boise
18. ~~J. Hodge - S. Ala.~~
19. B. McNeal - West Kent.
    (Jay Burson - INJ)
    ~~. St.~~
20. D. Hunter - N. Texas
21. J. Timberlake - Boston U
22. J. Lebo - NC

Two's

1A. ~~T. Lichti - Stanford~~
1B. ~~G. McCloud - FSU~~
2. ~~B. Irvin - Missouri~~
3. ~~R. Marble - Iowa~~
4. ~~B. Edwards - E. Carol.~~
5. ~~D. West - Villanova~~
6. ~~M. Cutwright - McNeese~~
7. ~~J. Martin - Murray St.~~
8. ~~J. Edwards - Ind.~~
9. ~~S. Haffner - Evansville~~
(10) J. Taylor - E. Ill.
11. C. Cheeks - Va Comm.
(12) R. Davis - Wyom.
13. R. Hollis - Houston
(14) M. Newton - Kansas
15. D. Spradley - Gonzaga
16. B. Dinkens - UNC Char.
17. W. Lancaster - Virg. Tech
18. S. Bucknall - N.C.
19. E. Brown - Miami

Our worksheet on the night of the draft.

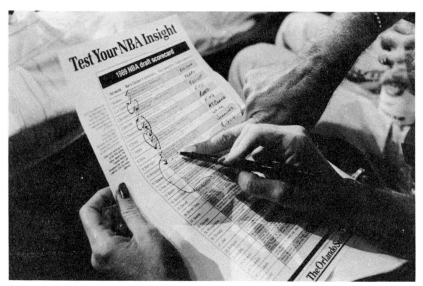

Who'd draft whom? Fans could test their own drafting skills by filling in a sheet in the Sentinel.

I retreated to a room just off our locker room, the players' wives' lounge, which had been set up as a draft control center. A TV monitor would show what was going on in New York and a large blackboard would keep up with the picks. A familiar draft team was seated around the table: Matty, Bobby, Bill du Pont, Gabe and me. The board was manned by Eric Dennis, our young assistant in charge of the scouting videos, and Jack Swope.

On the table were position rankings, information sheets and two phones connected to Danny and "Zoot Suit" Stanley in New York. Trainers Lenny Currier and Keith Jones were there with medical reports from the NBA on all the players. After an expansive search, we plucked Lenny from the Dodgers' organization as our head trainer. Keith joined us from the University of Minnesota to become the only black trainer in the NBA.

(Speaking of conditioning, another old friend from Philadelphia came to Orlando to work on player strength and conditioning. Pat Croce, perhaps the country's pre-eminent fitness expert, opened his own fitness center in conjunction with the Jewett Clinic in Winter Park. He's got a body by Fischer and is so optimistic that had he been on the

Titanic he'd have said no problem, we're just stopping for ice).

Picking first, Sacramento GM Bill Russell ended a long, tense pre-draft guessing game by taking Pervis Ellison. The LA Clippers took Ferry, who'd end up signing a lucrative one-year deal in Italy. We were sweating. Two of the Bulls' four-man list for the Corzine trade were gone. But third and fourth went as advertised: San Antonio took Sean Elliot and Miami took Glen Rice.

That touched off our first mini-celebration around the table. With No. 5 Charlotte now up and the remaining two players on Krause's list still available, the Corzine trade was assured. Charlotte took J.R. Reid and Krause nabbed Stacey King for the Bulls. Remember that if Reid hadn't come out as an underclassman, the Bulls likely wouldn't have had a shot at King, erasing the Corzine deal.

What a relief. We had an NBA center. He's not Bill Russell reincarnated. He's not Kareem Abdul-Jabbar. But he's a center who can play and make you competitive. Jack Swope hopped on a conference call with Irwin Mandel, the financial officer of the Bulls, and Joel Litvin of the league office, and we officially made the Corzine trade as the draft was unfolding.

Seated from left, Mark Acres, Sidney Green and Sam Vincent sign autographs for season-ticket holders.

At No. 7, Indiana took George McCloud. Dallas took Randy White at No. 8. Now came a pick vital to us. Washington had No. 9 and Minnesota No. 10 ahead of us. Still available were two of the three we most hoped would be there.

Washington took Hammonds. Now we were at the mercy of our fellow neophytes, the Minnesota Timberwolves, who had five minutes to decide our fate. We could only pray they wouldn't take Anderson. But I couldn't wait. I grabbed the phone and shouted to Danny to go over to the Timberwolves' table to see who they'd select. At least it might provide another minute or two before the commissioner announced their selection to begin studying alternatives.

Danny rubbernecked over the Minnesota guys, fortunately at the adjacent table, and returned to the phone. "Minnesota is taking . . . ," he said with a pause that sent us up the wall, " . . . Pooh Richardson."

The Timberwolves were about to flabbergast the basketball world by

The town was waiting to explode over a team. The arena crowd went wild as we announced picking Nick Anderson.

Nick Anderson, our first-rounder, embraces his mother at draft headquarters in New York.

taking UCLA point guard Pooh Richardson. We figured the logical picks would have been Anderson or Lichti. The Timberwolves would take one and we'd get the other. Pooh Richardson? We couldn't believe it. (After the draft, Musselman said they wanted to build around a lead guard, but a Minneapolis reporter wrote that Musselman looked like he'd just swallowed a bowl of cold gruel when he said it).

On the monitor we watched David Stern step to the podium and announce: "Minnesota . . . in their first college pick . . . selects Pooh Richardson." Maybe it was just my imagination, but it seemed David Stern had a most quizzical look on his face, as if to say, "Hey, I'm just as surprised as you fellas." Understand that Pooh may be a fine player. It's not like he was an unknown. But most everyone had him pegged later in the draft. Unexpected, to say the least. But now we had a free run at our man. Another celebration erupted in our little room. I exchanged a low-five with Bill du Pont, which is a pretty dramatic gesture for him. We formally took Nick Anderson and I scrambled out into

the arena to announce our selection to the crowd even before David
Stern could tell them on the big scoreboard screens over center court.
Matty went into the press room to discuss it with the media.

Two weeks later we learned that Denver made a frantic effort during
the early part of the draft to trade for Indiana's No. 7 pick and would
have used it to take Anderson. Thankfully, Indiana asked too much in
return — all-star guard Lafayette Lever — and Denver gave up. Hairpin turn No. 728 and we hadn't even realized this one was taking place.

The Minnesota press, which wrote the T-wolves whipped us in the
expansion draft, all agreed we came out ahead on the college draft.
Touche.

At the end of the first round the commissioner announced our Corzine trade. Matty and I switched roles. He went to discuss the trade
with the crowd and I went to the press room. Then we reconvened to
get ready for our second-round pick. Matty was ashen-faced.

"They booed me," he said, still blinking like a wounded puppy.

"You're kidding," I said. "Talk to me. What happened?"

"I'm serious," he said, his voice two octaves higher than normal.
"They booed."

"They booed what?"

"They booed the deal."

*May, 1989: Actual basketball
players attempting to make the
Magic roster at a camp at the
University of Central Florida.
The camp was closed to the
public, but some UCF students,
above, still figured a way to see
the players. At left, Wallace
Bryant gives me his phone
number just in case we ever
have need for a seven-footer. At
right, Matty Guokas is excited
to return to the coaching wars.
Here he tells two prospects
which way the basket is.*

"Whaddaya mean? We just made a great deal."

"Yeah? Well, they booed it."

Later, Bill Fay, Magic beat writer for the *Tampa Tribune*, said he knew what the problem was. He said the fans here still have an NFL mentality. Two second-rounders in the NFL are future All-Pros. They don't realize yet that second-rounders in the NBA are longshot gambles at best.

For days, writers around the country chose sides on the Corzine deal. George White of the *Sentinel* rose to our defense. Jan Hubbard of *The Sporting News* said we double dribbled. And so it goes.

I'd been out of the draft business for three years and quickly discovered it's the same wild, controversial world. But it felt great to be back.

Suddenly in the second round there was another pleasant surprise. Michael Ansley of Alabama had been the 37th and last player invited to the Orlando All-Star Classic two months earlier. Ansley had lit it up at a lesser camp in Portsmouth, Virginia, and Gabe called me late on the final night. "Nobody has the nerve to tell Ansley he can't come to the Classic. I know we're at 36, but can we get a 37th uniform and bring him down? I can't tell him no."

Ansley wound up making the All-Tournament team after averaging 14.6 points and 11.6 rebounds in three Classic games. Most people projected him as a late first-round or early second-round pick. But there he was, still unclaimed, as our second pick approached. We may have had minor surgery to thank. Michael had a cyst removed from his backside the day before the Chicago camp earlier that month and couldn't play. Had he played and sparkled as he'd done in the earlier camps in Portsmouth and Orlando, it's doubtful he would have still been available to us in the second round.

It all ended at 11 o'clock. Everything broke for us. The Corzine deal fell in. Nick Anderson was there. Getting Ansley was a nice break. I went to my car at midnight and found a little note stuck under the windshield wiper. "Great job!" it said. "Sid Cash." A perfect ending to a perfect day.

The next day still was full speed ahead. Nick Anderson flew in from New York and Cari Haught and her staff outdid themselves. At the airport were The Magic Girls, banners, Church Street Station's Dixieland Band, and Matty and me. It was as if the prime minister of Guatemala was about to arrive. Watching Matty greeting his No. 1 pick made me laugh; couldn't you just see Vince Lombardi doing that?

While Anderson was dealing with the media at Delta's Crown Room, Michael Ansley's flight arrived from Birmingham. We gave him the same reception, except this time Anderson joined the welcoming committee. Ansley stepped into this spotlight wearing only shorts, a T-shirt and sandals.

I said, "Michael, where's your bag?"

"Mr. Williams, I didn't bring one."

Our first crisis of the draft.

We had a major reception scheduled that night for our owners and sponsors at the swank Citrus Club which has never even *heard* of T-shirts and sandals. The first order of business was to take Michael by the Urban Gorilla men's store downtown to purchase a pair of slacks and shirt with a collar. Shoes? We ended up at Sam Behr's store, where they claim they can fit any human, including basketball players.

I was emcee at the reception, introducing each player to say a few words. I told the crowd that Reggie Theus had never met a shot he didn't like.

Reggie responded, "I heard all of Pat Williams' jokes in the fifth grade."

It was only a summer league game at UCF, but you'd never have guessed from this fan and player reaction.

I couldn't resist.

When Reggie's brief remarks were over, I said, "Reggie, three of the best years of your life were spent in the fifth grade."

Following the reception, most of the players who were not into Citrus Club hors d'oeuvres ended up eating barbecue at the Cheyenne Saloon. Meanwhile, Dave Corzine had just arrived from Chicago. He was hungry and coincidentally went to the same place. It was an all-Chicago reunion: Corzine, Sidney Green, Sam Vincent, Reggie Theus and Nick Anderson. They greeted Corzine like a long-lost brother. High fives and embraces all around.

"It was electric," said Eric Dennis, our video assistant.

Eric took all the players back to the airport the next day. By this time the whole city was in a frenzy over the Magic. As Eric stood among these skyscrapers in the lobby, it appeared everyone in the airport was staring at our new heros. Three little Filipino women came running over and started bowing. A well-dressed business executive sauntered by and said, "Welcome to Orlando. When's your next game?"

Ahem. It was the end of June. Our town was excited but it appeared we had a little NBA educating to do.

The next month was a flurry of activity — more player press conferences, contract signings, the release of our first season's schedule, the hiring of our TV announcers and sparring with agents over which rookies and free agents would attend our Summer League camp, a.k.a. The Darryl Dawkins No-Show II. Our first season, for so long a hazy image somewhere out there in the distance, suddenly drew into focus and the public picked up the scent.

Ticket activity surged anew. Ignited by the draft, coffeeshop conversation in formerly football-dominated Central Florida turned to basketball and increased to an excited clatter by the Summer League scrimmages against Miami, Charlotte and Atlanta in late July. The first two nights were played at Florida International University in Miami and featured the first-ever meeting of the Heat and Magic in what was already showing the classic signs of a spirited rivalry. Though the haughty South Florida media kept shrugging off the thought of a rivalry with the little bumpkin town up the turnpike and though Heat coaches downplayed the rivalry, the intensity of that first meeting, even in a summer rehearsal with rookies and free agents, was clearly apparent.

Players on both teams sensed the tone-setting importance and went at each other as if it were the seventh game of the playoffs.

"Who are we kidding?" one Heat marketing official said in a show of candor. "This is a rivalry and we want to win." An SRO crowd of 3,500 taunted the Orlando team with Mickey Mouse jeers and went out of their gourds when Heat star Rony Seikaly stuffed in the game's first two points. They were more subdued two hours later, filing out after we won, 105-103.

"That was fun!" gushed our Jerry Reynolds. Ansley, who had been up on the bench leading cheers during the final minutes, was still pumped up 20 minutes after the final buzzer. "That was like an Alabama-Auburn game!" he exclaimed. Even Matty, our bastion of detachment who was going to sit calmly and take notes at the press table, wound up pounding his fists, berating the referees and yelling instructions to our players. And I was as animated as Matty.

The rematch came three nights later after the "tournament" shifted to Orlando. Another sellout, this time with Magic fans screaming, applauding, and stomping their feet in mid-playoff frenzy at the University of Central Florida gym as our guys bopped the Heat, 102-78. The game was telecast live by Channel 2 — unprecedented for NBA summer leagues. Any doubt that the fans were into this now was erased when I treated our three daughters to a birthday breakfast the next morning in Winter Park. A guy on the sidewalk shouted out, "Great win last night!" Our waitress recognized me and went on and on about beating Miami. The people at the next table applauded.

When Cari Haught stopped off at the cleaners the clerk recognized her as a member of our staff. "Congratulations!" said the clerk. "For what?" Cari responded, just beginning to understand the fan fervor.

These were only rookie exhibitions, but we completed the sweep, winning four games and presenting ourselves with a huge trophy to the enthusiastic applause of our players. The atmosphere in that cramped locker room was, well, Magic.

I could sense it coming a week earlier when the transition from future franchise to basketball reality sank in on the first morning of the Summer League camp. There I sat in the bleachers of the tidy little gym on the UCF campus, soaking in the first official practice. Watching the players work, I was filled with a glowing mix of anticipation for the fervor that was about to capture this town and — even stronger — a montage of memories of all that had transpired in this grand adventure. I thought of the many heartaches and exultations as the fantasy became reality. I could hear Jimmy Hewitt's syrupy Southern voice on the phone that night three years earlier: "Bubba ... I've gone as far with it as I can go ... You come and head it up or we're not going to do it."

We had come up short on guards for the start of that camp, so Gabe pressed into service an old playground basketball crony from Philadelphia, Eddie McTague. Eddie, a paper products salesman and hoops junkie, happened to be in Orlando on vacation at Disney World. He relished the chance to put his moves on our pros, no doubt fantasizing about catching Matty's eye and winning a spot on the roster. But his wife called it off after Eddie had only one Walter Mitty day. "We're here on vacation," Mrs. McTague ruled, tapping her foot. "No more basketball."

Cling to that dream, Eddie. I can attest that, indeed, sometimes they really do come true.

1989-90
ORLANDO MAGIC

NAME	POS	HGT	WGT
Mark Acres	F-C	6-11	225
Nick Anderson	F	6-5	205
Michael Ansley	F	6-7	225
Terry Catledge	F	6-8	230
Dave Corzine	C	6-11	260
Sidney Green	F	6-9	220
Frank Johnson	G	6-1	185
Jerry Reynolds	G-F	6-8	206
Scott Skiles	G	6-1	180
Otis Smith	G-F	6-5	210
Reggie Theus	G	6-7	213
Jeff Turner	F	6-9	240
Sam Vincent	G	6-2	185
Morlon Wiley	G	6-4	192

BIRTHDATE	COLLEGE	PRO
11/15/62	Oral Roberts '85	2
1/20/68	Illinois '89	R
2/8/67	Alabama '89	R
8/22/63	South Alabama '85	4
4/25/56	DePaul '78	11
1/4/61	UNLV '83	6
11/23/58	Wake Forest '81	8
12/23/62	Louisiana St. '85	4
3/5/64	Michigan St. '86	3
1/30/64	Jacksonville '86	3
10/13/57	UNLV '78	11
4/9/62	Vanderbilt '84	3
5/18/63	Michigan St. '85	4
9/24/66	Long Beach St. '88	1

Terry Catledge — Bullets

Otis Smith — Warriors

Reggie Theus — Hawks

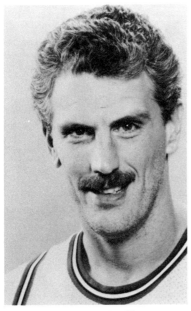

Dave Corzine — Bulls

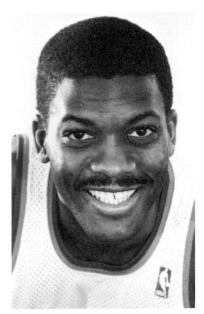

Sidney Green — Knicks

Sam Vincent — Bulls

Morlon Wiley — Mavericks

Mark Acres — Celtics

Frank Johnson — Rockets

Jerry Reynolds — Supersonics

Nick Anderson — U. of Illinois

Michael Ansley — U. of Alabama

Scott Skiles — Pacers

Jeff Turner — Italian league

AND SPEAKING OF MIAMI...

Another reason for Miami to hate me? Here's the "disguise" I wore to the summer league games there. I thought the whole scene was hilarious, but my old pals from the Heat looked at me as if I had the plague. This episode fit right in with my passion for humor, particularly one-liners. This interest was sparked in the late '70s when I heard the hilarious ex-Utah Jazz coach, Frank Layden, captivate audiences. Then I met Ken Hussar, a schoolteacher in Lancaster, Pennsylvania, and fellow one-liner addict. We've been collecting the best one-liners ever since. We can't get our fill. We've been deeply influenced by the most prolific one-line writer of all time, Bob Orben. So have a few laughs on my favorite NBA and new Florida targets.

MIAMI: A family moved into one Miami neighborhood the other day and was fired on by the Welcome Wagon.

MY TRIP TO MIAMI: The mayor gave me the key to the city and Billy Cunningham had the locks changed. I stood on the beach and the tide refused to come in. So I picked up a seashell and I heard a voice saying, "Williams, ya bum, get off the beach." I recognized the voice...it was David Stern's mother.

THE MIAMI HEAT: I've seen occupational therapy groups make more baskets than the Heat.

MIAMI DOLPHINS: Don Shula finally figured out what the problem is. The Dolphins are tipping their plays. Every time they break from the huddle, three of the backs are giggling and one is white as a sheet.

FLORIDA GATORS: There was a recent scandal on campus. Three football players were caught in the library.

FLORIDA STATE SEMINOLES: At FSU they don't give a football player his letter until he can tell which one it is.

MIAMI HURRICANES: Why do Hurricane graduates hang their diplomas from their rear-view mirrors? So they can park in handicap places.

TAMPA BAY BUCS: They've solved their problems by drafting a 5-6, 130-pound fullback. That's the exact size hole the offensive line opens. Every time they fake it to one halfback diving into the line, you can hear him crying out, "I don't have it! I don't have it!"

SUMMER IN ORLANDO: It's so hot I saw a dog chasing a cat. They were both walking.

WEATHER IN FLORIDA: Let a smile be your umbrella and you'll get a mouthful of rain.

WINTER PARK: There's a new camp in Winter Park for yuppie kids. It's Camp Gimmegucci. The main feature is an indoor lake. The kids stay up late at night telling ghost stories around the microwave.

BITHLO, FLORIDA: In Bithlo if you own a painted turtle they call you an art lover.

JEFF CLARK: Jeff is so tough he bowls overhand.

LARRY GUEST: No man is an island, but Larry Guest comes pretty close.

MY WARDROBE: Margie Varney of the Orlando Chamber calls me "the prince of polyester." She says, "Even priests think Pat is a dull dresser."

MICHAEL ANSLEY'S WARDROBE: Michael hates formal occasions. It's so tough to put cufflinks on a T-shirt. A real fashion plate, he's the only guy I know who wears a double-breasted T-shirt.

THE NBA: I can tell you what it's like working for the NBA. Picture a nervous breakdown with paychecks.

HAROLD KATZ: When I was with the Sixers, Harold gave me a sign for my desk. It read, "Like to meet new people? Like a change? Like excitement? Like a new job? Just mess up one more time!"

SEVEN-FOOT CENTER DAVE CORZINE: He spent the summer working as a lifeguard at Daytona. He can't swim but he can wade like mad.

MAKING MAGIC: This book is in its sixth printing. I sure wish the *Sentinel* had done the first five right.

MY WIFE JILL: Before Burdine's plans a sale, they always phone Jill to see if she's available. But she's doing a better job of keeping her bills down. She bought a heavier paperweight.

MICHAEL EISNER: Michael's neighborhood is so exclusive that the fire department has an unlisted number. The favorite restaurant is Pheasant Delite.

MY 12 CHILDREN: A man with 12 children is more content than a man with 12 million dollars. The man with 12 million dollars wants more.

DARRYL DAWKINS: He was a very big infant. He was born on June 1, 2 and 3. He learned yoga in the NBA by trying to get in and out of airline seats.

MAYOR BILL FREDERICK: I was at city hall and the mayor was making one of his decisions. I didn't actually see the mayor, but I did see the coin being flipped.

ICE HOCKEY IN ORLANDO: It'll never go. I once gave a hockey puck to Mayor Frederick and he spent the rest of the day trying to open it.

TIP LIFVENDAHL: Let's put this in perspective. All Tip wants from the newsroom is perfection, although he'll settle for more.

MAGIC MUSIC

The Magic braintrust decided early that what this team needed was a good fight song. Not the classic college fight song, but a more contemporary tune to fire up our fans. With no particular songs in our hearts at the time, we set out in January, 1989, to find one — and there occurred yet another of those hairpin turns. One afternoon in March, local songwriter and producer Glen Gettings of Ocoee and vocalist Ryan Kelly, a family friend, waltzed unannounced into my office for a live, impromptu performance of what they assured was the song we'd been looking for. You know something? They were right. We knew immediately the search was over. Here's the worksheet with the lyrics they handed us that day:

THERE'S A SPIRIT IN ORLANDO
THERE'S MAGIC IN OUR TOWN
THERE'S A HEARTBEAT POUNDING IN THE STREETS
ITS SO FANTASTIC AND OUT OF CONTROL
YOU CAN FEEL THE POWER UNDER YOUR FEET

ABRA-CADABRA...   RAZZ-A-MA-TAZZ...
SLAM DUNK...   OPEN SESAME...   GONNA SET THE SPIRIT FREE!
HOCUS-POCUS...   ALA-KAZAM...

ORLANDO MAGIC...   ORLANDO MAGIC...
ORLANDO MAGIC...   EVERYWHERE...
ORLANDO MAGIC...   ORLANDO MAGIC...
ORLANDO MAGIC...   ...   WATCH OUT... BEWARE... (interlude)
GONNA GET YA!

IF YOU COME TO OUR GREAT CITY
AND TRY TO TAKE OUR TOWN
IF YOU THINK YOU'LL WALK AWAY WITH VICTORY
YOU BETTER THINK TWICE, sucker
CONSIDER THIS...   POOF!   YOU'LL BE HISTORY!   You're History

ABRA-CADABRA...   RAZZ-A-MA-TAZZ...
SLAM DUNK...   SESAME...
HOCUS-POCUS...   ALA-KAZAM...   GONNA SET THE SPIRIT FREE!

ORLANDO MAGIC...   ORLANDO MAGIC...
ORLANDO MAGIC...   EVERYWHERE...
ORLANDO MAGIC...   ORLANDO MAGIC...
ORLANDO MAGIC...   ...   WATCH OUT... BEWARE...
GONNA GET YA!

(INSTRUMENTAL BREAK)

ABRA-CADABRA...   RAZZ-A-MA-TAZZ...
SLAM DUNK...   OPEN SESAME...
HOCUS-POCUS...   ALA-KAZAM...   GONNA SET THE SPIRIT FREE!

ORLANDO MAGIC...   ORLANDO MAGIC...
ORLANDO MAGIC...   EVERYWHERE...
ORLANDO MAGIC...   ORLANDO MAGIC...
ORLANDO MAGIC...   IN THE AIR...   WATCH OUT... BEWARE...
GONNA GET YA!   ...ORLANDO MAGIC!!!

THE ARENA

Dimensions and characteristics

☐ Square footage (all levels)...367,000
☐ Concourse width
    North/south...28 feet
    East/west...22 feet
☐ Building volume .... 17,800 cubic feet
☐ Clear height (floor to steel truss)...87 feet
☐ Clear span from upper seat to opposite upper seat
    Length...396 feet
    Width...300 feet
☐ Maximum seat distance to first seat on floor...........................130 feet
☐ Maximum distance to center of floor
    East/west..209 feet
    North/south...164 feet
☐ Exterior glass... 50,784 square feet
    (north/south)...46 feet x 280 feet
    Block (east/west) ....46 feet x 272 feet
☐ Skyboxes..26
    Square footage (each)...450
☐ Upper terrace north and south sides (each)...........16 feet x 270 feet
☐ Concession area.. 17,434 square feet
☐ Restroom fixture ratio (per guest)...1:74
☐ Ticket windows (at three locations)...20
☐ Kitchen facilities .... 8,500 square feet
    (equivalent to commercial level food preparation)
☐ Elevators 4
    Skyboxes..2
    Food and service 1
    Handicap..1

Centroplex area development

☐ Area ....81 acres
☐ Parking spaces 11,405
    On site..3,838

Off site	Exist	Planned
¼-mile radius	802	1,400
½-mile radius	1,712	2,300
¾-mile radius	1,353	—

THE BELIEVERS

In this book you've met the people who played leading roles in making the Magic a reality. But this story has some other stars — the 4,000-plus companies and individuals who paid for more than 10,000 season tickets, many before there was a franchise, an arena or any players. Without them there would be no Orlando Magic. They are hereby enshrined in this original season-ticket honor roll:

A

A. & T. ANTIQUES
ABC BUS
AC & CB INC.
A. D. ARNOLD CONSTRUCTION CO.
A HAIR EMPORIUM
A. J. FRIED CHICKEN & SEAFOOD
A-1 AUTO SALVAGE
ASSOCIATES INC. C.R.
AAA BUILDING SERVICES
AAGAARD BROTHERS
AAGAARD-JUERGENSEN
AARON PEST CONTROL
AARON SCRAP METAL
ABC AUTO PARTS
PETER ABDALLA
T. ABRAMS
DR. M. ABUFARIS
ACE TRIPPLER CLEANERS
ACI CORP.
THOMAS W. ACKERT
TERRENCE WILLIAM ACKERT
ACME OIL CO.
ACOUSTICAL DISTRIBUTORS
ACTION GOLF
ACTION NISSAN
ACTRON III
ADAM ENTERPRISES
CURTIS ADAMS
BOB ADAMS
BEN ADAMS
CAREY L. ADAMS
MARK D. ADAMS
DR. DAVID ADKINS
ADVANCED MAIL PROCESSING
ADVANTAGE GLASS & SUPPLY
ADWEL INC.
AGEMY ENTERPRISES
AGGRESSIVE APPLIANCES
AGNER AUTO PARTS
AGRI-STARTS
AIKEN & ASSOCIATES

AKERMAN SENTERFITT & EIDSON
AL'S ARMY STORE
ALAMO MEXICAN KITCHEN
ALAN B. KINGSTON D.M.D. P.A.
ALAN D. SIROTA D.P.M. P.A.
ALAQUA REALTY
ALARM SYSTEMS OF ORLANDO
DR. STEPHEN ALBERT
ALBERTSON INTERNATIONAL
ALCO TRUCK RENTAL
ALDEN EQUIPMENT CO.
ALEXIS RISK MANAGEMENT
   SERVICES
ALL AMERICAN TERMITE CONTROL
ALL AMERICAN EQUIPMENT RENTAL
ALL FLORIDA GLASS & MIRROR
ALL INTERIOR SUPPLY
ALL SERVICE APPRAISALS
ALL STAR PRINTING
ALLEN & ASSOCIATES
ALLEN BROWN & BUILDER P.A.
ALLEN ENGINEERING
ALLEN TROVILLON INC.
ALLEN'S CHEVRON
DR. JOHN J. ALLEN
DR. JOHN ALLEN
DWAYNE ALLEN
GLENN ALLEN
JESSIE ALLEN
KENDALL ALLEN
RICK ALLEN
ROBERT ALLEN
STEPHEN D. ALLEN
ALLIED METAL DOORS & FRAME
ALLSBROOK CONSTRUCTION
ALLSTATE REPLACEMENT PARTS
ARTHUR D. ALLY
ALRO METALS
ALTAMONTE OB-GYN
ALTAMONTE PEDIATRIC
   ASSOCIATES

KEITH ALTIZER
ALTON RAINBOC CORP.
ALUMA-TRIM INC.
ALUMINUM SERVICE
JOE ALVAREZ
AMALIE REFINING CO.
AMBER ELECTRIC
AMBRICO & CO. P.A.
HAMILTON-AVNET A.M.D.
AMDEV CORP.
AMERICA OUTDOORS CAMPING
AMERICAN COLOR
AMERICAN DOUGLAS METALS
AMERICAN DISTRIBUTOR OF
   JACKSONVILLE
AMERICAN INTERNATIONAL HEALTH
   & REHABILITATION
AMERICAN INTERNATIONAL RENT- A-
   CAR
AMERICAN MOBILE POWERWASH
AMERICAN PIONEER LIFE
AMERICAN PIONEER SAVINGS BANK
AMERICAN PAGING
AMERICAN RECOVERY SERVICES
AMERICAN SANITARY PARTITION
AMERICAN TITLE INSURANCE CO.
LEONARD AMES
JOHN AMICK II
MICHAEL W. AMMEN
AMOCO OIL CO.
MARK AMRHEIN
ANCHOR FINANCE CO.
RANDY ANDERSEN
DR. AXEL ANDERSON
JOHN ANDERSON
MIKE ANDERSON
DANNY ANDERSON
MARK C. ANDERSON
AVA ANDERSON
ANDREW B. THOMAS P.A.
ANDREW CONSTRUCTION

ANDREWS-BARTLETT & ASSOCIATES
RONALD ANDREYCHIK
KEVIN C. ANGERT
RAFAEL J. ANGULO
ERIC ANSCHUETZ
ROBERT E. ANSLEY JR.
ANSWERITE
DAVID ANTENUCCI
ANTHONY & VAUGHN
ANTHONY'S SALON
ROBERT ANTHONY
DON ANTHONY
PHIL ANTLE
JUDGE JOHN ANTOON II
APEX ROOFING
APOLLO HAIR BOND
SIXTO APONTE
APOPKA CHIROPRACTIC CENTER
STEPHEN APPEL
APPLIED CONCEPTS
RICHARD APTER
ARA LEISURE SERVICES
ARA-WOOD
ARBETTER HOT DOGS
DAN ARBUCKLE
GREGORY ARCHAMBAULT
JOHNNY ARCHER
ROBERT ARCHIE
ARCHWAY COOKIES
JIM L. ARD
SCOTT ARGO
ARLINGTON-HEIDMANN
WILLIAM ARLINGTON
LEON ARMSTRONG JR.
JOHN ARMSTRONG
ARNOLD MILLER D.O. P.A.
SAMUEL ARNOLD
C. JEFFERY ARNOLD
ROSANNE M. ARNOLD
ARRINGTON HOBBS & ASSOCIATES
ARTHUR ANDERSEN & CO.
ARTHUR YOUNG
ARTIZAN INC.
DAN ARTMANN
ARUTE & ASSOCIATES
JAMES ASH
JEFF ASHBY
GREGORY L. ASHCRAFT
ASHE INDUSTRIES INC.
ASHLAND CHEMICAL
ASHTON AGENCY
GENE ASKEW
ASSOCIATED TEMPORARY STAFFING
ASSOCIATED PRINTING & GRAPHICS
ASTRO MARKETING
ASTRO-VALCOUR INC.
AT&T
AT&T INFORMATION SYSTEMS
ATLANTIC CABINETS
ATLANTIC FOAM & PACKAGING
BILLY ATWELL
JOHN ATWOOD
AUDIO MEDIA PRODUCTIONS
AUFSEHER ENTERPRISES
S. M. AUGER
AUTONOMOUS TECHNOLOGY CORP.
EDUARDO AVELLANEDA
MIKE AVERILL
AVID INC.
LOUIS W. AVRIETT
AWNINGS BY CAREY
DR. DARRYL L. AYERS
AZTEC-PROPERTIES
AZTECH ELECTRONICS

B

B & B VENDING
B & H SALES
B & W CUSTOM STAINLESS
BASF

B. G. ADKINS CONSTRUCTION CO.
DR. B. R. BLAKEY
BSG ENTERPRISES
DR. NOAH A. BABINS
ALAN BACH
ROBERT BACH
BRUCE G. BACHAND
PAUL R. BACHAND
JEB BACHMAN
JOHN BADDERS
DR. RICHARD BAGBY
CHARLES BAILES
BAILEY OFFICE PRODUCTS
WAYNE BAILEY
FRANK BAILEY
CARL BAILEY
TIMOTHY J. BAILEY
BAKER & HOSTETLER
BAKER BROTHERS
DAVID E. BAKER CPA
W. J. BAKER II
DR. NORTON M. BAKER
DAVID A. BAKER
GREG BAKER
HART BAKER
RICHARD E. BAKER
RICH V. BAKER
RANDY BAKER
STEPHEN BAKER
YVONNE BAKER
BALCOR PROPERTY MANAGEMENT
BALDWIN-FAIRCHILD FUNERAL
   HOME
GARY BALL
JOHN BALLANTYNE
MERLE BALLARD
FRED D. BALTAZAR JR.
BAMSI INC.
BANANA BAY GROVE
BANCBOSTON MORTGAGE CORP.
BANDY AUTO SALES
BAR HARBOR LOBSTER CO.
JIM BARBER
PAUL BARBER
BERT BARCLAY
HERBERT W. BARCLAY
WILLIAM R. BARKER
DAVID BARKWILL
GEORGE BARLEY
DR. WILLIAM P. BARNARD
BARNETT BANK
TERRY BARNEY
BARNIE'S COFFEE & TEA CO.
BARR DISPLAY & FIXTURE
DR. BARRY A. LEVIN
BARRY NEAL CARPETS
LONGWOOD B. RUTENBERG HOMES
THOMAS JOHN BARRY
PAUL W. BARTLETT
JIM BARTOE
STEVE BARTON
BARTY REALTY
JOHN BASILE
IRA BASILE
PETER E. BASKAUSKAS
BASKETBALL ASSOCIATES
MIKE BASS
BATCHELOR FINE PHOTOGRAPHY
TIMOTHY O. BATES
WARREN W. BAUCUM
BAUMAN & PANZO M.D. P.A.
JUDITH BAUMANN
ED BAXA
CHARLES M. BAXTER III
BAY HILL CLUB & LODGE
BAY HILL REALTY
BOB BAYLEY
BDO SEIDMAN
BEACH AUTO BODY
BEACH PHOTO
JOHN BEASLEY
NORMA L. BEASLEY
WALT BEAVER
DAVID BECKER

JOHN L. BECKER
GUS BECKSTROM JR.
RICK BEELER
WILLIAM F. BEEMER
BEHE & UMHOLTZ
RONALD BEIGHLEY
STEPHEN BEIK
DANIEL R. BEISTEL
CARL BELCHER
BELL & IRWIN
R. BELL
SCOTT BELL
H. PAUL BELLINGER
BELLOWS TV & APPLIANCE
BELLSOUTH MOBILITY
W. BRIAN BELTON
KATHY BELYEA
BENDER CONSTRUCTION CO.
BENDER ROOF CO.
MARC BENIGNO
WAYNE BENNETT
ROSS BENNETT
BENNIGAN'S
CARL E. BENNINGER
BENT OAK GOLF CLUB
KENNETH BENTLEY
RAYMOND C. BERARD JR.
ARTHUR BERK
BERKSHIRE GROUP
GARY BERKSON
BERMAN SHAPIRO CRAWFORD & CO.
REID BERMAN
RICHARD J. BERNIER
MICHAEL BERNSTEIN
BEST AMERICAN HOMES
BEST CARPET CARE
BEST CONCRETE PLUMBING
   SERVICE
BEST FOODS BAKING GROUP
RENNEY BETRIS
WILLIAM O. BETTERTON JR.
BETZ ENTEC
BEVERLY B. MASON REALTY
GARY W. BEYMER
LINDA BIAS
BART BIBLER
BRENT W. BICKHART
STEVEN BIENEFELD
JOHN T. BIGALKE
BILL BROWN VOLKSWAGEN
BILL BRYAN SUBARU/SAAB
BILL KNAPP'S FLORIDA INC.
BILLIE HELLER & CO.
BILLINGS & CUNNINGHAM
ROBERT M. BININGER
BINNER EQUIPMENT CORP.
CHARLES BIRD
ROBERT A. BIRNHOLZ
THOMAS R. BISIENERE
DOUG BISSON
STEVE BITLER
BLACK ANGUS RESTAURANT
GOMER J. BLACK JR.
A. CLIFTON BLACK
BLACKADAR INSURANCE AGENCY
AL BLACKBURN
FRED BLACKMON
J. AL BLACKMON
BLACKTON INC.
KEITH A. BLACKWAY
PHILIP E. BLAKE CPA
R. MASON BLAKE
RICHARD E. BLANCHARD
DONOVAN C. BLANCHARD
CRAIG BLATTNER
ROY E. BLEDSOE
BRIAN BLEVINS
DON J. BLISS
DAVID BLONDELL
DR. ROBERT D. BLOODWELL
MICHAEL H. BLOUNT
BLUE RIBBON PLUMBING
ANNA JEAN BLUE
BLUMENAUER CORP.

EDWARD B. BLUMENTHAL
MARTIN BLY
BOB MCCLELLAN'S CHRYSLER
ENZO BOCCAROSSA
DEAN BODAGER
BOEBINGER INT. TRUCK SALES
JOHN BOHBRINK
ROGER A. BOLDIZSAR
CHUCK BOLT
DAN BONACCI
JAMES BONAR
JOHN BONNER
DONALD B. BOONE
SCOTT BOONE
DR. JAMES D. BOOTH
BORDEN INC.
PAUL J. BORDONARO
TODD BOREN
JACK S. BORLING
JOHN BORNMAN
DR. BURTON BORNSTEIN
THOMAS BOROUGHS
ALAN P. BOSMA
PERRY BOTWIN
STEVE BOURKE
THE REV. HERBERT L. BOWDOIN
JAMES BOWERS
SCOTT BOWERSOX
GARY BOWIE
ROBERT BOWIE
BOWLES REALTY
CHARLES (KERRY) BOWLES
MICHAEL BOWLING
BRUCE R. BOWMAN
DR. TIMOTHY BOWSER
CLARENCE BOWSER
BOWYER-SINGLETON & ASSOCIATES
JEFFREY A. BOYER
BOYLE ENGINEERING CORP.
DONALD J. BOYLE
KENNETH J. BOYLE
BILL BOYNTON
HAROLD J. BRACKETT
BRADFORD & FLETCHER
DR. BRADFORD W. PORTER
BILL BRADFORD
KEN BRADLEY
LLEWELLYN BRADLEY
LOUIS P. BRADY
BRAILE CHIROPRACTIC CLINIC
WAYNE BRANDT
BRANIFF
BRASS & SCHNEIDER
BRAUN CADILLAC
BLAZ BRAVAR
KEN BRAY
RONALD E. BRAY
DENNIS BRAZIEL
EDWARD F. BRENNAN JR.
ROBERT BRENNAN
TERRENCE BRENNAN
TIM BRENNAN
MATTHEW BRENNER
BRETT BLACKMON INC.
BREVARD BUILDERS SUPPLY
BREVARD POOLS
BREVARD RENTALS
BREVARD SERVICE CO.
BRICE BUILDING CO.
JOHN C. BRIGGS
CHARLIE W. BRINKLEY JR.
JIMMY BRINLEY
EDWARD BRINSON
RICK BRINSON
L. B. BRINSON
BRITT RUNION PHOTOGRAPHY
ROBERT BRITT
SHAWN TAYLOR BRITTON
GENE L. BROCK
JERRY L. BROCK
BOB BRONCATELLO
JEANELLE BRONSON
SHELDON BROOK
BROOKS BEAUTY SUPPLY

BROOKS STARLING
ED BROOKS
RICHARD BROOKS
JAMES S. BROOKS
THOMAS C. BROOMALL
PETER BROTSCH
BROWN & BROWN
BROWN KILLGORE & PEARLMAN
BROWN TRANSPORT CORP.
DR. C. H. BROWN
DANIEL S. BROWN
JACK BROWN
JAMES BROWN
KENNETH BROWN
RALPH BROWN
RONALD BROWN
KAREN M. BROWN
O. G. (TONY) BROWNELL
BROWNING PRESS
CHUCK BROWNING
BROWNLEE LIGHTING
CHARLES T. BRUMBACK JR.
ALAN BRUNS
RAY BRUSH
BRUTON BOULEVARD AMOCO
BRYAN AUTOMOTIVE GROUP
NIKI BRYAN
MARY E. BRYAN
RALPH P. BRYANT
WALTER BRYANT
GREGORY W. BRYANT
JOHN J. BUCH JR.
BUCK AN HOUR AMERICA
BUDDY FREDDY'S
BUDGET COURIERS
BUDGET RENT-A-CAR
BUENA VISTA PALACE
PATRICK BUFFA
GARY BUFFINGTON
BULL & BUSH
GARY J. BUNKER
BUNKY'S RAW BAR
DAVID BURCHETT
BARRY BURCZYK
MICHAEL BURDETTE
BURKE BALES & MILLS ASSOC.
GARY L. BURKEY
BILL BURLEIGH
WILLIAM BURNS
NICOLAS BURRELL
JIM BURROWS
JOHN W. BUSSEY III
BUTCH'S CAR CARE
DR. MICHAEL BUTLER
ROBERT BUTSCH
CHARLES BUTTERWORTH
ROBERT P. BUTTERY
BRETT BUXBAUM
BUY LOW AUTO PARTS
O. E. BYERS
DR. BILL BYRD
JOHN BYRD
TUCKER BYRD
JIM BYRNE
RICHARD BYRNE

C

C & C CRAFT
C & H PRODUCT GROUP
C & M CORE DISTRIBUTORS
C & S BANK
C & S DATA ASSOCIATES
C & S TRUST CO.
C & W TRUCKING
C. FERRARA P.A.
CP ENTERPRISES
CSH MINI #1
CWP ENTERPRISES
BARRY CABANISS
CABLEVISION OF CENTRAL FLORIDA
CABOT CABOT & FORBES

CHARLES J. CACCIABEVE
BRUCE J. CADWELL
WILLIAM A. CAIN
COL. JOHN CAITHNESS
PHILIP J. CALANDRINO
ANDREW P. CALANDRINO
R. W. CALCUTT
WILLIAM B. CALL JR.
CALLICO SPORTS
DR. JOSE CALLUENG
CALVIN COLLINS JR. M.D. P.A.
RITA CAMARATA
DOUGLAS CAMERON
CAMP DRESSER & MCKEE
LYNOR CAMP
ROBERT CAMPAGNONE
CAMPBELL'S SOUPS
DAVE CAMPBELL
BRIAN CANDELA
GARY CANEZA
GERONIMO CANLAS
VICTOR CANNON
CANTON-FLORAL PARTNERSHIP
BILL CANTWELL
CAPE PUBLICATIONS
RON CAPONI
ALBERT CAPOUANO
PAT CAPPABIANCA
GEO A. CAPPUZZELLO
CAPRICORN FOODS
TERRY CAPRON
CAPSMITH INC.
ANTHONY F. CAPUA
RENE CAPULONG
CAR STORE OF WEST ORANGE
CARBO DISTRIBUTORS
CARDELLO ELECTRIC SUPPLY
BRUCE CARDEN
MYRON CARDEN
CARDIOLOGY ASSOCIATES
CARDIOLOGY CONSULTANTS
CARDIOVASCULAR SERVICES
ROBERT CARDWELL
CARE UNIT OF ORLANDO
CAREY AYLWARD & O'MALLEY P.A.
CAREY LIMOUSINE SERVICE
BETTY CAREY
CARLMAN BOOKER PUBLIC
   RELATION
BARRY CARLSON
LINDA CARLSON
LISA CARLSON
CARLTON ARMS OF WINTER PARK
ROBERT CARMAN
CARMINE M. BRAVO P.A.
CARNATION CO.
DEBBIE CARPENTER
CARR & FINKBEINER P.A.
GARY CARR
J. MAC CARRAWAY
JIM CARROL
FRANK CARROLL
RICH CARROLL
CARSE OIL CO.
CARTER BELCOURT & ATKINSON
   P.A.
DR. JAMES E. CARTER
PHILLIP CARTER
DARYL CARTER
FRANK CARTER
LYNWOOD CARTER
THOMAS A. CARTER
T. J. CARTER
WILLIAM CARTY
AUSTIN CARUSO JR.
JIM CARUSO
STEPHEN CARUSO
JOE CARUSO
MARY GAIL CARUSO
REGGIE CARUTHERS
CASA GALLARDO
JOHN T. CASCIO
SHAWN A. CASEY
CASH & ASSOCIATES P.A.

JOHN CASH SR.
CASINO CONSULTANTS II
CASSELBERRY FAMILY PRACTICE
MARILEE CATALANO
JOHN CATHER
CATO STEEL CO.
CATTLE RANCH STEAK HOUSE
BRIAN CAUKIN
EUGENE B. CAWOOD
GLEN CAYS
CBIS
CDI CORP. SOUTHEAST
MICHAEL CECCHINI
PAUL E. CELANO
CELLULAR ONE
CEMCO
CENTER CONTRACTING CORP.
CENTER FOR PLASTIC SURGERY
CENTEX REAL ESTATE CORP.
CENTRAL BUSINESS MACHINES
CENTRAL FLA. FOOD MANAGEMENT
CENTRAL FLA. CARDIOLOGY
CENTRAL FLA. CARDIOLOGY GROUP
CENTRAL FLA. FORMS SUPPLIES
CENTRAL FLA. MARINE
CENTRAL FLA. PRESS
CENTRAL FLA. UROLOGY
   ASSOCIATES
CENTRAL FLA. RETINA
   CONSULTANTS
CENTRAL FLA. ORAL SURGERY
CENTRAL FLA. UNDERGROUND
CENTRAL FLA. NEUROSURGICAL
CENTRAL FLA. LINCOLN-MERCURY
CENTRAL FLA. MAGAZINE
CENTRAL FLA. TITLE CO.
CENTRAL NATIONAL BANK
CENTRAL PAINT & BODY SUPPLIES
CENTRAL SEAFOOD CO.
CENTRAL SERVICE CORP.
CENTRAL STATE LEASING
CENTRUST SAVINGS BANK
CENTURY 21 INC.
CENTURY REALTY FUNDS
CERAMICS UNIQUE INC.
CESAR F. BARO & CO. P.A.
CH2M HILL
EAN CHALOUPKA
CHAMBERLIN'S NATURAL FOODS
WILLIAM R. CHAMBERS
JOHN CHAMBLISS
DONALD CHANEY
GLEN N. CHAPIN
CHAPMAN & SON
CHARLES BROWN CO.
CHARLES MUSIC CO.
JAMES CHARLTON
JOHN CHASE
CHASTAIN'S RESTAURANT
CHATHAM STEEL CORP.
CHEMICAL CONTAINERS
CHEPENIK FALLER FINANCIAL
RICHARD CHERMAK
MARK CHERNEGA
GEORGE CHEROS
BOBBY D. CHESTEEN
DR. JOSEPH CHIARO
CHICAGO TITLE INSURANCE CO.
TODD CHILDRESS
HAL CHILDRESS
SCOTT CHISHOLM
NATHAN CHITTY
STEVEN L. CHITWOOD
LORA CHMIELEWSKI
BERT CHODOROV
CHRIS'S HOUSE OF BEEF
PAUL G. CHRISMAN
EDWIN P. CHRISTENSEN
PATRICK CHRISTIANSEN
KEN CHRISTOPHER
CHURCH STREET STATION
CIGNA
CINTAS
CITICORP SAVINGS

CITRICARE INC.
CITRUS WORLD
CJW & ASSOCIATES
CLANCY'S FRIED CHICKEN
CLARK FISHER ENTERPRISES
EDWARD CLARK
J. RODNEY CLARK
LARRY CLARK
OMER CLARK
RON CLARK
VERN CLARK
WILLIAM R. CLARK
CONNIE CLARK
STEVEN K. CLARKE
TOM CLARKE
CLASS ONE AUTO SALES
JOHN CLASSE
CLASSIC CARE CARPET CLEANING
CLASSIC HONDA
CLASSIC KITCHENS & BATHS
CLAYTON & ROPER APPRAISAL
CLAYTON'S REALTY
DONALD CLAYTON
CHARLES CLAYTON
TRACY CLAYTON
DR. TONY CLEMENT JR.
GREGORY R. CLEMENTS
RUSSELL CLEMONS
WAYNE CLEWIS
CLIFFORD NEIL ASSOCIATES
TOM CLIFFORD
MELODY CLIFTON
RON CLIMER
BRIAN CLINE
CLINICAL MEASUREMENTS
CLINICAL RESEARCH
   COORDINATORS
ED CLOSUIT
PATRICK J. CLOUGHER
VINCE CLOYD
CNA INSURANCE
CNL GROUP
COASTAL FOUNTAIN SERVICE
COBB & COLE
COCO DISTRIBUTING
CODE ELECTRICAL CLASSES
DR. HAROLD COE
ESTHER COFFIELD
MICHAEL R. COFFMAN
COGGIN-OSTEEN HONDA
DR. MICHAEL J. COHEN
DR. PHILLIP COHEN
JAY M. COHEN
COLDWELL BANKER
TOM COLE
COLEMAN RESEARCH CORP.
ROBERT L. COLEMAN
COLLIER AUTO SALES
COLLING & BEATTIE P.A.
CHARLES COLLINS JR.
CARL COLLINS
JAMES F. COLLINS
SHANNON COLLINS
COLONIAL AUTO PARTS
COLONIAL CAR RENTALS
COLONIAL CHURCH-NAZARENE
COLONIAL LIFE & ACCIDENT
COLONIAL PLAZA SHOE REPAIR
BRIAN COLSON
COM PRO
COMANCHE POTTERY
COMCOR CORP.
COMMERCIAL INDUSTRIAL
   PROPERTY
COMMONWEALTH INSURANCE
COMMUNICATION CONSULTANTS
COMMUNICATIONS SUPPLY CORP.
COMPUTER POWER SYSTEM
COMPUTERLAND
GREGORY W. COMSTOCK
COMVEST INVESTMENTS
CON SERV CO.
CONCEPTUAL FINANCIAL PLANNING
CONCORD CONDOMINIUMS

CONDEV PROPERTIES
JULIAN CONE JR.
THOMAS A. CONLEE
CONLEY & ASSOCIATES
JOHN CONN
STEVEN CONNELL
ROBERT G. CONNESS
EDWARD N. CONNOR
CONOLEY FRUIT HARVESTER
WILLIAM G. CONOMOS
CONSOLIDATED FREIGHTWAYS
CONSOLIDATED DISTRIBUTING CO.
CONSORTIUM PROPERTIES
CONSTRUCT TWO INC.
CONSTRUCTION ENTERPRISES
CONSTRUCTION COMPONENTS
CONSULTING SPECIALISTS
CONTAINER RENTAL CO.
CONTEMPORARY CARS
CONTEMPORARY CONSTRUCTION
CONTEMPORARY MORTGAGE
   SERVICES
CONTEMPORARY ROOFING
CONTEMPORARY BUILDERS
COOKSEY CORP.
COOL 105.9 FM
KEVIN E. COOLEY
RANDY COOMER
ROBERT COON
COOPER SIMMS NELSON MOSELY
ALAN COOPER
BOB COOPER
JOHN N. COOPER
JIM COOPER
ETHELEEN COOPER
COOPERS & LYBRAND
COORDINATED FINANCIAL SERVICES
RICHARD COPELAND
JIM COPELAND
STEVEN CORBETT
VERNON E. CORBIN JR.
SCOTT CORBIN
ALAN CORDILL
RAYMOND COREY
W. W. CORNELL
CORPORATE MANAGEMENT
   ADVISORS
CORRECT CRAFT
CORSO CONSTRUCTION
COTTER UHRIG ET. AL. P.A.
KEVIN COTTER
VERONICA COTTER
DR. C. RAYMOND COTTRELL
CHRIS COTTRILL
RAYMOND T. COUDRIET
COURTESY PONTIAC
COVELLI CLINIC P.A.
CHUCK COWAN
BRIAN COX
GARY COX
JOHN COX
RICK H. COX
THOMAS CRAGE
DAVID E. CRAIG
CRALLE-HALL MACK SALES
STEWART CRANE
GLENDA P. CRANE
PETER F. CRANIS
NEAL M. CRASNOW
CRAWFORD EQUIPMENT &
   ENGINEERING CO.
FRANK E. CRAWFORD
DEREK K. LAMAR CRAWFORD
GARY CRAWFORD
CREATIVE SIGNS
CREDIT BUREAU
CREDIT CARD SOFTWARE
DR. FRANK CRESPO
GARY CREWS
DALE CRILE
CRITERION CONSTRUCTION GROUP
CROSS TESSITORE & ASSOCIATES
RONALD CROSS
RICHARD CROUCH

CROWNE CONSULTING GROUP
CRUM & FORSTER COMMERCIAL
  INSURANCE
HOWARD CRUM
CRYSTAL POOL
LARRY CSONKA
CTL DISTRIBUTION
DR. R. CUBARRUBIA
JAMES CULBERT
BLAKE S. CULPEPPER
ROBERT CULTON II
GERALD CURENTON
REV. BILL CURL
ALAN CURRAN
CURRY CONTROLS CO.
CURRY TAYLOR & CARLS
TONY CURTIN
CLINTON CURTIS
PAUL CURTIS
MICHAEL CURTO
LARRY CUSHING
CUSHMAN & WAKEFIELD
CUSTOM BUSINESS FORMS &
  SYSTEM
CUSTOM FAB INC.
CUTLIP SERVICES
MIKE CUTTER

D

D & D SMITH CONSTRUCTORS
D & J SCOTT MANAGEMENT
D.C. JAEGER CORP.
D.G. O'BRIAN
JAMES D'AMICO
D'VINE DISTRIBUTORS
HUBERT O. DABNEY
DON DABNEY
KAREN DABOLISH
DAD'S COOKIES
ALFRED DAGON
CLAUDE DAIGLER
SCOTT DAIGLER
DAIRY FARMERS
MICHAEL A. DALFONSO
DALLAS MAVERICKS
MICHAEL DAMIANO
DAN TOWNSEND & ASSOCIATES
DANIEL L. ARNOLD M.D. P.A.
DANIELS LUMBER
DANIELS PUBLISHING CO.
JERRY W. DANIELS
JOHN K. DANIELS
SAM DANIELSON
DANIS PROPERTIES
SHOOK DANIS
CLAY DANNEL
SHERMAN S. DANTZLER
RICHARD E. DARDEN
JEFFREY J. DART
JOSEPH DASOVICH
MICHAEL J. DASPIN
DATA SPACE MANAGEMENT
DATA SUPPLIES
DAVGAR RESTAURANTS
DAVID A. SAWYER PLUMBING
DAVID GLICKEN LAW OFFICE
DAVID K. LUNDBERG P.A.
DAVID M. HAMMOND P.A.
DAVID W. POWERS M.D. P.A.
MARK DAVIES
DAVIS STUDIOS
BRADLEY DAVIS
ERVING E. DAVIS
ERDMON O. DAVIS
GARY DAVIS
GEORGE R. DAVIS
DAN DAWSON
DAYS INN WEST
DAYTONA BEACH COLD STORAGE
DAYTONA LINCOLN MERCURY
LUCIANO DE PAZOS

NICK E. DEAL
DEAN MEAD EGERTON
  BLOODWORTH
DEANGELIS & NATION
TOM DEBENEDICTIS
DEBRA INC.
DECICCIO & BROUSSARD P.A.
THOMAS DECOMBO
BRIAN D. DEGAILLER
GARY M. DEJIDAS
DELANEY TEXACO
BRIAN DELIA
ALBERT DELISLE
ERIC DELLA CIOPPA
DELOITTE HASKINS & SELLS
DELRIO NURSERY
DELTA AIR LINES
DELTA CAPITAL CORP.
DELTA SEARCH OF ORLANDO
DEMETREE BUILDERS
BERNARD H. DEMPSEY JR.
DONALD L. DEMPSEY
BOB DENIS
DR. ALAN DENNER
STEVE DENNISON
DENTON M. KURTZ M.D. P.A.
DEPENDABLE MORTGAGE CO.
DUMONT A. DERMON
DR. WILBUR DERSHIMER JR.
BRIAN DERSTINE
CLEON DERSTINE
MARILYN L. DESHIELDS
DESIGN HOMES
DESIGNLINE CUSTOM HOME STYLES
CARL DESMARAIS
LEONARD S. DESSERT
GUY DESTEFANO
MARLIN DETWEILER
DAVID DETWILER
GENE DEVANEY
GUY DEVANEY
THOMAS C. DEVLIN
DEWITT EXCAVATING
JAMES DEXTER
STEVE DIAMOND
RICHARD DIBARTOLOMEO
VICTOR DICE
DICK APPELBAUM CO.
DICK BENNETT MOTORS
ALLAN A. DICKEY
DAVID DIDAS
DOUG DIEBLER
DR. CARLOS DIEGUEZ
DIGIS PIZZA & SUBS
DAVID D. DILLMAN
JOSEPH E. DILUZIO
DISCOUNT WATERBED WAREHOUSE
DISNEY DEVELOPMENT CO.
DISPOSALL
DISTRIBUTOR SALES OF FLA.
DITTMER ARCHITECTURAL
  ALUMINUM
DIVERSIFIED OFFICE PRODUCTS
DIXIE ELECTRONICS ASSOCIATES
DIXIE OF ORLANDO
DIXIE SHOWER DOOR
H. R. DIXSON
MIKE DIZNEY
DODD & ASSOCIATES
JOHN MCKEE DOLAN
MICK DOLAN
BARARDI DOMINIC
DOMINION LANDSCAPE &
  MAINTENANCE
DON KABOL & ASSOCIATES
DON MEALEY CHEVROLET
DON REUDLINGER
DON SAUNDERS REALTORS
DONALD COMMUNITY SERVICES
DONALDSON LUFKIN & JENRETTE
JIM DONATO
DONNA BROOKS & ASSOCIATES
DONNELLY DIRECTORY
DOPSON-HICKS

DORA LANDSCAPING CO.
THOMAS DORMAN
DORN NASH CHASAN M.D. P.A.
DONALD DORNER
DONALD DORRIES
RICHARD DOSCHER
JEFF DOSTER
RICHARD DOSTER
WILLIAM E. DOSTER
BOB DOTHEROW
DOUBLES HOAGIES
DOUGLAS H. GLICKEN P.A.
CURTIS L. DOUGLAS
RALEIGH DOWLING
HAROLD DOWNING
DR PEPPER CO.
DRAGE DEBEAUBIEN ET. AL.
PATRICK DRAKE
DRANE INSURANCE AGENCY
DREXEL BURNHAM LAMBERT
LILA S. DRISCOLL
O. LOUIS DRISKELL
DRS. SWANSON SOWERS ET. AL.
DRUM SERVICE CO. OF FLA.
DSJ ENTERPRISES
PHILLIP DUBEAU
DUBSDREAD RESTAURANT
DULIN BROKERAGE CO.
DUNBARS RESTAURANT
KEITH DUNCAN
RICHARD DUNEGAN
DUNKIN DONUTS
WILLIAM DUNN
CAROL DUNN
ROBERT DUNNICAN
DUPONT CENTRE
D. E. DUPPENTHALER
AMY DUPREE
STEVE DURHAM
DURKEE AUTO MACHINE
RICHARD A. DUROSE
EILEEN DUVA
SAMMY DUVALL
SUSAN DYE
DYER RIDDLE MILLS & PRECOURT
JIM DYER
ROBERT DYER
WILLIAM T. DYMOND JR.

E

E. L. SNYDER & ASSOCIATES LTD.
E. L. WILLIAMS INC.
E. S. BARTLETT & ASSOCIATES
E-Z RIZER CHAIR CO.
DANIEL P. EAD
WILLIAM L. EAGAN
JAMES C EAGER JR.
GERRY EAGER
EAR NOSE & THROAT SURGICAL
  ASSOCIATION
EARTHCARE LANDSCAPING
EASLEY MCCALEB & STALLINGS
FRANK EATON
EATONVILLE FAMILY CARE
RICHARD A. ECKSTEIN CLUSFP
ED TAYLOR CONST.
EDDIE'S GULF CARCARE
VERNON G. EDGAR JR.
MIKE EDMONDS
TED EDMONDSON
EDWARD M. LIVINGSTON P.A.
JIMMY EDWARDS
SHARON EDWARDS
EESSI
JERRY EGGEBRECHT
EGP INC.
DAVID EHNSTROM
H. TERRY EICH
CARL L. EICHSTEADT JR.
JERRY S. EILER

ALAN B. EISEMAN
ADAM EISEN
ELDER HOLDER ET. AL.
ROBERT ELDER
STEPHEN ELDRIDGE
ROY ELIASSEN
ELITE PAINT & BODY SHOP
BILL ELLENBACK
ELLIOT SCHUMAN M.D. P.A.
ELLIOT W. COOPERMAN M.D. P.A.
E. LEE ELLIOT
RICHARD ELLIOTT
JOHN W. ELLIOTT
ELLIS CHEVROLET
DR. JOSEPH E. ELLIS
AARON ELLIS
J. E. ELLIS
ROSS ELLZEY
EMERALD PACKING CO.
CHARLES F. EMERSON JR.
EMPLOYEE REHABILITATION
ENGINEERING TECHNOLOGY
ENGLANDER TOYOTA
ENTELLUS TECH GROUP
EPOCH PROPERTIES
EQUITABLE REAL ESTATE
   INVESTMENT MANAGEMENT
CANDICE ERICK
ERNST & WHINNEY
LESLIE ERTEL
ARTURO F. ESPINOLA
ETERNA URN CO.
EUGENE SCHWARTZ M.D. P.A.
EVANS PROPERTIES
NEILL EVANS
W. KIM EVANS
JENNIFER L. EVANS
EXCELTECH
EXECUTIVE PRESS
EXECUTIVE RISK CONSULTANTS
DR. C. T. EXUM
EYEGLASS BOUTIQUE

F

F. MATUK M.D. P.A.
JERRY FADEM JR.
GEORGE R. FAENZA
DR. HARVEY FAHY
DONALD R. FAITH
JEFFREY FAITH
JAY L. FALK
FALKNER INC.
DAVE FALL
FAMILY PRACTICE ASSOCIATES
CLYDE FANT
RICHARD M. FAROTTO JR.
FASCO INC.
FAY TOOL & DIE
BILL FAY
GARY C. FAYER
PAUL FAZEKAS JR.
FEEDER TRUSS
LOUIS FEINBERG
MIKE FELDMAN
FELICETTI INC.
FENSTERMAKER COMMUNICATIONS
FERGUSON ENTERPRISES
STEVE FERNANDEZ
FERNCREEK PROPERTIES
JAMES W. FERRELL
STEPHEN FERRELL
FERRIS REEVES GALLERIES
DR. ROBERT T. FERRIS
TIMOTHY P. FERRIS
MIKE FESS
PAUL A. FESSENDEN
FGLM ENTERPRISES
FICO INTERIOR CONSTRUCTION CO.
FIDELITY COMMERCIAL PROPERTIES
FIDELITY TITLE & GUARANTY CO.
ROBERT M. FIFER

FINANCIAL RESEARCH GROUP
FINANCIAL SECURITY CORP.
FINFROCK INDUSTRIES
DAVID FINK
RICHARD FINNEGAN
FINNIE'S WRECKER SALES
FINWALL & ASSOCIATES INSURANCE
   INC.
FIRST FEDERAL SAVINGS & LOAN
FIRST MARKET INTERNATIONAL
FIRST SOUTHERN GROUP
FIRST UNION NATIONAL BANK OF
   FLA.
JOHN FISHBACK
FISHER ROBB INC.
FISHER RUSHMER ET. AL.
RICK FITZGERALD
FITZGERALD PROPERTIES
NANETTE FLEISCHMAN
FLEMING BLALOCK HIGGINS M.D.
   P.A.
FLEMING TRAMMELL
BRIAN FLEMING
GARY FLEMING
CARLTON FLETCHER
SHIRLEY FLETTER
FLEXIBLE COMPENSATION SYSTEMS
JOSEPH FLOOD
FLORIDA AUTO AIR
FLORIDA AUTO AUCTION
FLORIDA BALFOUR
FLORIDA BRACE CORP.
FLORIDA CARBONIC
FLORIDA CHURCH INSURANCE
FLORIDA COMMUNICATION
   CONTRACT
FLORIDA EMERGENCY PHYSICIANS
FLORIDA FOOD PRODUCTS
FLORIDA FOOD
FLORIDA FRUIT & VEGETABLE
   ASSOCIATION
FLORIDA GAS TRANSMISSION
FLORIDA HEART GROUP P.A.
FLORIDA HIGH LIFT CORP.
FLORIDA HOSPITAL
FLORIDA HOSPITAL ASSOCIATION
FLORIDA INTERNAL MEDICINE
FLORIDA IRRIGATION
FLORIDA LEAGUE OF FINANCIAL
FLORIDA MEDI-CO
FLORIDA MINING
FLORIDA NATIONAL BANK
FLORIDA OTOLARYNGOLOGY
FLORIDA OUTDOOR EQUIPMENT
FLORIDA PIZZA MANAGEMENT
FLORIDA POWER CORP.
FLORIDA POTTING SOILS
FLORIDA RANCH LANDS INC.
FLORIDA RESIDENTIAL
   COMMUNITIES
FLORIDA SKIN CLINIC
FLORIDA TERRAZZO
FLORIDA TECHNICAL COLLEGE
FLORIDA TRENCHER
FLORIDA UTILITY TRAILER
FLORIDA VETERINARY LAB
T. FLUCHRADT
BERNICE FLUKER
FLYNN & CO.
LINDA FOHL
NORM FOLDENAUER
FOLEY & LARDNER
JIM FOLSOM
FOOD SERVICE CONNECTION
SUE FORAND
CLARENCE FORBES
DRAKE FORD
RICHARDS FORD
FORE GOLF
KENTON J. FOREMAN
KEVIN R. FOREMAN
FORGET-ME-NOT FLORIST
BOB FORGIT
PHYLLIS FORGIT

JOHN F. FORMICA
FORNESS GRAHAM & COTTRILL
GUY FORSYTHE
VINCENT FORTUNA
FOSTER & KELLY P.A.
FOUNTAIN MOTORS
FOUNTAIN MOTOR CO.
FOUR GRAPHICS
MARK FOWLER
FOX & BREWER
JACK J. FOX
PETER FLINT FOX
ERNEST FRAGE
FRAILEY & WILSON
FRALEY & ASSOCIATES P.A.
FRANK FRANA SR.
THOMAS FRANCIS
MICHAEL R. FRANK
MITCH FRANK
TODD FRAPPIER
EDMUND L. FRAPPIER
TERRY FREDERICK
W. FREDERICK
JOHN FREDRICKS
FREEMAN DECORATING CO.
EDGAR F. FREITAG
HARRY FREITAG
STEVEN FREY
DANIEL S. FRIEBIS
FRINGE BENEFIT PLANS
BILL FRISBEY
FRITH & STUMP
FRITO-LAY
JAMES FRITZE
RON FROMAN
FRY HAMMOND & BARR
RICHARD FRY
BRIAN FUCILE
CHARLES H. FUGATE
ROBERT W. FULLER
TIMOTHY A. FULMER
PHILIP R. FULMER
FUNWAY HOLIDAYS FUNJET
KATHY AMICK FUQUA
ANDY FURIA
ROBERT W. FUSIK

G

GRG CONSULTING ENGINEERS
RICHARD H. GADAPEE
EDWARD GAFFNEY
GAGNIER HICKS ASSOCIATES
RICHARD GALLAGHER
GLEN H. GALLIVAN
GALLOWAY & ELERICK P.A.
BRIAN GAMAGE
GLEN P. GAMMA
GREG GANAS
ANTHONY GARAMELLA
BOB GARAPIC
JOSEPH GARDNER
ROBERT GARDNER
CHUCK GARDNER
RICHARD GARDNER
GARNER WINDOW & DOOR SALES
MICHAEL GARO
WILLIAM GARRITY
DR. JAMES GARVEY
GARWOOD & MCKENNA
GARY HURLBUT INSURANCE
   AGENCY
GARY M. WEISS M.D. P.A.
GARY W. DEVANE M.D. P.A.
GASTROENTEROLOGY ASSOCIATES
JOHN GATES
GATOR GRAPHICS
GATOR PROPANE
JOHN GAUDETTE
JEFFRY GAY
GAYLON BLACK FORD
GAYLORD & GAYLORD P.A.

HERB GEARTNER
THOMAS GEBERT
THOMAS GEGENHEIMER
DR. R. WILSON GELDNER
RAYMOND GELLEIN
GELLER RAGANS JAMES ET. AL.
GENERAL ELECTRIC SILICONES
GENERAL MILLS RESTAURANTS
GENERAL ROOFING INDUSTRIES
GENESYS
STEVE GENNETT
EDWARD GENTILE
JOHN A. GENTILELLA
LARRY GENTON
GENTRY INSURANCE AGENCY
GENUS ENTERPRISES
ROBERT GENZMAN
GEORGE BROWN & CO. P.A.
KENNETH B. GEORGE III
CHARLES GEORGE III
GEORGE J. ADLER P.A.
GEORGE NAHAS OLDSMOBILE
GEORGE W. EDWARDS D.M.D. P.A.
GEORGE W. LEWIS REALTY
HAL GEORGE
SCOTT GEORGE
GERARD & RIVERA
BOB GERHARD
KEVIN R. GERO
GERSCOVICH & ULCH M.D. P.A.
JOHN GETTEL
CHARLES D. GETTEL
GIBRALTER INSURANCE SALES
KURT GIES
GIFTS UNLIMITED
JAMES GILCHRIST
KENT GILL
RAYMOND GILMER
BYRON GILTZ
GERALD A. GITLES
DONALD E. GLASS JR.
GLASS SYSTEMS
HARRY GLASS
MATTIE GLASS
GLATTING LOPEZ KERCHER ANGLIN
FRED GLAZER
JAMES P. GLEASON
JOHN W. GLICK III
FREDERICK L. GLICK
GLOBE VALLEY NURSERIES
DAVE GLOCKER
LOIS GODBOLD
GOLD & DIAMOND SOURCE
DAVID R. GOLD
GOLDEN FLAKE SNACK FOOD
GOLDEN LOAF BAKERY
MICHAEL A. GOLDFINE
MARK GOLDSTEIN
GOLFPAC INC.
LYDIA M. GOMEZ
JOHN GONG
JESUS GONZALEZ
DAVID GOODE
GOODINGS MANAGEMENT
MARY E. GOODSON
JULIE MARTIN GOODWIN
GOPHER UTILITIES
SCOTT GORALNIK
MICHAEL J. GORDON
MITCHELL GORDON
STANLEY GORDON
ART GORDON
GORDONS TRANSPORT
DR. C. BRUCE GORDY
GORMAN AIR CONDITIONING
STEVE GORNEY
DUWAYNE GOSSETT
GOUCHENOUR INC.
GRACE & ANNE GLAVIN P.A.
OLIN GRACZYK
JAMES GRADDY
GRAHAM ASSOCIATES
JOHN GRAHAM
DINAH B. GRAHAM

GRAND CYPRESS RESORT
DAWSON GRANT
GRANTHAM DISTRIBUTING CO.
GRANTS FURNITURE CO.
GRAPHIC SYSTEMS
JEFFREY W. GRASTY
RANDY GRAVES
STEPHEN E. GRAVES
ROBERT A. GRAVES
GRAY HARRIS & ROBINSON P.A.
MIKE GRAY
GRAYBAR ELECTRIC
GRAYS APOTHECARY
JEFFREY GRAYSON
GREAT WESTERN MEATS
GREATER ORLANDO CHAMBER
RICHARD J. GREEN
SAMUEL S. GREEN
JAMES A. GREENE
SCOTT GREENWOOD
GREG HALE & ASSOCIATES
WAYNE GREGORY
STANLEY B. GREGORY
STEPHEN GRESEK
TIM GRETHER
WILLIAM C. GRIDLEY
GARY A. GRIEGER
WILLIAM GRIER
GARY GRIFFIN
JOHN GRIFFIN
DAVID GRIFFITH
MICHAEL L. GRIFFITH
GRIZZLY ENTERPRISES CORP.
MARSHA J. GROOME
KENNETH S. GROSS
GROSVENOR RESORT
GROUND CONTROL LANDSCAPING
GROVER BRYAN INC.
JACKIE GRUENLOH
GRUMMAN TECH SERVICES
GRUNAU FIRE PROTECTION
   SYSTEMS
DAVID A. GRZYB
GTE COMMUNICATIONS
GTE TELEGUIDE
BOB GUDINO
FRANK M. GUERCIO
JAMES GUERCIO
KEVIN W. GUFFEY
JOHN T. GUILFOYLE
WILLIAM T. GUINEY
PETER J. GULDEN
GULF ATLANTIC TITLE
GULF SEED
GULF STREAM POOLS
COULBY GUNTHER JR.
PAUL GURCIULLO
DAVID GURSKY
JOE GURTIS
GUS' POOL REPAIR & SERVICE
TERESA GUTHRIE
VANCE GUTIERREZ
BOB GWIZDALA
GYPSUM DEALER MANAGEMENT
   ASSOCIATES

H

H & H PRINTING
H & H PRODUCTS
H. F. MASON EQUIPMENT CORP.
H. J. HIGH CONSTRUCTION
HJ MARKETING
H. LEE COOPER C.P.A.
HTE
WILLIAM H. HAAR
HAAS BOEHM ET. AL.
JIM HACKETT
CHARLES W. HACKNEY
MICHAEL E. HADDAD
ED HADDOCK
SCOTTY HAGE

JERRY E. HAGOOD
LESLIE HAGUE
MICHAEL HAJEK
RUSSELL B. HALE
HAROLD HALEY
DR. FRED HALL
DONALD C. HALL
LARRY D. HALL
ROBERT HALL
SCOTT A. HALL
CATHERINE HALL
MICHAEL HALLIDAY
ROSS HALLOCK
BRUCE HALT
LAURENCE HAMES
JAMES L. HAMILTON
ALAN HAMILTON
DAN HAMILTON
GEORGE E. HAMLIN
JERRY HAMM
BILL HAMMOND
KENNETH R. HAMMONS
HAMPTON ENTERPRISES
JILL M. HAMPTON-KONG
ALBERT GRALAN HAMPTON
ARLIE J. HANCHEY JR.
STAN HAND
BILL HANDS
ROBERT HANDT
HANGING TREE NURSERY
HANGOVER HOUNDS
STANLEY HANIN
HANNAH MARSEE BEIK & VOGHT
ANDREW J. HANNIGAN
DON HARBIN
HARBOR CITY OIL CO.
RANDY HARBOUR
HARCOURT BRACE JOVANOVICH
HARDEE'S FOOD SYSTEMS
PAUL HARGETT
REA V. HARKINS
JULIAN B. HARLAN
HARMON GLASS OF FLORIDA
JERRY HARNE
DENNIS HARNEY
HARPER MECHANICAL
MARK HARPER
R. M. HARRELL
HOWARD HARRIS JR.
NORMAN HARRIS
MARTIN HARRIS
JOHNNIE HARRIS
DEBORAH HARRIS
KENNETH HARRISON
MICHAEL HARRISON
ROBERT HARRISON
RANDY HARRISON
JACK HARTIGAN
JEFF HARTMAN
ELEBIS HARVEY JR.
JIM HARVEY
JAMES R. HARVEY
M. R. HASS
WILLIAM C. HASSOLD
GARY D. HASSON
THOMAS W. HASTINGS
MARION F. HATCHER
N. V. HATEM
MICHAEL HAUGH
ROBERT HAVEN
HAWAIIAN TROPIC
GARY HAWKES
DR. ROBERT HAWKINS
KEVIN HAWKINS
RAYMOND HAYES
MICHAEL HAZELTON
ROBERT HAZEN
DOUG HEALEY
HEALTHCO INTERNATIONAL
DR. CHARLES W. HEARD JR.
DAVID HEARD
JOHN M. HEARIN
NED HEATH
HEATHROW LAND & DEVELOPMENT

MARY-JANE HEDDEN
DAVID W. HEDRICK
RAYMOND A. HEERS
JOHN HEINE
LAWRENCE HEINKEL
MARTHA A. HEINRICH
PAUL B. HEINTZE
FRANK HEINZ
HELLER AND ROEN
HELLER BROS. PACKING CORP.
THOMAS R. HELLER
DANIEL HELMAN
ALAN HELMAN
JOHNNIE HELMS
HELP U SELL OF S. ORANGE
WAYNE L. HELSBY
COL. L. JACK HEMPLING
DEBORAH A. HENDERSON
BILL HENDRICH
LEWIS HENKEL
GLENN HENNIG
MERV HENNING
THE REV. JAMES B. HENRY
HERBERT HALBACK
HERFF JONES CO.
JIM HERMAN
JULIO A. HERNANDEZ
WILLIAM HERNANDEZ
WILLIAM HERNDON JR.
MARK HERR
BILL HERRING
HERTZ EQUIPMENT RENTAL
JIM HEWITT
JAMES HEWITT
ROBERT W. HEWITT
R. T. HIBBARD
HICKMAN & WHITE
HICKOK & ASSOCIATES
RALPH M. HICKOK
ANTHONY HICKS
BYRON S. HICKS
GMC HIGGENBOTHAM BUICK
JOHN HIGGINS
ROBERT HIGGINS
HIGH REACH CO.
DONALD HIGHMILLER
CAROLYN K. HILAND
SAMUEL C. HILL III
GEOFFREY HILL
MICHAEL HILL
RANDY LEE HILL
W. DAVID HILL
DELENE HILL
HILLDRUP MOVING & STORAGE
HILLSHIRE FARM & KAHN'S
HILTON INN FLORIDA CENTER
MARSHALL HINSON
RONALD HIRSCH
ROGER HIRSCHY
HIS STORES FOR MEN
ALFRED L. HISS
WILLIAM S. HIXON
GARY HOAG
SAMUEL L. HOARD
ROBERT L. HOCK
HODGE HOMES
HODGES BROTHERS ROOFING
THOMAS W. HODGES
CLARENCE HODGES
JOSEPH D. HODGES
HERMAN C. HODGES
BRUCE HODGSON
NELSON L. HOEPPNER
CHARLES HOEQUIST
SUSAN HOFFMAN
AUTREY HOFFMANN
DAVID HOLBROOK
DR. RODNEY F. HOLCOMB
KURT J. HOLFTST
HOLIDAY BUILDERS
HOLIDAY INN INTERNATIONAL DR.
HOLIDAY INN E. OF DISNEY
HOLIDAY INN

INTERNATIONAL AIRPORT HOLIDAY
  INN
HOLLAND & KNIGHT
BENJAMIN J. HOLLAND II
ALLEN HOLLAND
TOM HOLLEY
HOLLINGSWORTH REALTORS
TOM HOLLINGSWORTH
SUSAN HOLLINGSWORTH
DAVID HOLLINS
HOLLIS ENGINEER INC.
JOHN W. HOLLOWAY
HOLMES REGIONAL MEDICAL
  CENTER
JOHN V. A. HOLMES
JAMES G. HOLMES
HOLT SURVEYING
BRIAN J. HOLT
PHILLIP HOLT
HOMAN'S PROFESSIONAL SERVICES
RUBY C. HOMAYSSI
HOME BUILDERS ASSOCIATION
HOME INSURANCE CO.
CHARLES M. HOOD III
PHYLLIS A. HOOD
WILLIAM M. HOOKS
DR. ROBERT T. HOOPER II
HOOPER PARTNERSHIP
MIKE HOOPER
HOPE FOUNDATION
HOPKINS CONTRACT HARDWARE
MABEL P. HOPKINS
JACK D. HOPPENSTEDT JR.
DAVE HORNER
LARRY HORNSBY
BERNICE HOSEY
GLENN T. HOSKIN
HOTEL ROYAL PLAZA
MICHAEL HOULIHAN
JEFFREY T. HOUSE
HOWARD JOHNSON DOWNTOWN
HOWARD JOHNSON FOUNTAIN PARK
HOWARD NEEDLES ET. AL.
ROGER HOWARD
KEN HOWARD
BLAIR HOWARD
KEN A. HOWDER
DAN HOWELL
JOHN HOWELL
HOWMEDICA
HPS PRINTING PRODUCTS
FRANK HUBBARD
WILLIAM D. HUBLER
HUDSON CONSTRUCTION
THOMAS HUDSON
KATHY HUDSON
DANIEL HUFFMAN
HUGHES INC.
HUGHES SUPPLY
HUGHES TOWING & RECOVERY
JOHNNY HUGHES
WILLIAM P. HUGHES
JOHN P. HUGHES
HUMANA HOSPITAL-KISSIMMEE
BRUCE HUMPHREY
LARRY J. HUNDLEY
MICHAEL D. HUNT
HUNTER CHEMICAL & FORMULATING
HUNTER INSURANCE AGENCY
CHARLES M. HUNTER
BRADLEY HURD
REX A. HURLEY
HUSK JENNINGS OVERMAN
BUDGE HUSKEY
HUTCHESON CORP.
KEITH HUTSELL
WILLIAM HUTTENHOWER
HYATT REGENCY GRAND CYPRESS
HYMAN LAKE ESQ.
TERRY A. HYMAN
MICHAEL HYNES

I

IBHW
PATRICE A. ICARDI
I CAN'T BELIEVE IT'S YOGURT
IMC FERTILIZER
IBM CORP.
IGI MARKETING
INDUSTRIAL CONTRACTING CO.
INDUSTRIAL ENGINEERING CO.
INDUSTRIAL DYNAMICS
INDUSTRIAL ELECTRIC CO.
CHRIS INGERSOLL
J. CHARLES INGRAM
INLAND CONTAINER
INSTRUMENT SPECIALTIES
INSURANCE RISK SERVICES
INTEGRATED SOFTWARE
  RESOURCES
INTEGRATED PLANNING SERVICES
INTEGRATED SOFTWARE SYSTEMS
INTERACTIVE SERVICE CORP.
INTERNATIONAL ANALYTIC CORP.
INTERNATIONAL SPEEDWAY CORP.
INTERSCAPE SYSTEMS
INTERSTATE BATTERY
INTERSTATE INSURANCE AGENCY
INVESTMENTS BY GMC
ALLEN D. IRVINE
MICHAEL D. ISAACS
DR. JOHN L. ISLER
ITEC PRODUCTIONS
IVAN LEFKOWITZ P.A.
IVEY'S
RAY IVEY

J

J & M AUTO GLASS
J. B. BOOTH ELECTRIC
J. BARRY BOYD M.D. P.A.
J. C. PENNEY CO.
J. J. MCCLELLAN INSURANCE
  AGENCY
JM'S HANDBAGS & ACCESSORIES
J. P. CAL ASSOCIATES INC.
J. ROLFE DAVIS INSURANCE
JSM SALES CO.
JTS ENTERPRISES
JV RESURFACING
JWF SALES CO.
DAVID JACKLITCH
JACKSON B. LONG
DR. CONSTANCE E. JACKSON
J. JACKSON
TIM T. JACKSON
J. R. JACOBS
DON JACOBS
THOMAS W. JAEGER
DENNIS JAFFE
JAL CHEMICAL
JAMES ALLEN SCOTT P.A.
JAMES B. GREENE & ASSOCIATES
JAMES COATES & ASSOCIATES
JAMES E. SLATER P.A.
JAMES H. WADE JR C.P.A. P.A.
JAMES O. EUBANK II P.A.
JAMES RIVER CORP.
BENJAMIN T. JAMES SR.
BILL JAMES
DENNIS JAMES
MARK JAMES
JAMMAL & ASSOCIATES
JAMZ-102 FM
JAN SAN BARINEAU
MICHAEL S. JANECZEK
ERIC JANSSEN
DR. PAUL C. JANSSON D.V.M.
CHESTER JAWORSKI
JAYMONT REALTY

JDT LANDSCAPING & IRRIGATION
JEFF GROTTO MASONRY
DAN JEFFERS
JEFFERSON SMURFIT CORP.
TONY JENKINS
JOHN JENNINGS
DON JERNIGAN
JEROME ADAMS M.D. P.A.
JERRY DAVIS LANDSCAPING
JERRY'S CUSTOM FURNITURE
JEWETT ORTHOPAEDIC CLINIC P.A.
JIM KRAGH & ASSOCIATES
JIM PLESS & CO.
JIM RATHMANN CHEVROLET
JIM TAYLOR CORP.
JMB PROPERTY MANAGEMENT CO.
JMC ENTERPRISES OF BREVARD
JOBES AUTO AIR
JOE'S BARBER SHOP
JOELSON CONCRETE & PIPE
JOHN F. MOORE, CHARTERED
JOHN G. CAREY M.D. P.A.
JOHN H. QUINN INVESTMENTS
JOHN J. GREENE TRUCK BROKERS
JOHN K. FUSSELMAN O.D. P.A.
JOHN M. BRODNAN M.D. P.A.
JOHN W. BISHOP D.D.S. P.A.
JOHNSON & CO.
JOHNSON & JOHNSON
A. G. JOHNSON JR.
JAMES H. JOHNSON
JERRY W. JOHNSON
KEVIN JOHNSON
MARC JOHNSON
RAY JOHNSON
RON R. JOHNSON
ALVIN JOHNSON
DAN JOHNSON
EBBON C. JOHNSON
CHAPIN JOHNSON
ROBERT JOHNSON
CARROLYN M. JOHNSON
NANCY E. JOHNSON
LILLIAN M. JOHNSON
SHIRLEY JOHNSON
JOHN JOHNSTON
ROBERT JOHNSTON
TONY A. JOHNSTON
LAWRENCE W. JOHNSTON
DARRYL W. JOHNSTON
BERRY JOHNSTON
DAVID JOHNSTON
THOMAS JOLLIFF
JOMAC OF ORLANDO
JACK A. JOMINY
JON M. HALL CO.
JONES AMUSEMENT CORP.
JONES CLAYTON CONSTRUCTION
DR. JAMES R. JONES JR.
WILLIE F. JONES JR.
AUSTIN JONES
B. JONES
BRELON S. JONES
GREG JONES
GREGORY L. JONES
JEFF JONES
JOHN JONES
MICHAEL JONES
ROGER JONES
TAD JONES
W. KEN JONES
MARGARET JONES
F. GRAHAM JORDAN
JOHN JORDAN
JOSEPH C. BROWN M.D. P.A.
JT'S PRIME TIME
JUICES & BEVERAGES
RICHARD JULIAN
JUNG BLOSCH & SCEARCE
JUNIOR ACHIEVEMENT
GUY JUSTINIANO

K

KKACO CONTRACTING CO.
MICHAEL H. KAHN, ESQ
E. JOSEPH KAISER
ELIZABETH KAISER
JOHN KALINOSKY
MIKE KAMENOFF
DAN KAMINSKY
DAVID KAMINSKY
DR. HARVEY KANSOL
R. CRAIG KANT
HAL KANTOR
KEVIN KAPKE
DR. BARRY J. KAPLAN
CAS J. KARBO
JIM KATT
DARRELL KATZ
N. KAUFMAN
KARL KAUTERMAN
KAY GREEN DESIGN &
    MERCHANDISE
CHRISTOPHER KAY
MICHAEL KAY
DR. JOEL KAYE
KAYS RESTAURANT
KAZECK & ASSOCIATES
JOHN KINGMAN KEATING
TIM KEATING
COBBY KEDERICK
JOHN KEEFE
ALLAN E. KEEN
SCOTT KEENA
HAL KEENE
JAMES W. KEETER
ROBERT KELLAR JR.
LOUIE KELLER
DAN KELLER
KELLEY'S POOL SPECIALTIES
CLARENCE L. KELLEY
RON KELLEY
KELLY SERVICES
KELLY'S MOBIL
KENNETH M. KELLY
FRED KEMP
KEMPER BUSINESS SYSTEMS
THOMAS KEMPER
KEN & WALT'S A/C & HEATING
KEN RUMMEL CHEVROLET
KEN-MAR
JAN KENDRICK
KENNEDY CONCRETE
KENNEDY DRUGS
JOHN RICHARD KENNEDY
JAY KENNEDY
CHARLINE KENNEDY
KENNETH P. COFFAE D.D.S. P.A.
KENTUCKY FRIED CHICKEN
MIKE KEOTAHLIAN
WILLIAM C. KERCHER JR.
KERNS & ASSOCIATES
DOUGLAS A. KERNS
JIM KERNS
WENDELL "GENE" KERR
SALLY D. M. KEST
NADIR "FRANK" KHAN
KHS & S. CONTRACTORS
GRANT KIMSEY
WILLIAM KINANE
KINCO OF CENTRAL FLORIDA
STEVE KINDER
KING AND BLACKWELL
CLYDE KING JR.
DARRELL W. KING
JOHN C. KING
LUKE B. KING
KINGSWOOD APARTMENT MOTEL
KIRBY RENTAL SERVICE AND SALES
GEORGE KIRCHGASSNER
KIRK MARKETING GROUP
GEORGE KIRK
KIRKEY & ASSOCIATES

JUDGE THOMAS R. KIRKLAND
CRAIG E. KIRKLAND
THOMAS J. KIRKPATRICK
KISSIMMEE SPRING WATER CO.
KISSIMMEE ELECTRO
KITTINGER BUSINESS MACHINES
    INC.
EDWARD KLEIMAN
EDWARD KLEIN
JERRY KLINE
KAREN KNAPP
T. KEVIN KNIGHT
ANDERSON KNIGHT
KNUDSON & MCGREAL P.A.
KOALA DEVELOPMENT CORP.
KOBRIN BUILDERS SUPPLY
PAUL KOEGLER
KOGER PROPERTIES INC.
THOMAS R. KOHLER
KOIVU RUTA & CO.
STEPHEN KOKOSKA
DR. IRVING KOLEN
MIKE KOLLER
KOLODINSKY & BERG
TED KOLVA
KIMBERLY KOPPERUD
AL KORENEK
GARY KORNFELD
ED KOUGH
ALAN D. KOZY
MARK KRACHT
DR. B. N. KRAMER
SUMNER KRAMER
F. RICHARD KREPAK
H. C. KRESGE JR.
ROD KRIVI
FRANK KRUPPENBACHER
PETER G. KUCHAR
DUANE KUCK
HOWARD KUEHN
WALTER H. KUHRT JR.
KURT WHITLOCK ASSOCIATES
LARRY KURTZE
MICHAEL KURTZWEG
DONALD K. KUSIAK
JOHN F. KUTZER
KUYKENDALL INSURANCE AGENCY

L

L & L ROOFING
L. J. BAR CATTLE RANCH
L. T. ACOSTA
EDGAR J. L'HEUREUX
LA AMISTAD FOUNDATION
LA PALOMA LANES
LA RUE & BERNARDINI
LABELLE FUR CO.
LABOR FORCE OF MID FLORIDA
STEVEN M. LABRET
VINCE LACAVA
CHARLES P. LACORTE JR.
MONTY LAFABER
JEFFRY J. LAFOND
DENA LAFRAMBOISE
LAKE AUTOMOTIVE
LAKE BUTLER GROVES
LAKE HOWELL ANIMAL CLINIC
LAKE NONA CORP.
ROLAND J. LAMB
LAMBERT CORP.
MARK LAMOTTE
MARK LANDAU
LANDIS GRAHAM & FRENCH ET. AL.
LANDQUEST INC.
LANDRETH INC.
HENRI LANDWIRTH
JAMES M. LANE
LANEY & LANEY P.A.
DR. JEFFREY N. LANG
MARGARET LANG
LANGFORD RESORT HOTEL

A. E. LANGLEY
DAVID P. LANIER JR.
JAMES A. LANIUS
DONALD LANKIEWICZ
DAVID W. LANMAN
DAVID LANSING
LAPIN SEPTIC TANK SERVICE
COL. P. J. LARRICK
LARRY H. BEATY INC.
PAUL D. LARSON JR.
SCOTT LARSON
OMAR LARSON
LAS OLAS BEACH CLUB
BOB LASAGE
LASER PHOTONICS
D. GARY LASHLEY
MITCHEL LASKEY
ARNOLD J. LASOTA
ROY LASSITER
PETER LATHAM
LATHAN CONSTRUCTION CORP.
JOHN C. LATHROP
JAMES D. LATIMER
JOHN H. LATSHAW JR.
LAUREL OAKS HOSPITAL
KENNETH M. LAUVER
BRUCE LAVAN
MALCOLM LAVENDER
LAW OFFICE OF JOE T. CARUSO
LAW OFFICE OF WM. FERNANDEZ
LAW OFFICE OF ANDERSON HILL
LAW OFFICES OF TERRENCE
    ACKERT
BRIAN J. LAWLOR
FRANK LAWRENCE
WILLIAM LAWTON
LAWYERS SOUTHERN TITLE
LAWYERS TITLE INSURANCE CO.
ZED LAYSON
GARY LAZAR
LE CORDON BLEU
ROBERT LEACOCK
RICK LEATON
DAVID H. LEBIODA
TODD LEDA
RICHARD LEDBETTER
DR. H. C. LEDBETTER
LEDFORD MAYFIELD & OGLE
LEE ADLER M.D. P.A.
LEE CHIRA ENTERPRISES
RANDOLPH M. LEE JR.
LEE VISTA CENTER
MARTIN LEE
SCOTT LEE
LOOMIS C. LEEDY JR.
JIM LEFFEW
GLENN A. LEFFLER
HOWARD LEFKOWITZ
ED LEINSTER
LEISURE BAY
LEISURE TIME FANCY VANS
LEISURE WAY INC.
HAL LELLE
FRANCIS LEMAY
KENNETH J. LENGYEL
LETSINGER PRODUCE
LEVANS CATERING SERVICE
LEVER BROTHERS CO.
DAVID LEVERETT
NORMAN E. LEVESQUE
DR. MITCHELL LEVIN
LAWRENCE LEVINSON
KENNETH D. LEVITT
LEWARE CONSTRUCTION CO.
DENNIS W. LEWIS
JAMES S. LEWIS
LARRY LEWIS
ROBERT S. LEWIS
TODD LEWIS
BEN LICIARDELLO
LAWRENCE L. LIDFELDT
LIFECO INVESTMENT GROUP
LIGONIER MINISTRIES
BILL LILES

ROGER LILES
JAMES W. LILLY
LARRY OR JANET LIMMEL
LINCOLN PROPERTY CO. OF FLA.
NANCY LINDBORG
RAYMOND LINDEMANN
LINDER INDUSTRIAL MACHINERY
GUY LINDER
CARL LINDGREN III
LINDSLEY ASPHALT CO.
JOE LINGAFELT
JOHN LINGO
JAY LIPELES
BRIAN LIPMAN
LIPTEN & CO.
GLENN LISTORT
LITCHFORD CHRISTOPHER
LITHOGRAPHICS INC.
DEL LITTLE
KELLAND LIVESAY
LUIS LLANOS
LLOYD & ASSOCIATES
LLOYD JONES FILLPOT &
    ASSOCIATES
LLOYD'S FURNITIRE CO.
LMG PRODUCTIONS
EDWARD LOBNITZ
LOCHRANE ENGINEERING INC.
WARREN LOCKEBY JR.
LOFT ENTERPRISES
DAVE LOGSDON
BLAIR LONG
C. W. LONG
DAVID F. LONG
LONGWOOD LINCOLN-MERCURY
LONGWOOD SHELL
LONGWOOD TOYOTA
BRYAN K. LOOKENOTT
AL LOOTENS
ERNIE G. LORD
LOREN STAKE & ASSOCIATES
DR. JAVIER LORENZ
RAYMOND J. LORENZI
PAUL LOTT
LOUIS H. LAUTERIA C.P.A.
LOVELACE ROBY & CO.
LOVVORN & ASSOCIATES
JAMES R. LOWE III
C. R. LOWERY
JOSEPH LOWMAN
LOWNDES DROSDICK ET. AL.
LUBET & BLECHMAN
MARK E. LUCAS
PAUL LUCAS
ERIC W. LUDWIG
CARL LUECK
CHERYL A. LUNA
FRED LUNDQUIST
SAM LUPFER
CHARLES LUSCUKIE
JERRY R. LUSK
JERRY LUXENBERG
DONALD A. LYKKEBAK
GEOFFREY LYNCH
JAMES R. LYNCH
LYON & MCMANUS

M

M. A. BRUDER & SONS
M. C. ARNOLD CONSTRUCTION
MCT CONSTRUCTION
M. CARTER GREEAR D.D.S. P.A.
MER & ASSOCIATES
M. G. RUSSO & ASSOCIATES
M. J. PETER & ASSOCIATES
MABEL GROVES
MAC PAPERS
MACAIONE CO.
RICK D. MACE
JAMES MACGREGOR
MACK PRECAST CORP.

CHARLES MACKEIGAN
JEFF MACKEY
GARY R. MADDOX
RANDY MADDOX
MADDUX SUPPLY CO.
MADER SOUTHEAST
ROBERT MADERER
MADIGAN MCCUNE & ASSOCIATES
RICHARD MAFFEI
JAMES W. MAGEE
WILLIAM B. MAGEE
PAT MAGGIO
MAGIC BUTLER
MAGIC LIMOUSINE
MAGIC PRODUCTIONS
RALPH MAGINO
DR. G. BROCK MAGRUDER
RONALD MAGRUDER
MAGUIRE VOORHIS & WELLS
MAHER OVERCHUCK & LANGA
EDWARD G. MAIER
MAIN STREET INVESTMENTS
MAINS-GRIMES ASSOCIATES
OSCAR MAISONET
MAITLAND DRUG STORE
MAITLAND ORTHOPEDIC CLINIC
MAITLAND WINTER PARK PLUMBING
MAJIC MARKETS
TAMMY MAJORS
MAKEPACE INC.
ANNE E. MALARICH
DR. PAUL MALUSO
MAMA B'S
ROBERT MANDELL
STANLEY MANDRESH
BENEDICT MANISCALCO
HOWARD MANISON
EDWIN R. MANN
STEVEN MANSFIELD
GEORGE MANTZARIS
MANUCOR LEASING
CLOYD MANUEL
MANZO & PRAVER P.A.
ROBERT MARCHOCK
MARY L. MARCUCCILLI
JEFFERY MARCUS
DR. GERALD C. MARDER
MARGARETTEN & CO.
HENRY M. MARINO
MARKEL MCDONOUGH & O'NEAL
MARKER COMMUNICATIONS
MARKET DEVELOPMENT GROUP
MARKETING PROFILES
CHRIS MARLETTE
MARLIN MANUFACTURING
WILLIAM S. MAROON
MARRIOTT EDUCATION SERVICES
MARRIOTT ORLANDO WORLD
    CENTER
ROBERT MARRON
DR. ELLA MARSH
KEVIN A. MARSHBURN
MARTIN MARIETTA ELECTRONIC &
    MISSILE SYSTEMS
DR. SAMUEL MARTIN
J. MICHAEL MARTIN
WILBUR MARTIN
WILLARD F. MARTIN
GROVER MARTIN
GEORGE A. MARTIN
KEN MARTIN
WAYNE MARTIN
CAROL MARTIN
PAUL MARTINEZ
LARRY MARTINSON
MARTLET IMPORTING CO.
MIKE MARTONE
MARVIN SEHNERT & ASSOCIATES
MARVISTA
JERRY MASK
J. CHENEY MASON
STEPHANIE MASON
MASS ELECTRIC CO.
MASSEY ALPER & WALDEN P.A.

MASTER CRAFT BUILDERS OF N. FLA.
MATEER HARBERT & BATES
WILLIAM G. MATEER
JOHN MATERNI
DOUG MATHEWS
PAT MATNEY
VICTOR MATSKO JR.
MATTHEWS FLYNN ET. AL.
SANDRA M. MATTHEWS
ROBERT C. MATTHIAS
RON MAULDEN
DR. D. A. MAURER
MAURY L. CARTER & ASSOCIATES
ERIC MAWYER
MAXWELL HOUSE COFFEE CO.
MICHAEL MAXWELL
ALLEN MAY
ROBERT G. MAYBERRY II
JAMES MAYNES
PERRY MAYO
ROBERT MAYO
DAVID MAYS
GRAHAM MAYS
KEN MAZIK
ANGELO J. MAZZA
JEFF MAZZOLI
R. MCADAMS JR.
MCALLISTER & ASSOCIATES
BEVERLY MCBRYDE
THOMAS J. MCCABE JR.
HOWARD MCCABE
RANDALL MCCALL
GREG MCCARTER
MCCARTHA & ASSOCIATES
MCCARTHY LAND CO.
TERRY MCCARTHY
RON MCCARTNEY
WILLIAM MCCARTNEY
RAY MCCLEESE
JANE MCCLELLAN
W. R. MCCLELLAND
MARION S. MCCLENDON
DENNIS MCCLUNG
SAMUEL MCCLURE
HARRY K. MCCONNELL
BARRY MCCONNELL
JACK MCCONNELL
HUTSON E. MCCORKLE
J. MIKE MCCOY
THOMAS T. MCCOY
MCCREE INC.
S. R. MCDANIELL JR.
W. F. MCDERMITT
MCDEVITT & STREET CO.
DAVIS & CO. MCDIRMIT
MCDONALD'S CORP.
GLENN MCDONALD
ED MCDONALD
ED MCDOUGALL
BOBBIE MCDOWELL
DAVID MCDUFFIE
JIM MCGEE
RICK MCGINN
ED MCGINNIS
PAUL T. MCGINNIS
JOHN MCGIVERN
WILLIAM C. MCGOWAN
MCGRIFF SEIBELS & WILLIAMS
DAVE MCGUIGAN
WILLIE MCHELLON
GLADYS MCILHENNY
MCINERNEY FORD
ALLEN C. MCINTOSH
DONALD MCINTOSH
JOHN MCKAY
MCKEE CHRYSLER PLYMOUTH
THOMAS MCKEE
JOHN MCKENNA
SUSAN K. MCKENNA
ALEXANDRA MCKENTLY
SEAN MCKEON
MAC MCKINLEY
THOMSON MCKINNON

JOHN E. MCLAIN III
MICHAEL D. MCLAREN
MCLAUGHLIN & ZIMMERMAN
DAVID MCLEOD
ROBERT MCLUCAS
EDWARD MCMILLIN
JON MCMILLIN
WILLIAM A. MCMILLION
MCNAMARA PONTIAC INC.
THEO MCNEIL
ROBERT MCNICHOL
C. HOWARD MCNULTY
JOHN MCQOUN
RICHARD D. MCRAE
JAMES MCTEAR
RICHARD F. MCWILLIAMS
ANDREW MEACHUM
BILL MEAGHER
MEARS TRANSPORTATION GROUP
JOHN MEARS
MECHANICAL SERVICES
LEONARD MECKALVAGE
MEDCO REVIEW
MEDICAL CENTER RADIOLOGY
    GROUP
MEDICAL MARKETING
MEDICAL SOCIETY SERVICES
MEDIEVAL TIMES
MEDTRONIC INC.
KEN MEEHAN
JOSEPH T. MEEHAN
DR. DOUGLAS L. MEIR
KEVIN MEISEL
MELBOURNE INTERNAL MEDICINE
ROBERT MELTON
CHARLES E. MELVIN
MELWEB SIGN CO.
GERALDINE E. MENUEY
CRAIG MENZIES
LARRY MERCER
JOHN MERIC
MERIDIAN CLUB OF WINTER PARK
JAY MERIDITH
MERIT FASTENERS
PATRICK MERLET
WILLIAM MERRALL
MANNY MESSEGUER
J.G. MESTAN
METCALF & EDDY
METROPLEX COMMUNICATIONS
ROD METZ
DR. ROBERT A. METZGER
PAUL MEYER
MEYERS & MOONEY P.A.
MEYERS BAKERY
MICHAEL REEP DRYWALL
MICHAEL ZAMORE M.D. P.A.
JOSEPH MICHALAK
JOSEPH E. MICHNIEWICZ
MICKEY D. HOWE ENTRPRISES
MICKIE'S GIFT SHOP
MICRONET SYSTEMS
MID CONTINENT ENERGY
MID-STATE AUTOMOTIVE
DON MIERS
BOBBY MILES
EUGENE MILEY
STEPHEN M. MILEY
MILL-IT CORP.
JIM MILLAR
MILLER & EINHOUSE
MILLER BREWING CO.
MILLER POOLS CONTRACTING
MILLER-SELLEN ASSOCIATES
BOB MILLER
MICHAEL MILLER
TOM MILLER
CARROLL MILLER
J. WAYNE MILLER
MITCHELL A. MILLER
KENNETH MILLER
ROBERT MILLER
MICHAEL A. MILLER
STEVE MILLER

MILLS & NEBRASKA
BERRY MILLS
ERNEST MILLS
THOMAS MINELLA
DR. NORBERT L. MING
RAYMOND MING
MARIO MIRANDA
MISSION INN RESORT
MITCHELL BUILDING CONTRACTORS
MITCHELLS FUNERAL HOME
STUART MIZARHI
MIZO-HILL INC.
MO-CAT INC.
MOBILE OIL CORP.
MOBILE X-RAY
BOB MOHS
FRANK MOLETTEIRE
MARY MOLETTEIRE
PAUL MOLETTEIRE
RICHARD MOLETTEIRE
MOLTON ALLEN & WILLIAMS LTD.
DONALD MONACO
DR. PETER MONROY
FERDINAND MONTES JR.
TIM MOON
JOE MOONEY
MOORE PAINTING
BRAD J. MOORE
D. E. MOORE
JEARL MOORE
PERRY MOORE
WILLIAM MOORE
ALICE MOORE
WALTER JOSE MORALES
MORALL & CAREY
HECTOR MORE
CRAIG MOREHOUSE
STEVEN WALTER MOREIRA
MORGAN & COLLING
FRANK MORGAN
TIMOTHY R. MORGAN
GARY W. MORGAN
KEVIN L. MORGAN
ANDREA MORGAN
SCOTT MORPHIS
MORRIS R. CARTER M.D. P.A.
FRANK MORRIS
KENNETH L. MORRIS
SELENA MORRIS
DENISE MORRIS
SHERWOOD MORRISON
ROBERT E. MORROW
LEROY D. MORTON
DR. PATTERSON MOSELEY
MOSS GLICKSTEIN ET. AL.
WILLIAM E. MOSS JR.
BILL MOSS
RICHARD MOSS
MOTORS SECURITIES CORP.
DAVID MOUERY
MR. AND MRS. T. P. LUKA
MR. AUTO INSURANCE
MR. B'S OF EATONVILLE
FRANK BORGON
JOHN STERCHI
MEL R. MARTINEZ
MICHAEL CONOVER
ROBERT WILSON
STEREO & VIDEO
STEVE HOVDESVEN
WM. M. SLEMONS III
SHARON ABNER
PAUL MUELLER
PAUL G. MULLEE JR.
BRIAN MULLEN
MULLER KIRKCONNELL LINDSEY
DR. W. J. MULLER
MULLINS SHELL SERVICE
MULTICOM INC.
ALEX MUNROE
MURATA ERIE NORTH AMERICA
RICHARD D. MURDOCK
JAMES MURELL
BILL MURPHY

JOHN L. MURPHY
TAZE MURPHY
TIM P. MURPHY
WILLIAM J. MURPHY
MURRAY PORTER ROYER
TIMOTHY H. MURRAY
WILLIAM MURRAY
TIM MURRAY
FRANK MURRAY
GUY MURTONEN
BEN MUSICK
JACK MUSUM
RICHARD MYATT
DAVID MYERS
MARY MYERS
EDWARD C. MYSLINSKI

N

BARRY R. NAGER
LEONARD NALL
J. ALLEN NANCE
DR. MITCHELL M. NASS
NATIONAL BEVERAGES
NATIONAL BANK OF COMMERCE
NATIONAL RISK MANAGEMENT
  SERVICES
NATIONAL SUPPLY
NATIONWIDE ADVERTISING
  SERVICES
NATIONWIDE WHEELCHAIR LIFT
NATURE'S TABLE
GARY NAVRATIL
KURT NAVRATILVA
NBA PROPERTIES
NCNB
NCNB REAL ESTATE LENDING
  DIVISION
NCNB TRUST
NEAL P. PITTS P.A.
STUART NEAL
GEORGE NEDER JR.
DAN NEEDHAM
ASHER NEEL
WILLIAM J. NEEL
NEILSON & ASSOCIATES
KYLE NEISLER
JAMES R. NEITZEL
NELSON INVESTMENT PLANNING
MICHAEL NELSON
RONALD NELSON
ALBERT NELSON
DAVID NELSON
GEORGE A. NEUKOM III
NEUROLOGY CONSULTANTS
NEW JERSEY NETS
NEW LEAF FOLIAGE
N. SMYRNA BEACH CHRYSLER
  PLYMOUTH
NEW YORK LIFE INSURANCE CO.
DR. THOMAS NEWELL III
DAN NEWHALLER
NEWLON & CO.
JOHN NEWSHAM
JAMES M. NEWTON
DONALD NEWTON
GLEN NICHOLS
SCOTT D. NICHOLS
STEVE NICHOLSON
PAUL D. NICOLINI
MICHAEL NIEMANN
BRIAN NIEMI
BRUCE NIERENBERG
NIGHT OWL GRAPHICS
JOHN NISSENZONE
NOBLE ENTERPRISES
NOBLE UNLIMITED
JEFFREY T. NOBLE
JOE NOECKER
TIM NOELL
DR. ROGER NOFSINGER
ROYAL W. NOFTSKER

GEORGE K. NOGA
NORMAN BROTHERS NISSAN
NORTH BREVARD CHILDREN
  MEDICAL CENTER
NORTH LAKE FOODS
NORTHWEST AIRLINES
WILLIAM K. NORVELL JR.
LOUIS NOSTRO
NOVA SALES
LEONARD J. NOVAK
ROBERT J. NOVAK
RICK NULTY
DR. LESTER NUNALLY
GORDON S. NUTT

O

O. F. NELSON & SON'S NURSERY
O. V. WILLIAMS & ASSOCIATES
O! GRAPHICS
O'BRIEN & HOOPER P.A.
AUSTIN C. O'BRIEN JR.
JOHN F. O'BRIEN
PATRICK O'BRIEN
SARAH O'BRIEN
PATRICK O'CONNER
ROBERT O'HALLORAN
MARK M. O'MARA
O'NEAL TAVENNER & THOMPSON
O'NEIL LEE & WEST
MICHAEL O'QUINN
FRANK O'REARDON
MAURICE O'SULLIVAN
E. OF FLORIDA
TOM OAKIE
MATTHEW E. OAKLEY
OAKRIDGE GUN RANGE
OAKWOOD FARM
OB & GYN SPECIALISTS P.A.
DENNIS D. OBURN
OCOEE ANIMAL HOSPITAL
OERTHER FOODS
FRED OETTEL
OFFICE AUTOMATION
JESUS OLAVARRIA
CLAYTON L. OLESEN JR.
DAVID OLSEN
GREG OLSON
TERRY OLSON
R. A. OLSSON
ROBERT J. OLSZEWSKI
OLYMPIA INSTRUMENTS
ALEC OMBRES
OMEGA FOODS
OMNI GRAPHICS AGENCY
OMNI INTERNATIONAL HOTEL
OMNI TALENT GROUP
BERT ONG
CHARLES P. OPP
ORANGE BUICK
ORANGE COUNTY CHEMICAL
ORANGE COUNTY SPECIAL
  OLYMPICS
ORANGE LAKE COUNTRY CLUB
ORANGEWOOD PRESBYTERIAN
  CHURCH
ORLANDO AIRPORT MARRIOTT
ORLANDO AUTO SALES & LEASING
ORLANDO CENTRAL PARK
ORLANDO CONTRACTING
ORLANDO DODGE
ORLANDO DRIVE MEDICAL CENTER
ORLANDO FORD NEW HOLLAND
ORLANDO GARCIA-PIEDRA M.D. P.A.
ORLANDO LIMOUSINE SERVICE
ORLANDO MAGAZINE
ORLANDO MARRIOTT-
  INTERNATIONAL
ORLANDO ORTHOPAEDIC
  CONSULTANT
ORLANDO REGIONAL MEDICAL
  CENTER

ORLANDO REGIONAL MAGNETIC
ORLANDO TECHNOLOGY
ORLANDO TOOL & FASTENER
WILLIAM S. OROSZ JR.
JAMES V. ORR
MICHAEL J. ORR
PETER ORSBURN
NEIL ORZO
TOM OSBORNE
OSCEOLA FINANCIAL CORP.
KARL OSHMAN
JON A. OSTERBUR
E. HOWARD OSTROM
ROBERT OTTENS
DANIEL OUELLETTE
OUR VENTURE
OVERHEAD DOOR CO.
JENNINGS L. OVERSTREET
THOMAS OVERTON
ROGER E. OWEN
WILLIAM OWEN
OWENS & MINOR
J. SAM OWENS JR.
CHARLES OWENS
LEE M. OWENS
OXFORD DEVELOPMENT CORP. INC.
OYLER CONSTRUCTION CO.

P

PAS RADIOLOGY
PCSG LEASING CO.
P. J. BERGERON CONSTRUCTION
VICKI PABLE
PACE INSURANCE
PACE-WILLIAMS & CO.
JEFF PACHA
PACIFIC POOL DISTRIBUTORS OF
  FLORIDA
PACIFIC POOLS OF ORLANDO
JOE PADAWER
EMIL P. PAIGE
BILLY PAINTER
STEVEN A. PALIS
PALM CASUAL FURNITURE
ANTHONY PALMA
ERIC PALMER
MATTHEW S. PALMER
DIANNE PALMER
PANNING LUMBER
ROBERT F. PANNING
JOE PANZL
TONY PAPAS
DR. HARRY R. PAPPAS
PARK PLACE HOSPITAL
JOSEPH PARK
PARKER BOAT CO.
PARKER JOHNSON OWEN ET. AL.
E. GERALD PARKER R. P.H.
WILLIAM H. PARKER
RANDY PARKER
DENNY PARKER
RUDY PARKER
BENJAMIN A. PARKER
JOEL PARKER
ANNIE L. PARKER
PARKVIEW INVESTMENT CO.
PARMELE & ASSOCIATES
EDWARD PARNELL
JOHN PARRETT
SIDNEY H. PARRISH
PARSONS CONSULTANTS
ROBERT PARTLOW
ROBBY PASCHALL
STEVEN PASICK
JOSEPH PASSIATORE
DR. NICHOLAS PASTIS
PAT'S PROMOTIONS
CARL PATIN
PATRICK AIR FORCE BASE
PATTERSON & GUNTER
JEFFERY D. PATTERSON

MARK R. PATTERSON
T. C. PATTERSON
CHARLIE PATTERSON
WILLIAM D. PATTON
RUTH PATZ
PAUL FANNIN & ASSOCIATES
PAUL W. WATERS
GLEN PAWLOWSKI
PAYCHEX INC.
PAYROLL PLUS
PDR ARCHITECTS
PEACHES ENTERTAINMENT
RICHARD J. PEARCE
PEAT MARWICK MAIN & CO.
ALAN D. PECK
MICHAEL PECORALE
PEDIATRIC ASSOCIATES OF
    ORLANDO
ASHLEY PEEPLES
PEGRAM ENTERPRISES
PEISNER & CO. P.A.
MIKE PENNEY
PEPPERIDGE FARM
PEPSI-COLA SOUTH
JOHN PERCY
PERKINS FAMILY RESTAURANTS
CHRISTOPHER K. PERRY
KEN PERRY
JOHN E. PESCHAU
EMMETT B. PETER III
MARK PETERS
JERRY PETERSEN
TIM A. PETERSEN
PETERSON OUTDOOR ADVERTISING
ERIC M. PETERSON
PETROLEUM EQUIPMENT
    CONTRACTOR
WRAY PETRY
WILLIAM PETSCHEL
JOHN PETTINARI
VINCENT PETTINATO
JOHN PETTIT
DALE PETTUS
JERRY PEZZEMINTI
MICHAEL PHILLIPPY
PHILLIPS AUTOMOTIVE
GEORGE N. PHILLIPS
STEPHEN B. PHILLIPS
DOUGLAS J. PHILLIPS
MIKE PHIPPS
PHOTO CHEMICAL SYSTEMS
PETER PICCIANO
DOM PICCOLO
PICERNE DEVELOPMENT CORP.
GREG PICKARD
WILLIAM R. PICKERING
WILLIAM PICKERING
MARVIN PICKETT
GERALD PIERCE
ED PIERZYNSKI
STANLEY PIETKIEWICZ
THOMAS J. PILACEK
PILLAR-BRYTON PARTNERS
PILLAR-BRYTON CO.
TARA PINCHAL
FATHER NELSON W. PINDER
PINE CASTLE MEMORIAL CHAPEL
THOMAS H. PINEL
PINKERTON & LAWS CO.
RAYMOND J. PIRINO
ROBERT PITINO
JOSEPH PITTMAN
GLENN PIZZARELLA
RONALD A. PIZZUTI
PLANTSCAPE HOUSE
PLEASURAMA USA
FRANK PLEZIA
PLOTKIN COHEN & EADS M.D. P.A.
PLUMASTERS PLUMBING
PNC COMMERCIAL CORP.
BOB POE
ROGER POETTER
TERESA F. POGUE
POINCIANA MOBILE HOME PARK

WILLIAM POLESCHUK
GENE POLINO
DR. ROBERT POLLACK
POLYMETRICS
DAVID POLZER
ROBERT POOLE
SCOTT G. POPE
ROBERT POPP
JAMES POSEY
POST BUCKLEY SCHUH & JERNIGAN
POST LANDSCAPING
WILLIAM POST
STEVEN POSTILL
WILLIAM C. POTTER
THOMAS R. POWELL
ISAAC L. POWELL
POWER CONCRETE PRODUCTS
PRECISION DODGE
PREMIER BEVERAGE
PRESTIGE LUMBER
PRETTY PUNCH SHOPPETTES
VINCENT PREZIOSI
PRICE & PRICE
PRICE WATERHOUSE
C. NORMAN PRICHER
DR. JEFFREY PRICKETT
HENRY PRIEST
PRINCE BUSH MANAGEMENT CO.
PRINT FILE
PRINTING USA
DAVE PRITCHETT
PRO STAFF PERSONNEL SERVICES
PRO TEK SERVICES
JAMES G. PROCTOR
RICK PROCTOR
MARTY PROCTOR
PROFESSIONAL LAND SURVEYING
PROFESSIONAL CONSULTING
    ASSOCIATES
PROFESSIONAL ENGINEERING
    CONSULTANTS
PROFESSIONAL MOVERS
PROGRESSIVE OFFICE SYSTEMS
PROGRESSIVE COMMUNICATIONS
PROUD MOMENTS IN SPORTS
DAVID PROVENZANO
PRUDENTIAL-BACHE
PRUDENTIAL ORLANDO GROUP
NORMAN PRYOR
PRODUCTIONS ELEGANTE PTA
PUBLIC BANK
PUBLIX SUPER MARKETS
PUCKETT & VOGEL
ED PUGHE
PURE POWER
WANDA PURYEAR
BRIAN PY
DAVID PYECHA
RON PYWELL

QUALAX INC.
QUALITY STONE & MASONRY
QUANDT AYER ENTERPRISES
QUARTERBACK CLUB
STEVE QUATTRY
QUICK FRAME CONSTRUCTION CO.

R & E FOODS
R & M DEVELOPMENT
R & R METRO INSURANCE
R & R SUPPLY CO.
R. B. ATKINS ENTERPRISES
R. DOUGLAS STONE & ASSOCIATES
RED TRUCK LINES
R. J. CONSTRUCTION CO.
R. P. WELKER PLANTS

RSR MANAGEMENT CORP.
R. W. BECK & ASSOCIATES
R. W. PHIPPS & CO.
R-L ENTERPRISES
RABBIT BUS LINES
BRENT RABORN
CARL W. RACIOPPI
BILL RADAM
VINCE RADASKIEWICZ
SHAWN RADER
RADIO SHOP
JULIUS RAFF
DR. FRED RAFFA
DR. CHRISTOPHER RAFFERTY
VICTOR RAGUCCI
DAN RAICEVICH
RAKER & ASSOCIATES P.A.
RALPH KAZARIAN AUTO INSURANCE
DOUG RALPH
MARK RALPH
SCOTT RAMPENTHAL
TIM RAMSBERGER
DR. ROBERT K. RAMSEY
CHARLES RAND
RANDALL KNIVES
RANDALL PLUMBING
MARTIN RANFT
JOE RANIERI
MIKE RAPP
PHOEBE RAPP
DR ARTHUR S. RAPTOULIS
WILLIAM H. RASHID
DAVID RASMUSSEN
CRAIG W. RAWNSLOY
RAX RESTAURANTS
GLEN W. RAY
RICHARD RAY
GARY R. RAYMOND
PAUL RAYMOND
RONALD R. RAYMOND
RON RAYMOND
RAYSWAY
RE/MAX 200 NORTH REALTY INC.
REALTY APPRAISAL CONSULTANTS
RECREATIONAL SERVICES NTC
RECREATIONAL FACTORY
    WAREHOUSE
RED LOBSTER INNS
RED SNAPPER
ALZO REDDICK
REED MOTORS
MICHAEL D. REED
TERRY REED
DAVID REES
REEVES SUPPLY
REFLECTIONS
REGENCY MAZDA
REGIONAL ORTHOPAEDIC
    ASSOCIATES
JEFFREY S. REICH
DONALD L. REID
ERIC REID
MIKELL REID
MIKE REID
DR. JACK REINHARDT
MICHAEL C. REINMAN
RELIABLE PEAT CO.
RELSI INC.
BELVIN REMBERT
RENEE STEIN & CO.
RENSELEAR DEVELOPMENT CORP.
IVAN REPASS
SANDY REPPERT
REPUBLIC PACKAGING OF FLORIDA
JAMES RESCHKE
RESIDENTIAL BUILDING SUPPLY
RESORT POOL MANAGEMENT
RESORT WORLD MANAGEMENT CO.
RESTAURANT ADMINISTRATIVE
    SERVICES
JAMES REUS
REX HUFFMAN & ASSOCIATES
REX-TIBBS CONSTRUCTION
MARK A. REYES

JOE REYNOLDS
RHEINAUER'S AT RUTLANDS
JERRY RHIND
PAUL RHINEHART
RHS CONSTRUCTION
RICH-UNITED CORP.
RICHARD A. CLARIDGE P.E.
RICHARD CHACE JR. D.D.S. P.A.
RICHARD RHODES P.A.
JOHN RICHARDS
K. A. RICHARDS
JAN RICHARDSON
RICHESON & BROWN P.A.
GENE RICHTER
THEODORE J. RICKETTS
ERIC RIDENER
SUSAN RIEBEL
JOHN RIFE
BARRY RIGBY
STEPHEN RIGHI
KARL E. RIGHTER
G. ALLIE RIGNEY
ROBERT K. RIGSBY
C. F. RILEY
THAD RILEY
RIMMER ENGINEERING
DAVID A. RIMPO
RINGHAVER EQUIPMENT CO.
STEVE RISNER
GEORGE RITCHIE
MICHAEL D. RIVERS
JEANELLE RIVERS
PAUL P. RIVOSECCHI
ROADWAY EXPRESS
ROBB & STUCKY
SUE ROBERSON
ROBERT A. DELORENZO BUILDERS
ROBERT A. LIEBERMAN M.D. P.A.
ROBERT C. YOUNGMAN M.D. P.A.
ROBERT J. BUONAURO P.A.
ROBERT J. DORFF M.D. P.A.
ROBERT L. EDGERTON D.D.S. P.A.
ROBERT P. SALTSMAN P.A.
ROBERT P. SCHIFFER M.D. P.A.
ROBERT PELLARIN D.D.S. P.A.
ROBERT T. BOWLES & ASSOCIATES
ROBERTS TRANSFORMER
DICK ROBERTS
DAVID A. ROBERTS
ROBERTSON & WILLIAMS P.A.
BOB ROBERTSON
ROBINSON'S PHARMACY
JAMES C. ROBINSON
DANNY C. ROBINSON
JOHN ROBINSON
ROBERT L. ROBINSON
JOSEPH M. ROBINSON
KEVIN ROBINSON
DAVID L. ROBINSON
RON ROBINSON
MICHAEL ROBSON
ROCHE INC.
ROB ROCK
ROCKET OIL CO.
MARK RODE
DR. FIDEL RODRIGUEZ
E. M. RODRIGUEZ
BOBBY ROESCH
ROBERT ROESCH
MARION S. ROESCH
ROGER HOLLER CHEVROLET
ROGERS & ASSOCIATES
ROGERS & DOWLING P.A.
ROGERS & FORD CONSTRUCTION
SHIRLEY A. ROGERS
MICHAEL ROGIER
ROH CONSTRUCTION & REPAIR
STEVEN ROHLFING
ROLAND CORP.
CHARLES ROLLASON II
ROLLINS RENTAL PARTY WORLD
RONALD E. REYNOLDS INC.
RONCHETTI CONSTRUCTION
RONNIE H. WALKER P.A.

RONNIE'S RESTAURANT
ROOF MANAGEMENT SERVICE
ROOF REPAIR SPECIALISTS
ELIZABETH ROPER
BRUCE ROSE
JOHN W. ROSE
ROSEMONT REALTY
ALLAN ROSEN
ED ROSENBLATT
EMERY H. ROSENBLUTH JR.
EDWIN E. ROSS
MARK ROSS
NEDD ROSS
RONALD ROSS
WILLIE J. ROSS
NANCY ROSSMAN
RICHARD ROST
ROTECH MEDICAL CORP.
ROBERT A. ROTHBERG
KEN ROTTMAN
STAN ROUSE
ROBERT B. ROWE
JULIANA ROWE
STANLEY BROTHERS ROYAL CUP
ROYAL JEEP EAGLE
ROYAL OLDSMOBILE
RSN INC. dba ARBY'S
EDWARD RUBACHA
RENO RUBEIS
RICHIE RUBIN
RUBY BUILDERS
SUSAN RUBY
JIM RUDDY
WILLIAM RUFF
DAN RUFFIER
RUMBERGER KIRK ET. AL.
GREGORY RUSE
RUSSELL PONTIAC-BUICK
RICK RUSSELL
JOHN B. RUSSELL
TIMOTHY J. RUSSELL
MICHAEL RUST
GERALD RUTBERG
MARTY RUTKOVITZ
RUTLAND'S
RYAN & ASSOCIATES
BUD RYAN
MICHAEL RYAN
TRUDY RYAN
RYDER TRUCK RENTALS

S

S & S FENCE
S & W KITCHENS
SAI ELECTRONICS
SET CONSTRUCTION
SFG PROPERTIES
S.I. GOLDMAN CO.
JOE SACCO
SAFECORP ENTERPRISES
SAFETY EQUIPMENT CO.
FRED SAFFER
MAXINE SAGER
BUD SAHINA
DALE SALATICH
HAROLD SALE
SALESTAR INC.
SALON VIENNA
DENNIS SALVAGIO
SAM PATTERSON TRUCK BROKERS
ALBERT SAMPEY
TERRY SAMUELS
SAN-ANGEL INN
DAVID SANBORN
SANDEFUR HOLDING CO.
JOE SARDANO
RICK SARGENT
JOSEPH SARJEANT
SASSER & WEBER P.A.
NANCY SATTERFIELD
GERARD SAULNEY

SAUNDERS DEVELOPMENT CORP.
NIKKI SAUNDERS
JAMES D. SAURMAN
JOHN SAWAYDA
TOM SAWYER
CAROLYN SAWYER
SCAN DESIGN INC.
SCANLON CORP.
WAYNE SCANTLING
STEVE SCHABER
MARK SCHAEFER
BOB SCHAFER
BOB SCHAMBERGER
SCHANTINI & ASSOCIATES
LINDA SCHEELE
SCHENCK CO.
SCHIEFER-DECKER PROPERTIES
STEVE SCHIFF
JOHN SCHNECK
DICK SCHNEEBERGER
DONALD SCHNEIDER
DR. KENNETH SCHNEIDER
MARK SCHNEIDER
T. G. SCHNETZER
DR. JAMES SCHOECK
ROBERT SCHRAMM
STEPHEN SCHREIBER
JOHN SCHULTZ
DUANE SCHULTZ
DR. PAUL D. SCHUMACHER
MIKE SCHUSTER
NANCY PORT SCHWALB
DR. W. SCHWARTZ II
DR. KERRY SCHWARTZ
KENNETH SCHWARTZ
RICHARD SCHWARTZ
CHARLOTTE SCHWARTZ
JAMES SCHWARZROCK
SCHWEIZER INC.
EDWARD J. SCHWOB SR.
DANIEL L. SCINTO
TERRY SCOTT
SCREEN ROOMS BY J
JOHN A. SCRIBNER
JOHN SCRUGGS
MATTHEW SCUSSEL
AL SCUTTE
SEA PINES REHABILITATION
  HOSPITAL
SEA RAY BOATS
SEABOARD FARMS
SEAGRAM BEVERAGE CO.
SEALY MATTRESS CO.
SEARLE LABORATORIES
RALEIGH F. SEAY JR.
PATRICIA SECRIST
SECURITY NATIONAL BANK OF
  OSCEOLA
SECURITY TITLE & GUARANTY
BRADLEY SEFRIED
RICK SEGAL
DR. MATTHEW SEIBEL
TIM SEIBERT
RICK SEIFERT
WILLIAM A. SELF
SEMINOLE DENTAL CENTER
SEMINOLE FORD
SEMINOLE ORTHOPAEDIC
  ASSOCIATES
SEMINOLE SURGICAL SPECIALISTS
SEMORAN FOOT CLINIC P.A.
SEMORAN MANAGEMENT CORP.
SEMTRONICS
SENCO OF FLORIDA
SENTINEL COMMUNICATIONS CO.
SERAFIN SHURM & ASSOCIATES
RICK SERFOZO
SERVPRO OF APOPKA WEKIVA
SESCO INC.
FRANK SESS
SEVILLA ROOFING CONTRACTORS
SEWELL PLASTICS
DOUG SEYMOUR
STANLEY SHADER

MICHAEL D. SHAFFER
JOHN SHAHINIAN
GEORGE SHALLCROSS
SHAMROCK DEVELOPMENT CORP.
SCOTT F. SHAPIRO
DR. MITCHELL SHAPIRO
RONALD SHAVER
STEVE SHAY
DONALD A. SHEA
SHEEHAN MARKETING
GLENN M. SHEEHAN
LINDA SHEETS
SHEFFIELD ENGINEERS &
    ASSOCIATES
SHEILA G. MILLAR P.A.
CHARLES J. SHERIDAN
WAYNE SHERIDAN
WILLIE SHERMAN JR.
SHERWIN WILLIAMS CO.
JOHN SHIPE
R. L. SHIPP
J. R. SHIREK
JOSEPH SHIRER
SHIRT CELLAR
SHIVELY COMMUNICATIONS
MR & MRS D. F. SHOEMAKER
TOM SHOQUIST
SHORELINE CARPET SUPPLIES
THOMAS SHOSTAK
SHOWALTER FLYING SERVICES
SHOWTIME SERVICES CORP.
SHREVE SURFACES
WADE SHRIVALLE
SHUCKER'S OYSTER BAR
JOHN A. SHUGHART JR.
ROBERT R. SHULL
SHUTTS & BOWEN
PATRICIA SHUTZ
CRAIG SIBLEY
RUSS SIBLEY
JAMES SIDLEY
HOWARD SIEGEL
MICHAEL SIGMAN
SIGNATURE PRODUCTS
SIGNGRAPHICS CORP.
SIHLE & WILLIAMSON
BARRY SIKORSKI
SIMMERMON & MORGAN P.A.
DR. LELAND D. SIMMONS
MICHAEL C. SIMMONS
MARK SIMMONS
GREG SIMMONS
MANUEL SIMOES
PETER SIMONINI
BARBARA SIMPSON
MIKE SINGLETARY
SIVAD SERVICES CORP.
CHRISTOPHER SKAMBIS
TIMOTHY SKELDON
GEORGE W. SKELLY
ALAN SKELTON
RUSSELL E. SKINNER
PAUL SKONSKY
STEVE SLACK
ROBERT SLANE
SLAUGHTER BROTHERS
ROBERT SLONE
JEFFREY R. SMALL
JAMES F. SMALLEY JR.
SMATHERS PLEUS ADAMS ET. AL.
WILLIAM S. SMITH III
SIDNEY SMITH III
BILL SMITH JR.
KENNETH L. SMITH JR.
SMITH LYONS APPRAISAL
SMITH SCHODER & ROUSE P.A.
SMITH'S NURSERY
ARCHIE SMITH
ANDRE SMITH
CHRISTOPHER L. SMITH
C. WILLIAM SMITH
DAVID V. SMITH
DOUGLAS SMITH
GENE P. SMITH

JEFF SMITH
JOHN SMITH
JIM SMITH
KEVIN SMITH
MICHAEL R. SMITH
MIKE SMITH
ROBERT E. SMITH
THOMAS SMITH
TODD SMITH
VICTOR SMITH
WILLIAM SMITH
ROBERT SMOLEY
SMYTH LUMBER
MIKE SMYTH
SNODGRASS HARDWARE
EDWARD SNOEYENBOS
ROBERT SNOW
RICHARD A. SNYDER
LARRY SNYDER
JAMES T. SNYDER
RANDALL SNYDER
SOBIK'S SUBS
SOFTWARE DESIGN GROUP
SOIL & MATERIAL ENGINEERS
SOLITE CORP.
SOLOMON F. SCHICK & ASSOCIATES
MARK SOLOMON
SONITROL
SONOCO PRODUCTS CO.
MICHAEL SORDELET
SCOTT SORENSON
LOUIS A. SORRENTINO III
RICHARD P. SOUCY
MARY K. SOUDRETTE
SOUTH BREVARD PHYSICAL
    THERAPY
SOUTH ORLANDO BUSINESS
    SERVICE
SOUTHEAST APPRAISAL
    ASSOCIATES
SOUTHEAST BANK
SOUTHEAST DEVELOPMENT &
    CONSTRUCTION
SOUTHEAST MEDICAL PRODUCTS
SOUTHEAST BANK N. A.
SOUTHEASTERN INVESTMENT
    PROPERTIES
SOUTHEASTERN MUNICIPAL BONDS
SOUTHEASTERN CLINICAL
    RESEARCH
SOUTHEASTERN FREIGHT LINES
SOUTHEASTERN HARDWARE
SOUTHERN BELL TELEPHONE CO.
SOUTHERN CLASSICS
SOUTHERN FURNITURE TRANSPORT
SOUTHERN GENERAL PRODUCTS
SOUTHERN IRRIGATION &
    MAINTENANCE
SOUTHERN MANAGEMENT SYSTEMS
SOUTHERN STATES GLASS
SOUTHERN WINE & SPIRITS
SOUTHERS & SOUTHERS
    LANDSCAPE
SOUTHLAND CONSTRUCTION
SOUTHLAND DISTRIBUTION CENTER
PAUL SOVRAN
TROY SOWERS
DANIEL SOYER
SPACECOAST PATHOLOGIST
GERALD SPANIOL
SPARKS COOPER & LEKLEM P.A.
HERMAN F. SPATH
SPECIALTY MAINTENANCE
BOB SPECTOR
GABRIEL E. SPECTOR
SPEED INDUSTRIES
HOWARD SPEIGEL
JAMES C. SPEIGNER
DAVID C. SPENCE
SPENCER EDENS INSURANCE
    AGENCY
J. TODD SPENCER
WILLIAM SPIGNER
SPIRIT TRAVEL CORP.

SPIRITS SPORTS BAR
ART SPLENDORIA
TOM SPLIT
WILLIAM C. SPOONE
JAMES SPOONHOUR
SPORTS PAGE OF ORLANDO
JIM SQUILLANTE
SRI ENTERPRISES
PHILLIP ST. LOUIS
LCDR. SAMUEL E. STAATS
STAGE DOOR II
STAINLESS & SANITARY FITTINGS
MARK STALDER
STANDARD POOLS
DR. THOMAS A. STANFORD
STANLEY DOOR SYSTEMS
BOB STANLEY
STEVE STARDY
STARKE LAKE STUDIOS
STARKS FUNERAL HOME
STARLING MANUFACTURING
JOSEPH STARLING
RONALD STARR
STATE ELECTRIC CO.
STATE FARM INSURANCE
ELYNOR STAUFFER
RICHARD STEALEY
STEAM PLUS
RONALD R. STEARNS
DONALD E. STEEDLY
JACK H. STEELE
HUBERT STEELEY
KENNETH L. STEEVES
ROBERT STEGER
CLIFF STEIN
WILLIAM STEIN
STENSTROM MCINTOSH ET. AL.
STEPHEN BROOKS M.D. P.A.
STEPHEN L MILLER REALTY CORP.
GAIL STEPHENS
SAM STEPHENS
C. DAVID STEPHENS
STERN BUILDERS
MATT STERN
STEVENS & PETERS P.A.
DR. ROGER STEWART
RUSS STEWART
STEWARTS ELECTRIC MOTORS
STIEREN CONSTRUCTION
STINSON CARPETS
MARK STIPULKOSKI
JOHN STOCKHAM
STOCKMAN HARNESS
JAMES G. STOKES
MELTON STOKES
BRIAN STOKES
STEPHEN STONE
JAMES STONESTREET
ALEX STOROSHENKO
SUE ELLEN STORY
STOUFFER FOOD CORP.
STOUFFERS ORLANDO RESORT
ROBERT J. STOVASH
STRAWN AND OLIVELLA
JAMES STREICH
PERCY STRIBLING
STAN W. STRICKLAND
IRENE STRITZEL
R. JAMES STROKER
MIKE STROLE
STROMBERG CARLSON
STROMBERG-CARLSON CORP.
DAVID C. STRONG
TED STRONG
STRUCTURED INFORMATION
    SYSTEMS
MARY ELLEN STUART
SUCCESS UNLIMITED OF FLORIDA
SULLIVAN & ASSOCIATES
MELISSA SULLIVAN
JOHN SULLIVAN
MICHAEL J. SULLIVAN
THOMAS R. SULLIVAN
LISA L. SUMMA

JOHN SUMMERLOT
ANTHONY L. SUMMERS
ROBERT SUMPTER
SUN BANK NA
SUN CHARM RANCH
SUN COAST SUPPLY
SUN LOVERS OF CENTRAL FLORIDA
SUN MACHINE
SUNARHAUSERMAN
SUNBELT ENVIRONMENTAL
    SYSTEMS
SUNBELT SYSTEMS CONCEPTS
SUNDANCE TALENT AGENCY
SUNDIAL BEACH TOWEL
SUNFLOORING
SUNRISE CATERING
SUNSHINE BUILDING &
    DEVELOPMENT CORP.
SUNSHINE GREENERY
SUNSHINE NETWORK
SUPERIOR PRINTERS
SUPERIOR TRIM & DOOR
SUPPLY ROOM
SUTER AIR CONDITIONING
DAVID W. SUTHERLAND
JOHN SUTPHIN
MICHAEL J. SUTTER
SVERDRUP SOUTHERN GROUP
SWANN & HADDOCK
RICHARD SWANN
DAVE SWANSON
SWEET PAPER SALES CO.
JOHN SWIFT
SYSCO FOOD SERVICES
SYSTEM SOFTWARE DESIGN
SYSTEMARK INC.

T

T. G. LAGRONE & ASSOCIATES P.A.
TEC HOMES
TGI FRIDAY'S
T. G. LEE FOODS
T. H. LITTLE ELECTRICAL
TJM DEVELOPMENT CORP.
T. P. HENRY INC.
TSG INC.
TACO BELL
TACO CITY
TACO SUPPLY
ERNEST TAFOYA
LEE TAKAHASHI
WAYNE TALBOTT
ROBERT TALLEY
TAMAR INNS
JOHN TANNER
FRED TANZER
TAPCO INC.
TY TARBY
JOHN TASKER
TAYLOR APPRAISAL CO.
TAYLOR DISTRIBUTORS
TAYLOR PRECAST
DEREK A. TAYLOR
MICHAEL J. TAYLOR
JOHN TAYLOR
JIM TAYLOR
COMER TAYLOR
JOE TAYLOR
ROBERT H. TAYLOR
ERIC TAYLOR
CINDY L. TAYLOR
TCI INSURANCE AGENCY
TEAK ISLE
TECHNITRONICS INC.
TED MANOS M.D. P.A.
LOU TELFEYAN
VANCE TEMPLE
BRUCE TEMPLIN
TEMPORARIES UNLIMITED
TENNIS SPECIALISTS
TERRY'S ELECTRIC

BOAKE TERRY
FRED G. TESSIER
TEST & BALANCE CORP.
PAUL W. TEUFEL
TEXICO REFINING & MARKETING
TGC INC.
THAT'S SPORTS INC.
THE A.G. MAURO CO.
THE ADVERTISING WORKS
THE ALLEN GROUP
THE BRAGA ENGINEERING CO.
THE BUG HUT
THE BYWATER CO.
THE CALIBRE CO.
THE CONTINUING EDUCATION
THE DENTAL SPECIALISTS
THE ELECTRONICS SHOP
THE EVANS GROUP
THE EXCHANGE
THE FIRST F. A.
THE FLOORING CENTER
THE GREATER CONSTRUCTION CO.
THE HAMILTON GROUP
THE HOUSE OF SEAGRAM
THE HOUSEHOLDER CORP.
THE HUSKEY CO.
THE INVESTMENT COUNSEL CO.
THE JONES CO.
THE KIRCHMAN CORP.
THE LANDMARKS GROUP
THE LEARNING CENTER OF
    ORLANDO
THE MAGIC SUITE
THE MARTIN BROWER CO.
THE MARTIN COMPANYS OF
    DAYTONA
THE MEDICK AGENCY
THE NEWPORT GROUP
THE NORTHWESTERN MUTUAL LIFE
THE OLIVE GARDEN
THE ONIONSKIN PARTNERSHIP
THE PEABODY HOTEL
THE PREDOT CO.
THE PRINTING PALACE
THE REMINGTON CO.
THE ROOFING CO.
THE TRIGG CO.
KARL THEILE
THOMAS A. MOORE P.A.
THOMAS C. LAWTON D.M.D. P.A.
THOMAS E. LYNCH
THOMAS G. CANE P.A.
THOMAS J. LIPTON
THOMAS W. RUFF & CO.
JAMES THOMAS
WILLIAM THOMAS
WILLIAM THOMAS
DALE E. THOMAS
JIM THOMAS
SHIRLEY M. THOMAS
JOY THOMAS
ROBERT THOMPSON
RANDY E. THOMPSON
JEAN E. THORNTON
RICHARD N. THRASHER
E. REID THURBON
MIKE THURINGER
MATT THURSAM
TIBBITTS INC.
ROB TIERNEY
TILDEN LOBNITZ & COOPER
BILL TILLARD
DR. DON T. TILLERY JR.
TIM CASTELL INSURANCE AGENCY
TIM WEBBER CATERING
TIMBER PRODUCTS CO.
TIP TOP ROOFING CO.
FRANK TOBIN JR.
GLENN TOBIN
DR ANTHONY P. TOCCO
TODD PERSONS COMMUNICATIONS
MARK S. TOMASSI
TOMPKINS INVESTMENT GROUP
DR. RANDY S. TOMPKINS

TONY MARINO'S
TOOTSIES
TOP TILE & MARBLE WORKS
GREGORY H. TOPPER
JOSEPH A. TORRES
TOTAL AUDIO VISUAL SERVICES INC.
STEPHEN P. TOTH
TOUCHE ROSS
TOWNE REALTY
JOHN TRACY
TRADITIONAL FLOOR COVERING
TRAIL LINCOLN-MERCURY
TRAILER SALES
TRAMMEL CROW CO. RESIDENTIAL
TRAMMELL CROW CO. COMMERCIAL
TRANSCONTINENTAL DAIRY
    PRODUCTS
TRANSPORTATION CONSULTING
ROBERT E. TRAPP
ERNIE TRAYHAM
GREGORY D. TRAYNOR
CONNER TRENT
TRI-CITY ELECTRICAL CONSULTANT
TRI-W-RENTAL
TRIBUNE MEDIA SERVICES
TAMARA L. TRIMBLE
TRIPLE G. DAIRY
MICHAEL TRIPP
ERNEST E. TROBAUGH
RICHARD J. TROCK
D. A. TROIANO
TROPIC CRAFT ALUMINUM
    FURNITURE
TROUTMAN WILLIAMS ET. AL.
J. L. TRUETT
TRUFFLES & TRIFLES
WALTER TRUMBO
J. BOWMAN TRUMBO
TTI II INC.
TTI TRESTRON
TUBESALES
TUCKER & BRANHAM
GARY TUGGLE
THOMAS TUKDARIAN
TULINO ENGINEERING
TUPPERWARE HOME PARTIES
RICK TURNAGE
TURNER CONSTRUCTION
TURNER MEDICAL BUILDING
    SERVICES
N. JAMES TURNER, ESQ.
JAMES TURNER
GARY TURNER
DAVID B. TWEEDELL
JACK TWIGG
TWIN DRAGONS RESTAURANT
TWO GUYS TIRES

U

UBR PROPERTIES
U. S. TRADE DISTRIBUTORS
UCF COLLEGE OF BUSINESS
DR. EDWARD UHLEMAN
ULTIMATE MOTOR WORKS
MICHAEL UMSTEAD
UNITED AMERICAN BANK
UNITED CONTRACTING
    ENTERPRISES
UNITED ENTERPRISES ORLANDO
UNITED FINANCIAL GROUP
UNITED HOSPITAL SUPPLY CO.
UNITED MEDICAL CORP.
UNITED RESOURCES
UNITED TELEPHONE SYSTEM
UNITED TROPHY MANUFACTURING
UNIVERSAL ENGINEERING
    SCIENCES
UNIVERSAL STUDIOS
UNIVERSAL PARTS WAREHOUSE
UNIVERSITY BEHAVIORAL CENTER
JIM UPCHURCH

UPS TRUCK LEASING
JAMES URBACH
JAMES I. URBACH
GLEN UREY
UROLOGY ASSOCIATES P.A.
USAIR
USG SOUTHEAST
USPA & IRA
TODD UTTAL

V

V. J. GROWERS SUPPLY
VALCON
VALENCIA COMMUNITY COLLEGE
JOHN VALERINO
DR. MICHAEL J. VALLILLO
CRAIG VAN SLYKE
VANASSE HANGEN BRUSTLIN
TODD VANDEBERG
VICTOR L. VANDEN OEVER
MICHAEL VANDERSLICE
JACK H. VANHART
BRIAN VANN
VANNICE CONSTRUCTION
ROBIN VANSWEARINGEN
VANZANTE ENTERPRISES
PAT VARAN
JACK VARASSE
VARIABLE ANNUITY MARKETING CO.
A. MICHAEL VARNEY
LANCE A. VARNEY
VAUGHAN PRESS
FRANK VAUGHT
LEX VEECH
VEIN CLINIC OF CENTRAL FLORIDA
PETER C. VENEZIA
PETER J. VENTURA
VERGASON & JOHNS ADVERTISING
VERSATRON PRECISION
VESTAL & CO.
VEYTEC INC.
TIM VICKERS
VICTOR GAMMICHIA D.D.S. P.A.
VIDEO COMMUNICATIONS
GEORGE J. VIELE
VILLAS OF GRAND CYPRESS
VINCENT AGENCY
ROGER P. VINCENT
LUIS VIRGILIO
DENNIS VISCONTI
GREG VISSERING
VISTANA RESORT DEVELOPMENT
VISTANA RESORT
VITAL SIGNS
VNA HEALTH CARE GROUP
STEVEN VOGEL
VON WALDNER BAIL BONDING
DWIGHT VOTAN

W

W. J. MILNER CO.
W. M. PHILIPS JR. M.D. P.A.
W. RILEY ALLEN P.A.
W. W. FAGAN & CO.
BERTHA WADE
DONALD WADSWORTH
ROBERT WAGNER
STEVEN R. WAGNER
TOM WAGNER
EVELYN J. WAGNER
DR. ALFRED WAHNISH
ROYCE B. WALDEN
WALKER FOIL
WALKER MILLER EQUIPMENT CO.
JOHN WALKER
NATHANIEL WALKER
RON WALKER
MARCELLE WALKER

ROBERT WALKER
DARLENE WALKER
JAMES C. WALL
NANCY M. WALL
WALLACE ELECTRONICS
DAVID WALLACE
WALLCOVERING INC.
DOUG WALLER
GARLAND WALLER
JAMES WALLS
KEVIN S. WALLSHLAEGER
JOHN WALSH
P. JAMES WALSH
RON WALSH
WALT DISNEY WORLD
WALT DISNEY WORLD CO.
JOEY WALTERS
GROVER WALTON
WALTREE CONSTRUCTION
DR. DENNIS WARD
TOM WARD
DON K. WARE
GORDON WARK
BILL WARREN
DR. D. E. WARSETT
DORIS D. WASHINGTON
WASHINGTON MILLS
WASMAN COLOR PRODUCTION
MICHAEL WASS
WASTE MANAGEMENT OF ORLANDO
BRIAN P. WATERHOUSE
WATERLINE PRODUCTS
WATERMAN MEDICAL CENTER
WATSKY & CO.
ROY WATSON
CLINT WATTS
P. D. WATTWOOD JR.
WAYNE AUTO FIRE SPRINKLERS
WAYNE DENSCH INC.
WDBO 580 AM
WDIZ 100 FM
ED WEATHERWAX
LESSIE WEAVER
DR. HOWARD WEAVERS
DR. RICHARD J. WEBER
JACK WEBER
RICHARD WEBER
WEBSTER'S FURNITURE
GEORGE WEIRICH
MAE WEISMAN
HERBERT WEISS
DAN WELBAUM
WILLIAM A. WELBORN
HUGH C. WELCHEL III
WELLS GATTIS ET. AL.
LESTER WELLS
DOUG WENDT
DENNIS WERNER
WESCO REALTY
WESH-TV CH. 2
BOB WESLEY
HUGH WESSINGER
HARRY WEST
JUDITH B. WEST
TERESA K. WESTERMAN
WESTINGHOUSE ELECTRIC CORP.
WESTSIDE SERVICES
WET 'N' WILD
WEYERHAEUSER
WEYERHAEUSER CO.
WFTV INC. CH 9
WHARTON SMITH INC.
WHEELER INC.
DONALD G. WHEELER
JAMES WHEELER
JIM WHEELER
ROBERT C. WHEELER
WHITAKER DOROUGH & WHITAKER
WILLIAM B. WHITAKER II
DAN P. WHITAKER
GREGG B. WHITAKER
KEN WHITAKER
PHILIP P. WHITBY
WHITE BUFFALO HOLDINGS

ERNEST WHITE JR.
WHITE ROSE DEPARTMENT STORES
WHITE'S BLUEPRINT SERVICE
WHITE-HAN INC.
DR. GEORGE WHITE
DR. GREG WHITE
BRUCE WHITE
DAVID WHITE
GARY M. WHITE
JAMES L. WHITE
LARRY WHITE
MALCOLM WHITE
NORMAN B. WHITE
W. GARNETT WHITE
DAVID WHITESCARVER
TOM WHITESEL
ELLIOTT WHITTON
LEWIS A. WIBLE JR.
KENNETH P. WICK
MICHAEL WICKWIRE
KEVIN J. WIEDECKER
JON WIERDA
W. F. WIESE
CURT WIGGINS JR.
LINDA WIGGINS
HOWARD WIGGS
WIGINTON FIRE SPRINKLERS INC.
WILCOX & ASSOCIATES
RONALD M. WILCOX
CHARLES D. WILDER
DWAYNE WILHAM
WILKERSON LUMBER
JAMES G. WILLARD
WILLIAM B. GARRARD CORP.
WILLIAM G. SELLERS
WILLIAM H. CROSS & CO.
WILLIAM J. SHEAFFER P.A.
WILLIAM LETOURGEN ENTERPRISES
WILLIAM M. THOMAS MASONRY
WILLIAM SPARE ET. AL.
WILLIAMS BROTHERS MAZDA
WILLIAMS CONTRACTING
WILLIAMS CO.
WILLIAMS SMITH SUMMERS
WILLIAMS WILLIAMS & WILLIAMS
ALFRED E. WILLIAMS
DENNIS WILLIAMS
EDWARD WILLIAMS
EDWARD D. WILLIAMS
GERALD WILLIAMS
MARK WILLIAMS
RICH WILLIAMS
KENNETH M. WILLIAMS
WARREN WILLIAMS
T. DARRYL WILLIAMS
DARYL W. WILLIAMS
JERRY WILLIAMS
ROBERT D. WILLIAMS
DARRYL WILLIAMS
WALTER WILLIAMS
MARTIN WILLIAMS
BRENT WILLIAMS
CHRISTOPHER WILMONT
WILSON ICE ENTERPRISES
WILSON WHEELER & SCHMIDT
WILSON'S CONCRETE SERVICE
WILSON'S SHOE STORE
JON M. WILSON
RONALD L. WILSON
MICHAEL W. WILSON
RICHARD WILSON
ROBERT WILSON
HARIETTE WILSON
DR. A. G. WIMER III
THOMAS WINDRAM JR.
DALE D. WINEINGER
WINGATE INC.
BRUCE WINNER
WINTER PARK ANESTHESIA
WINTER PARK BLUE PRINT
WINTER PARK UROLOGY
    ASSOCIATES
WINTER PARK BLUE PRINT

WINTER PARK CHAMBER OF
   COMMERCE
WINTER PARK MEMORIAL HOSPITAL
DR. THOMAS F. WINTERS
DEAN WINTERS
FRANK WINZIG
KARL J. WIPPERFURTH
STEPHEN WIREMAN
A. E. WISNE
DORIS WITTIG
WKCF-TV CH. 68
WOFL-TV CH. 35
G. CHARLES WOHLUST
LAWSON L. WOLFE
NORM WOLFINGER
LAWRENCE G. WOLLSCHLAGER JR.
GEORGE WOLLY
BILL WOOD
CHARLES WOOD
FRANCIS P. WOOD
ROBERT V. WOOD
WOODLAWN MEMORIAL PARK
BRUCE WOODRUFF
WOODS REHABILITATION SERVICE
RICHARD WOODS
WOOLFORK MORRELL & WILLIAMS
WOOLPERT CONSULTANTS
COUNCIL WOOTEN JR.
ED WOOTEN
ROBERT WORMAN
PAMELA LEE WRAY
KITTY WRENN
HENRY WRIGHT
GARY E. WRIGHT
LERRIL P. WRIGHT
ROBERT WRIGHT
TRUDI WRIGHT
WSSP 104 FM
WYATT ANDERSON CONSTRUCTION
WYMORE OB-GYN SPECIALISTS
M. WYNN III

ZIMMER POSTER SERVICE
ZIMMERMAN SHUFFIELD ET. AL.
ROBERT ZIMMERMAN
ZINK PUBLISHING
DR. AND MRS. WILLIAM P. ZINK
COL. HARRY ZIPPER USAF RET.
VICTOR ZOLLO JR.
JOE ZORNIK
RAY ZUAZO
CARLIS ZVEJNIEKS

X

XPERT TUNE INC.

Y

GEORGE A. YANOVITCH
WAYNE YARBER
CHRISTOPHER S. YAWN
ERIC YEADON
YELLOW FREIGHT SYSTEM
KAY M. YEUELL
MICHAEL D. YODER
STEPHEN YOST
KENNETH YOUMANS
YOUNG COMMANDOS
JAMES YOUNG
NED YOUNG
TIM A. YOUNG
LORETTA YOUNG
DONALD YOUNGS

Z

Z. L. INVESTMENTS
DON ZABEL SR.
HOWARD L. ZACHMAN JR.
ANN T. ZAYA
CHARLES ZEGELBONE
KEITH P. ZEITLER
JIM ZENGARO
ZEPHYRHILLS BOTTLED WATER
CAROLYN ZEULI
AL ZIFFER
ARMAND E. ZILIOLI

INDEX